Weather
for
Sportsmen

Weather for Sportsmen

A NEW KIND OF BOOK FOR SAILORS AND ALL OUTDOORSMEN

THORN BACON

MOTOR BOATING & SAILING BOOKS

NEW YORK

To the memory
of my Father and to Mother
who never lost the faith.

A MOTOR BOATING & SAILING BOOK

Copyright © 1974 by The Hearst Corporation
959 Eighth Avenue, New York, N.Y. 10019
Library of Congress catalog card number: 74–21668
ISBN 0–910990–12–3
This book was designed by
William Bossert
Composition, printing and binding by
American Book–Stratford Press,
Saddlebrook, N.J.

Acknowledgments

THE NUMBER of people who have graciously consulted with me in the preparation of this book are so many that it would be impossible to list them all. In gratitude and thanks, however, I must single out those individuals whose expenditures of time and patience far exceeded the helpfulness and courtesy normally extended to a writer preparing a specialized book.

To the U.S. Coast Guard, especially to the men at the Galveston, Texas, Station, may I express my thanks; not excluding Admiral W. J. Smith, Commandant U.S. Coast Guard, and Captain V. J. Mitchell, Chief of Boating Education, who made my visits to the Coast Guard facilities at Galveston and New Orleans possible, and who opened the Search and Rescue investigation files for my use; also to A. J. Rohlfs, Marine Supervisor, National Weather Service Marine Center, New Orleans; Davis Benton, Chief Meteorologist, National Weather Service, Galveston; and Norman Prosser, Chief Principal Assistant Meteorologist, Denver, go my special thanks for enduring what must have seemed endless questioning; and to Miss Lisabeth Brimm and John P. Pollock, I owe a debt of gratitude. To Rear Admiral R. A. Keating (Ret), I wish to say thanks for helpful suggestions based on the wisdom gained through more than a quarter of a century as a U.S. Navy navigator. Finally, there are too many others to say thanks to here, but I must acknowledge the cooperation and guidance of the people in the Weather Section of the National Aeronautics and Space Administration at Houston.

Preface: Doing Something About the Weather

YOU LOVE the outdoors—the sea, the sky, your favorite lake or river, the part of the trout stream where you were lucky once. You feel a part of that outdoors. It isn't so much that you feel you own the bay or the hills; rather, it's that they own you.

To be a part of the outdoors is to know the weather. You want to feel the east wind in your face, watch the scudding clouds, and say "Rain this afternoon," and be right. You want to know which side of the Sound is the right one to take in your boat this weekend, which is like knowing where the water won't be so rough. You want to know *when* the fog will lift, where the signs of nature are that tell you about:

storms
clouds
winds
rain
fog
fishing

and when it's safe to go out, when it's prudent to hug the shore or stay in harbor.

You are a sailor, a camper, a fisherman, the owner of a canoe, an open runabout, or a 40-foot cruising boat. You may be planning on buying a snowmobile. You perhaps go hunting every fall. Indeed, all these words may describe you if you're like many outdoorsmen. You are part of the water, the hills, the beach. You want to feel that you are part of the weather.

This is what Thorn Bacon has written about . . . the outdoorsman's weather. Some of his ideas are as contrasting as the changeable moods of the sky itself. At first you may think he's spoofing you about nature's signs and the old rhymes from 1722. Again, you may feel like it's sort of rough going to figure out weather patterns and how they move from west to east. You didn't plan on learning the science of meteorology.

Yet, you already know part of it. You know that a big anvil-like cloud means a thunderstorm, high winds, and appropriate carefulness. After you have followed Bacon through some of the explanations, you'll see much more in the clouds, you'll know much more what the simple available instruments can tell you, and most of all, you'll be able to follow the weathercasts in newspapers and on the air.

On the air? One friend of mine was sailing in a small boat on a Saturday afternoon, listening to a nearby ball game on his portable radio. When the announcer told about the high gusts churning up the stadium, he realized there was a squall line somewhere near. He looked for it, took down his sail in time, and avoided a capsizing. It takes a touch of wisdom to *do* something about the weather.

So much for Mark Twain and "but nobody ever does anything about it." Here are some things you can do about your weather. Let's say in ten days time you're set for a cruise in your boat, a camping trip, or a fishing trip into a wilderness area. You can clip the daily newspaper weather map for a week, and watch the lows and highs and fronts moving toward you. You can pay special attention to the same signs on your telecast weather program, even making a note or two. You can write down which radio stations have complete weather information at which hours, and put the notes with your portable radio. You can watch your barometer, several times a day, and note what the pattern of movement is before your vacation starts.

And you can put all this together with Thorn Bacon's lore from many years of camping and fishing and boating, and be your own weatherman on location for a few days, without the television, without a miniature weather station of your own, without a lot of scientific knowledge. You can use one of his chapters at a time; you can keep a weather log, or just learn to always notice which direction the wind is blowing from. That's one of the real marks of an experienced outdoorsman. It helps him to pitch a tent, build a campfire so the smoke won't be a nuisance, or plan an afternoon's sail. Oh, at first the novice can hardly tell where the wind is from. And then he doesn't know which way north is.

But *you,* you'll do better than that. Like many another outdoorsman, you have already started balancing a little practical weather watching with a little reading. You listen to the old hands in the boat yard, and know whether they're right or not.

Speaking of the old hands in the boat yard: there was a time, and it was long ago, when my family and I drove into the yard of the City Island Yacht Club one Saturday morning, with bags full of food and drink, ready for a weekend of boating. But a wise old gentleman, known to many people over the decades, took time out to talk with me for a few minutes. The wind was a little damp and chilly, and Eddie Quest made an observation: "It's blowing from the East, and it will be cold and wet all day, and most of tomorrow. I don't think you want to go out this weekend."

I listened, and knowing Eddie Quest had been around Cape Horn before he settled down to running boat yards and advising sailors about their rigging, I listened well. We didn't go out. Sure enough, it rained and blew for two days.

I realized Eddie knew how to tell the real weather just by noticing which way the wind was coming from—and eventually I realized a special wisdom. For that part of the country, at the Western end of Long Island Sound, that's the first rule: if it starts blowing from the east, be cautious. You don't have to figure out what *every* direction means, just that Easterly is enough to start on. Later on, as Thorn Bacon tells you, there are a score of other signs that are worth a little thinking about, to tell what the fish will be doing, or when to take an extra sweater along.

It's the best part of the outdoors, the weather is, and the only thing you can do about it is understand it and work with it.

John R. Whiting

Introduction

MANY BOOKS have been written about the weather, but there is very little non-technical material in print. The reader who seeks to learn about weather by reading the sky, winds, the motion of the tides, the shape of the clouds, soon becomes discouraged when confronted with terms like Adiabatic Lapse Rate (rate of decrease of temperature with height), or Frontolysis (the process leading to the disintegration of a front). Most everyone has a natural interest in the weather, but few of us have the mathematical training or the patience to wade through the dry, textbook language of modern meteorology which has eliminated the romance of weather from its jargon.

There is a profound and delightful difference between skillful personal weather observation and the meteorological accuracy of the professional weatherman whose forecasts are based upon computerized data from all over the world.

A common complaint of the trained meteorologist is that he seldom gets a chance to look at the weather. The daily bread of his eyes is not the moving sky but the machines in his insulated office that receive coded information from weather sensing stations he may never have seen in person.

In the course of researching this book, I have talked with dozens of weathermen, many of whom confessed that they once thought that delving into the anatomy of raindrops, or measuring the frightening energy in a tornado, would be as exciting as the crackle of thunder that enthralled them as children. When they understood what I hoped to accomplish in this book, I detected a wistful desire among these men to participate themselves more fully in rediscovering the great legacy of weather lore that has largely been discarded or forgotten. It is much more fun to watch a squall line forming, knowing in advance how the winds will shift, than being a closeted architect of weather equations.

This, then, is not just another weather book on the changing state of the art in weather analysis. Rather it's a new sort of book in the respect that it is selective of those facts (and theories) that the sportsman requires as a guide to better, more enjoyable, boating, fishing, camping, and sailing. As a weather guide, the book's purpose is to teach the sportsman how to forecast tomorrow's weather, and to help him learn about the mechanics of the atmosphere. But more importantly, by having an understanding of how the weather makes up, changes, is born and reborn in moody cycles, the sportsman should gain a greater sense of self reliance, and hopefully, the good feeling of having penetrated some of the mysteries about our endless weather.

There are countless clues and guideposts which nature has placed at our disposal, as aids in anticipating changes in the weather and as helpful hints in natural navigation. These clues were well known by our forefathers, earlier explorers, and the pioneers among such perceptive primitives as the American Indians and the Polynesians.

But it only has been in the recent past few years that the science of meteorology has taken cognizance of this treasury of weather-wise facts. Old ideas, once debunked as foolish weather sayings, are now being reevaluated. Many folklore prophecies have been proven true, and form the basis of a whole new body of weather information.

Much of this information is not readily available to the sportsman. It resides in the vast environmental data files of the National Oceanic and Atmospheric Administration; in the largely uncorrelated researches being undertaken at dozens of major universities all over the world, covering subjects as seemingly disparate as volcano analysis, fish migration, salinity ratios in the seas, biological rhythms in animals, detection of water currents, wave propagation, magnetism in raindrops—the list is staggering.

In this book the sportsman will find answers to many questions that have puzzled him. Certainly, as a dedicated fisherman, I have been puzzled on many occasions as to why fish feed voraciously on certain days and pass up the best you can offer them on others. As science is learning, there are sound reasons for this selectivity. Part of the explanation lies in the weather around us. And that is the trouble. We are so used to our weather that we take it for granted. Seldom do we stop to think how all-embracing it really is; how totally related are the earth, sea and sky, and how the combined effects of this relationship dictate a cyclic behavior in every living thing. The fish that fail to rise on certain days do so because they are responding to some environmental clue that we have either failed to apprehend or have overlooked.

Thus, here you will find methods of observing and interpreting the evidence of how the interplay of weather factors affects the feeding habit of fish—how stratification of water and its temperature determines the depths at which different kinds of fish lie, drift, or swim.

Everybody's heard the adage that lightning never strikes in the same place twice. Is this true? Lately, meteorologists have been deliberately triggering lightning at sea. Their fascinating discoveries about the nature of uninvited electricity have provided some startling new information about lightning protection for boating sportsmen.

Can you recognize interfaces in water where fish congregate, and where the hunting skin diver will often find his best kills?

Did you know there were more then 5,000 boating accidents in the United States in 1973, with over 1,000 fatalities, a large number attributed to failure of the boat operator to anticipate or act wisely in view of prevailing weather conditions? Through the cooperation of the U.S. Coast Guard, accident reports based on official U.S.C.G. Search and Rescue Missions are analyzed in this book. Existing weather at the time of accident is examined, commentary offered and conclusions of error drawn—all to the purpose of making boating safer.

Clouds, tides, currents and waves, questions and answers about the weather sayings of old sailors, why fish bite and why they don't, heavy weather antics explained, using nature's signs to predict the weather—these are some of the subjects treated in this book. It is a book for all readers who have a compelling curiosity and a warm feeling for this old weather-wreathed earth. It is for the pleasure boatman who speculates in awed wonder at the glorious sight of twin rainbows in the sky—for the seasoned skipper who knows as well as a bowline knot the shape and meaning of every cloud in the sky, but can't identify them by name, and it is for the weather novice who would aspire to know more than the thought expressed by Shakespeare: "In nature's infinite book of secrecy, a little I can read." Finally, it is for all the good and wonderful people who look at the sky and are worried because on some days it is dimmed by civilization's dust, and they ponder how long it will remain true that the sky is the only part of the world man will not change because he cannot.

Contents

CHAPTER ONE

Folklore Sayings
of Sailors and Fishermen

IT IS A SHAME that so many of the old American weather sayings have been lost. Through disuse, they've simply disappeared from our language. At one time many of these colorful prophecies were printed in almanacs. But hundreds of these shrewd observations coined by sailors, farmers, woodsmen and fishermen were never printed in any form. They were simply passed down from one generation to the next by word of mouth, as part of the rich heritage of living philosophy that reflected an everyday concern with weather in America.

Not too long ago, I presented an editor friend with an outline for an article which I wanted to write for his magazine. It was to be called *Folklore of American Weather*. I warned him in advance that it had already been turned down by another editor whose remark was that Americans do not want to learn about the weather, or read about weather folklore, they just wanted to know whether or not it will rain tomorrow. He added, also, that it was too philosophical.

I liked best this objection the editor advanced for politely refusing the article, for like many of us, he had become too civilized to place himself in the primitive role of our far-removed ancestors who as tribesmen or as seed gatherers came to know intimately the warnings of wind and cloud and the signs of the moon. Later our ancestors turned to verbalizing their weather observations and raising gods to intervene for them against the elements. But the language of reason and its opposite, superstition—which has often been too little or too much of nothing—inevitably found its most perfect, or craftiest expression on the tongue of some cunning explicator whose facility with words recorded not the truest but the catchiest weather proverbs, and they survived in error. This one is from the English:

> *Frogs croak before a rain,*
> *But in the sun stay quiet again.*

The error was compounded when men from other nations who spoke different languages changed these lines of foolishness, not because of arrogance, but because in their tongue the last two words in each line did not rhyme. But the sailors and hunters turned farmers still clung to those traditional proverbs whose testing had proved, at least in a majority of times, that they could be relied upon to forecast the weather with reasonable accuracy.

The editor who did buy my *Folklore of American Weather* article agreed with me that it was important to separate the weather-wise proverbs from those which are patently ridiculous, and which fit into the jackass jingle category. He also shared with me the conviction that most people have an abiding interest in the weather, and while many may not wish to learn the sophisticated mechanics of weather making, most everybody likes to be weather-wise, and likes to test the accuracy of old weather sayings, especially if in the testing they can learn something that is both practical and useful.

The point to remember about folklore prophecies is the fact that they are generally regional in origin, but at the same time may hold true for other localities. The National Weather Service lumps most of them into the category of "single space" forecasting. Single space forecasting refers to all the weather you can see, from horizon to horizon. But since we all live in a single space, or travel from one single space to another, our present locality is the one we are concerned about.

Now, the real value of these homely sayings is that they give definite information for any single space you happen to be occupying. If you consider that the National Weather Service can predict and plot what is happening over the horizon—a high or low pressure area moving in—but cannot promise exactly what will happen in a specific locality or single space, then reliable folklore sayings indeed become valuable.

I stress the word reliable, for I have spent many hours with meteorologists to verify the accuracy of the folklore sayings printed here. Those that were doubtful I threw out. Those remaining here meet the test of meteorological accuracy, and the explanations given for them reflect that if the old timers didn't know the reason why, for example,

When the moon wears a halo
Around her head, she will cry
Before morning and her tears
Will reach you before tomorrow,

they were at least weather-wise enough to know it was going to rain.

Following, then, are time-tested folklore sayings, portents that have the stamp of approval of modern weather science. They are divided into two categories: Sailors' Weather Sayings and Fishermen's Folklore Prophecies.

SAILORS' WEATHER SAYINGS

Mackerel Skies and mare's tails
Make tall ships carry low sails.

If high-flying cirrus clouds are few in the sky and resemble wisps in a curled broom or a mare's tail in the wind, this is a sign of fair weather. Only when the sky becomes heavy with cirrus or mackerel clouds—these are cirro-cumulus that resemble wave-rippled sand on a beach—can you expect a storm coming. There is an exception to the above, however. If cirrus clouds form as mare's tails with the hairs pointing upward or downward, the probability is for rain, even though the clouds may be scattered.

Lightning from the west or northwest will reach you.
Lightning from the south or southeast will pass you by.

This is a true saying, if you live in the north temperate zone: Lightning comes hand in hand with storm clouds, and thunderheads always loom over the horizon from the west or northwest, and usually move east. So lightning anywhere from the south or southeast will pass you by.

Red sky at morning—
Sailors take warning;
Red sky at night—
Sailors' delight.

There is a simple explanation for this ancient and quite reliable proverb. Actually, it probably originated before the time of Christ, but not a few people are surprised to find it in Chapter 16 of Matthew. Christ is quoted as having said: "When it is evening, ye say, It will be fair weather; And in the morning, It will be foul weather today, for the sky is red and lowring."

The red sunset alluded to by Christ was the sun viewed through dusty particles in the air, the nuclei necessary for the formation of rain. This air probably would reach an observer the following day. Since weather tends to flow west to east in most places, if tomorrow's weather appears to the west as a line of wetness, the sun shining through the mass appears as a yellow or greyish orb. On the other hand if the weather lying to the west is dry, the sun will show at its reddest.

Some professional weathermen might take exception to this simplified explanation by pointing out that various forms of air pollution reduce the dependability of this ancient proverb. The question weather scientists are still trying to solve is what kinds of dust in polluted air form the nuclei suitable for the formation of raindrops. It is, however, true that the smear on our skies created by industrial smoke, and automobile fumes, do tint the sunlit air with unnatural colors—red, yellow, or even a billious green. It also is true that this old saying is basically quite reliable, particularly when you have removed yourself from the visible evidence of air contamination. Red sky in the morning is caused by the rising, eastern sun lighting up the advance guard of high cirrus and cirrostratus, which will be followed later on by the lowering, frontal clouds. Red sky at night—a red-tinted sunset—often derives from the sky clearing at the western horizon, with the clouds overhead likely to pass before the night is done.

Rainbow in morning
Sailors take warning;
Rainbow toward night
Sailors' delight.

This also is quite an old weather jingle, and a little reasoning, particularly in view of the explanation above, would tell you it is true.

As we learned, storm centers usually move from the west. Thus, a morning rainbow would have to be viewed from its position, already in the west with the sun shining on it from the east. The storm would move in your direction and you could confidently expect rain. However, an evening rainbow, viewed to the east would tell you that the storm has already passed. The following, another old seafarer's saw about rainbows, is certainly worth remembering because it is almost infallibly true:

Rainbow to windward, foul fall the day;
Rainbow to leeward, rain runs away.

This one is so chock full of common sense an explanation hardly seems necessary. If a rainbow is behind or with the direction of the prevailing wind, then you can expect its curtain of moisture to reach you. But if the rainbow appears to the lee of the wind, then you know rain has already passed and the grey line of showers is receding, moving away from you.

Winds that swing against the sun
And winds that bring the rain are one.
Winds that swing around the sun
Keep the rain storm on the run.

This old saying is based on the direction a weathervane is pointing, but observing a flag will do as well. It means that a wind that changes its direction so it moves from east to west, as the sun moves, almost always issues in clear skies. But a wind that changes against the sun's movement, blowing first from the west, then the east, brings dirty weather with it.

A backing wind says storms are nigh;
But a veering wind will clear the sky.

Backing and *veering* are terms that describe changes in wind direction relative to an observer using the horizon as a clock: A wind direction that changes clockwise—blowing, for example, first from the south, then southwest, then from the west, is a veering wind. A wind that changes its direction in a counter-clockwise fashion is a backing wind—from south through southeast to east, let us say. This folklore observation generally refers to storms running in a southerly direction.

Shape and color of the moon as indicators of coming weather changes have long been a subject of controversy, mostly among those meteorological experts in whose rankling opinion the moon has no appreciable control over the weather beyond a very small tidal effect on the atmosphere. But for now, let's be content with the observation that as far as weather portents are concerned, the moon is one of the most visible and absolutely reliable signs of weather change. It is not so much the moon's influence that makes the following sayings ring with truth, as it is other atmospheric modifications that influence the moon's appearance.

Sharp horns on the moon threaten high winds.

When you can clearly see the sharp horns or ends of a crescent moon with your naked eye, it means there are high-speed winds aloft which are sweeping away cloudforms. Inasmuch as these high winds always descend to earth, you can predict a windy day following.

When a halo rings the moon or sun
The rain will come upon the run.

Halos are excellent atmospheric signs of rain. The sun setting with a whitish or pale yellow color indicates that it is shining through tomorrow's weather. In the U.S., and most other places, weather tends to flow from west to east. Thus a pale sun indicates rain. If the air to the west is dry, the sun appears red. Halos around the moon after a pale sun confirm the advent of rain, for you are viewing the moon through the ice crystals of high cirriform clouds. When the whole sky is covered with these cloudforms, a warm front is approaching, bringing a long, soft rain.

Let's look at two other halo proverbs, which at first reading may seem to be contradictory:

A halo around the sun indicates the approach of a storm within three days, from the side which is the most brilliant.

Halos predict a storm at no great distance, and the open side of the halo tells the quarter from which it may be expected.

These two sayings are more explicit in their forecasting and deserve an explanation. As cirrus and cirrostratus fronts push across the sky in the region of the sun, the halo first appears and subsequently becomes brightest in that part of the arc from which a low pressure system is approaching. Later, the halo becomes complete and the light is uniform throughout. As the storm advances, altostratus clouds arrive and obliterate the original, and for a time, the brightest part of the halo—that is, the side nearest the oncoming storm. Both proverbs are true, but refer to different times in the life history of the halo.

It is also true that when halos are double or triple, they signify that cirrostratus clouds are relatively thick, such as would be the case in a deep and well-developed storm. Broken halos indicate a much disturbed state in the upper atmosphere, with rain close at hand.

Now, to put any confusion at rest about the forecast persistence of rain by the appearance of sun and moon halos, the U.S. Weather Service has verified through repeated observations that sun halos will be followed by rain about 75% of the time. Halos around the moon have a rain forecasting accuracy of about 65%.

When the far lighthouse stands sharp in thinning air,
The weather promise is for warm and fair.

This is false. Landlubbers, and sailors too, are often misled by a clear day when the sky is sharp and far-away objects appear close and distinct. Look for rain the day following such a high level of visibility, particularly along coastlines. Reason: In good weather, salt water evaporates fast and this causes a haze which obscures or smudges the sharp outline of the horizon, causing low visibility. Unstable air, however, diffuses the salt haze, creating the illusion of distant points looming closer. Sure as can be, it will rain within 24 hours. The correct version of this proverb reads:

The further the sight,
The nearer the rain.

When boat horns sound hollow,
Rain will surely follow.

Anyone who has spent any time around boats knows the truth of this time-honored prophecy. Nor do you have to be sitting on a piling in a marina to notice the unusual sharpness of sounds on certain days—the more penetrating sound of a bell ringing or voices that carry longer distances are signs of the acoustical clarity when bad weather lowers the cloud ceiling toward earth. The tonal quality of sound is improved because the cloud layer bounces the sounds back, like the walls of a canyon echo a cry. When the cloud barrier lifts, the same sounds dissipate in space. Another (English) version of this saying goes like this:

Sound traveling far and wide
A stormy day does like betide.

This suggests that you actually can hear bad weather approaching, say, when a faraway train whistle is audible when normally it would be faint. The reason the sound carries farther is because the whistle was blown under a lowering cloud ceiling whose extending barrier may not have reached your position yet.

Counterclockwise round a low,
The whistling wind will sink and blow.

High and low pressure (which will be discussed in another chapter) are the keys to understanding this weather saying. For the present think of high pressure as being represented as a mountain of density and air will flow from the mountain high to a valley of low pressure. If it were not for the Coriolis force (another term with which you will become more familiar), any object sliding down a mountain would follow a straight line into a valley of low pressure. However, and this is where amateur weather buffs run into trouble, if you were to whiz down a mountain representing a high pressure contour on a pair of roller skates, your track downward would describe descending circles in a *clockwise* direction. In other words, winds of "high pressure" spiral down the sides of a mountain to the left, while winds of low pressure flow *counterclockwise* inside the valley or depression. This low pressure veering to the right is the result of the Coriolis force at work.

Perhaps this can be made clearer if you pretend that you are standing at the North Pole with a bow and arrow. When you let loose with an arrow aimed at a target located at the equator, the arrow would describe a straight flight. But the target would have moved with the rotating earth to the right. If instead, you fired an arrow from the equator at a target stationed on the North Pole—you guessed it—it would miss too, bearing left, instead of right of the mark.

So the winds of a high, which are normally composed of cold, dense, Polar air, are subject to the right deflecting Coriolis force in the Northern Hemisphere, while winds of a low spiral counterclockwise downward, as if descending to the bottom of a well. The point to remember is that winds of lows act like the warm moist air of Southern Hemisphere latitudes, veering to the left.

Now, because winds of low pressure describe counterclockwise circles, it is an easy matter for a person to locate the nearest storm area. Simply face into the wind and point with your arm to your right. If a low pressure area is coming from the west, say San Francisco, at a rate of 400 miles per day, and you live in San Antonio, Texas, it should reach you in about four days. A good exercise is to follow a low pressure area you've discovered by this method on a weather map.

The wind always favors the shore at right angles.

Even a good many experienced sailors seem uninformed about this fact. And it is one that has been the cause of not a few accidents. As one Lake Michigan weekend sailor once told me, "the wind blows the same way near the shore as it does a mile or so out." Not wishing this gentleman any embarrassment, his statement is quite misleading. Wind, whether onshore or offshore, almost always blows at right angles to the land. If an onshore breeze is striking the shoreline at an angle, it tends to shift so that its direction is straight in, or in the case of an offshore breeze straight out. This can be easily tested, for as you approach the shore, you will encounter a wind shift line—the wind changes and its orientation is more direct or at right angles to the land. This is a good rule of thumb to follow; the reason for it has to do with the interchange of heating and cooling explained in Chapter 2.

FISHERMEN'S FOLKLORE SAYINGS; TRUE OR FALSE?

There is probably no body of American folklore so jam-packed with misconceptions, gullibil-

ity, superstition, plain foolishness and downright lies as the collection of sayings—mostly myths—that have sprung out of the mouths of our ubiquitous fishermen.

If there are any common denominators or failings that adequately characterize the optimistic creatures with bait bucket and line, they would have to be found in this paraphrase of Mark Twain: Persons attempting to find a motive for fishing will be prosecuted; persons attempting to find a worm of truth in most fishing proverbs will be banished; persons attempting to find a plot in fishing methods will be shot.

However, notwithstanding the fact that the majority of fishermen's folklore sayings represent a gullibility and inconsistency that would put a fish to shame, here are, nevertheless, some real nuggets of information among those fishing proverbs that have survived scientific weeding out:

When smoke curls down and ditches reek,
The wise angler heads straight for the creek.

This saying indicates that humid air has flowed in, accompanied by a lowering of atmospheric pressure. The previous high pressure of fair weather has kept odors in ditches, creeks and swamps close to the ground. But when the pressure lowers, these captive smells are released and there is a richer, more pungent smell to the fields, streams and to the tiny marine life upon which fish feed. Actually, this proverb should be used in connection with the next one, because it explains certain behavioral characteristics of fish during times of low pressure.

Before a rain the fishes rise
And nimbly catch incautious flies.

As was pointed out in the foregoing, a lessening of atmospheric pressure releases captive odors, but people also react. Corns ache, old wounds throb, human nerves complain due to a greater dehydration of tissues. Fish react, too, by developing sudden activity. The biometeorologists don't know exactly why a falling barometer affects feeding habits of fish, but they've come up with two deductions.

One is that a fish, no less than a human, responds to atmospheric pressure. In water it is subject to the same 15 pounds per square inch as a human in his airy environment, plus the pressure of the water depth in which it is swimming.

Figure 6—1

Whether fish detect changes in air pressure as extra pressure in the surrounding water or as changes in the equilibrium of gases in the water is not yet accurately known.

It is known that a fish feels the pull of gravity and reacts to it in the manner by which it maintains its state of fluid balance by inflating or deflating the air sac which lies along its backbone to compensate for continual variations in atmospheric and water pressure. This continual adjustment is, however, an unconscious function, just as humans take shallower or deeper breaths, depending on existing physical conditions. This compensatory inflating and deflating, it is believed, also triggers feeding responses. In other words, it is one of the many diurnal rhythms to which fish respond instinctively.

But fish do get restless, excited by weather changes. The other fascinating conclusion about low pressure effects on fish is that, like humans, when fish are frightened or nervous, they eat. One recent study of overweight people disclosed that they cannot distinguish when they are really biologically hungry.

Applying this to fish, we come up with this observation: Fish often don't know when they're hungry either. A falling barometer apparently triggers, not appetite, but nervousness. Sensing

the change in its fluid environment brought on by increased pressure, the fish reacts to some signal or life rhythm. Why, exactly, an impending rain

Figure 6—2

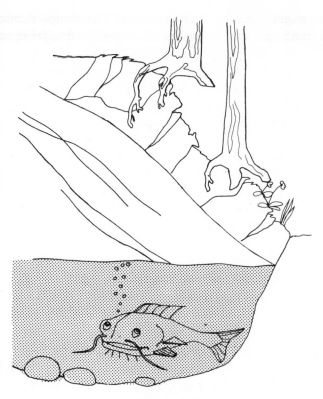

Figure 6—3

Wow, the river's rising! That means a real smorgasbord will come downstream, soon.

storm induces this false feeding, we don't know, but it does.

Channel catfish hold a banquet after a rain.

This saying has a great deal of merit. Weather-wise fishermen who run trot lines have profited by this knowledge for years. They know that a rainfall "chums" for them, releasing from up-stream drowned insects, worms, grubs—a variety of edibles that float downstream. It would be wrong to say that channel cats only feed after a rain, but it is certainly true that they feed much better when the water level rises. Rain upriver raises the level downstream, so the cats feed. A falling barometer is the best guarantee for a catfish fry.

When the moon is round and bright
Sore-mouth fish refuse to bite.

This is pure hokum. I've included this saying in this collection of fishing proverbs for the sole purpose of discrediting it in print. As far as I can discover, it is an Old South saying, as disreputable, and without foundation, as the one follow-ing. Apparently, it derives from the mistaken

belief that the rays of the full moon have a deleterious effect upon the brains of fish (lunacy) and this in turn induces a general leth-argy in the fish which affects its feeding habits. As to why a full moon would cause a fish to develop a sore mouth, I have not been able to find out, even after discussing the matter with at least a score of fishermen, who, notwithstanding the fact that they ardently believed a full moon does indeed cause fish to have sore mouths, could offer not one single reason for their conviction. Still, despite all evidence to the contrary, many fishermen are adamant that a bright round moon makes a sore-mouthed fish.

It's poor to fish that time of year
When "dog days" are looming near.

This is another one of those surviving folklore superstitions without any basis in fact. This de-rives from the South and is attributed to the fact that during, and after the Civil War, the period starting about July 26 and lasting about five weeks, was under the influence of Sirius the dog star. Since this period spanned some of the sum-mer's hottest weather, including periods of drought when people living in poor sanitary con-ditions were struck by the plague, the idea spread that illness came with the appearance of the Dog Star. People avoided the water, particularly, feel-ing fish were contaminated, and the eating of them would bring on madness.

Fish during dark of the moon,
Home with a fat string soon.

If we weigh the overwhelming evidence of thousands of fishermen who attest to better luck fishing in the dark, this saying has to be true. But aside from experience there are some sound ex-planations that fishing may consistently be better during certain hours of the night.

One is that fishery biologists have verified that some species prefer darkness so that they do not betray their movements to other predator fish. Another explanation has to do with the way all living organisms gain information about time and how they should react to it. This time sensing falls under the heading of invisible circadian rhythms (taken from circadies, "around a day") or time cycles, which underlie most of what we assume to be constant in the world around us. Though we cannot see nor feel them, we are nevertheless surrounded by rhythms of air pressure, sound, light waves, electromagnetic fields, and gravity—rhythms which animals, fish, trees and plants are far more attuned to because these living things still occupy a natural habitat.

As long ago as 1936 John Alden Knight wrote a book entitled *The Modern Angler,* in which he presented a theory that minor or major feeding times of fish corresponded to relative positions of the moon, earth and sun to one another at any given time of the year. Subsequently, Knight began publishing a pamphlet which he called *Solunar Tables,* of which 38 annual editions have now been issued. At that time, the science of biometeorology was still in its infancy, and the theory that Knight guessed at has been enlarged and largely verified by thousands of fishermen who swear by it, though it has not been scientifically tested.

Briefly, Knight's idea was that the sun and the moon exert a tidal pull upon the earth. And at certain times when the sun and moon are in the right juxtaposition—often during the dark of night with little or no lunar illumination—fish will feed voraciously. But they also feed just as hungrily during times of moon brightness.

We now know this much: All living organisms gain information about time and how they should react to it through a variety of atmospheric rhythms. The central nervous systems of plants and animals act as a kind of storage battery-receiver-transmitter. Say a variation in earth's magnetism or gravitational pull is recorded. By a process as yet not completely identified, memory cells in an animal's brain weighs this information and advise a course of action—feeding activity or a lull, or a danger signal to seek refuge.

In other words, for any geographical location, there is a continuous variation of atmospheric rhythms—the electromagnetic field, sound, light waves, and gravity, etc., in time. The fact that some fish may bite more readily in the dark of the moon may indeed be due to the fact that they are using murky water to camouflage themselves from predators, but it is also certain that intensities of light also trigger behavioral responses about which the average fisherman knows very little.

When humidity rides on the low tide,
The fisherman bestirs himself.

This saying refers to two atmospheric phenomena already discussed. Humid air signifies a lessening of atmospheric pressure, and things smell more pungently, alerting fish to the presence of insect and marine life. Too, low tide has always been a good time to fish because many denizens of the sea are captive in tidal pools until released by the next high tide.

Fish nose out an angler more quickly before a rain.

Many veteran fishermen will scoff at the answer for this one. But the saying happens to be true. It has been proved that fish not only can

Figure 6—4
Whew, there's something down here that smells deader than yesterday's mackerel!

detect various odors, but they give off certain odors that can be detected by other fish. This being so, it is more than plausible that during a period of low pressure, when odors are more distinct, fish will certainly smell a fisherman more plainly, if he is sweating, which is likely to be the case during the humidity of pre-storm conditions. The human skin is protected by a thin layer of a horny substance (the corneum) that is deader than yesterday's mackerel, and is apparently repugnant to a fish.

The biologists tell us that minnows can detect the presence by smell of a predator fish. Also, many types of fish can detect by lingering traces which other fish have recently vacated a space of water. Then why shouldn't a fish become excited, alarmed by the human odor? I know of one fisherman who believes so thoroughly in the olfactory abilities of fish that he wears skin-tight rubber gloves when skewering a worm on a line or cutting bait. It goes without saying that when fly fishing for trout or salmon, he will not enter the water without waders. It only remains to say that smell influences the fish profoundly. It directs many of its movements, and also often guides it to food. Low pressure enhances the odor of things, and since in fish the sense of smell is so highly developed that they can detect diluted substances—as low as several parts per billion in water—why shouldn't the alien human smell make them cautious and wary?

Fishing's better on the windward side of the stream.

There seems to be a rule, at least among some fishermen, that they catch fish on their terms, rather than those of the fish. This insistence that fish should accommodate the angler is fine if you like to stand on the edge of a bank and simply hold a pole in your hand as a brief resting place for dragonflies and other itinerant insects. However, the smart fisherman takes into consideration the effect of wind and rain on surface fishing and plans his strategy accordingly.

Rain and winds have a distinct bearing on when fish enter shallows. Though the leeward side of a lake or stream may be more pleasant on a windy day, the fish will generally be feeding on the windward side, from which the wind is blowing, where wave action stirs up morsels of food from the bottom, and where wind-driven insects are liable to strike the water. The rain "chums"

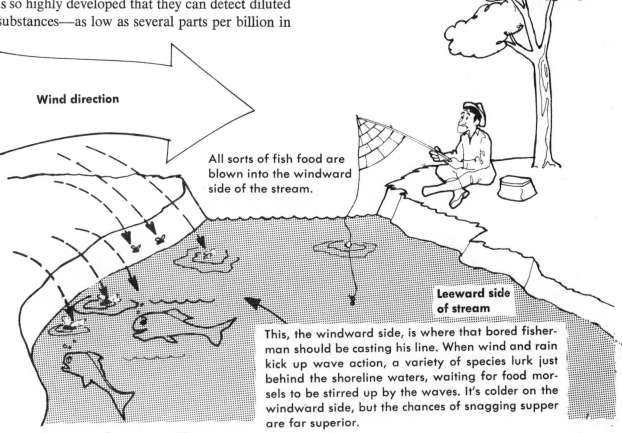

Wind direction

All sorts of fish food are blown into the windward side of the stream.

Leeward side of stream

This, the windward side, is where that bored fisherman should be casting his line. When wind and rain kick up wave action, a variety of species lurk just behind the shoreline waters, waiting for food morsels to be stirred up by the waves. It's colder on the windward side, but the chances of snagging supper are far superior.

Figure 6—5

for you, washing food into streams and lakes, alerting the fish to feed. Lake trout, Northern pike, largemouths, walleyes are just a few of the varieties that lurk just back of these turbid shoreline waters waiting for the food stirred up by windwave action. There is no question but that the windward side of a lake or stream is wetter and usually colder, but the results outweigh the discomfort. Remember, too, that following a downpour gamefish in a lake move into shoreline waters—the runoff from windward grassy slopes and banks contains a variety of edibles.

The majority of the weather proverbs that you have read in this chapter have to do with whether or not it will rain. They will make even better sense to you when you know how cloud formation takes place—the first step in becoming weatherwise.

CHAPTER TWO

All About Clouds

CLOUDS are the sculpture of the skies. Stop and think about this statement for a moment, please. Better still, if there is a window handy, step up to it and look out. If the sky is perfectly cloudless, imagine how dull it would be if it were forever to remain that way. Without movement, the sky would be faceless, a blank canvas of bland, blue stillness.

The prospect of unending cloudless sunshine is as unnerving as it is incompatible with the weather, but the idea serves to illustrate the obvious point I wish to make: Clouds give the sky its variety and character. Of course if this, and their rainmaking ability, were the only reasons for clouds, we could dispose of the evaporation, condensation, precipitation cycle quickly and go on to other things. But there are many reasons for clouds, and a knowledge of what these reasons are—of what clouds accomplish in the whole grand scheme of weather—can be of inestimable value to the sportsman.

Too, clouds are the concrete expression of the vital daily cycle of heat exchange around the earth, without a grasp of which no clear understanding of the mechanics of weather can ever really be mastered.

Poets, who as a rule, wouldn't know a cumulonimbus from an altostratus, have been dramatizing cloudforms from the time since man first became expressive enough to communicate his thoughts about the awe-inspiring heavens, and, whether they knew it or not, in words that display special insights into the function and purpose of clouds.

Shelley characterized cloudform in this way:

I am the daughter of Earth and Water,
   And the nursling of the sky;
I pass through the pores of oceans and shores;
   I change, but I cannot die.

A scientific interpretation of Shelley's lines would tell you that clouds are products of heat and atmospheric water. The sun's heat evaporates millions of tons of water into the air daily. Lakes, streams, forests, oceans, animals, trees and plants transpire water vapor (gas) in steadily ascending streams. As this moist, warm air rises, it cools slowly to the point where its relative humidity (water vapor content) reaches 100 percent. Cooled, the water vapor changes by condensation into visible moisture—clouds or fog. The elemental cycle is completed when clouds return moisture to the land and sea in liquid form, as precipitation.

"I change, but I cannot die."—this is the definition of a cloudform and the secret of cloud birth—the process of changing moisture from invisible gas into visible water droplets.

Two lines from a sonnet by another poet of the sky, James Thompson, contain some important clues about cloud behavior:

And of gay castles in the clouds that pass;
Forever flushing round a summer sky.

What about castle-like formations? Do they tell us anything? With practice it is possible to forecast summer weather reasonably accurately six hours in advance by observing cumulus clouds, particularly if you keep an eye trained on the development of their topmost regions. Towers of cumulus clouds, resembling fuzzily outlined castles or turrets—often three linked together—portend storms or heavy showers. There is less probability of a storm if these cumulus clouds do not build their castles in the air.

There are ten basic cloud types, as listed in the Cloud Classification Chart later in this chapter. These ten, which everyone who aspires to read the weather should memorize, were codified by Luke Howard, an English manufacturing chemist, in 1803. Since that time, science has taken some seven-league steps in the conquest of cloud knowledge, and Howard's slender classifications have been ponderously enlarged by weather experts who are constantly running into difficulties in arriving at a nomenclature that will satisfy aviation meteorologists, government environmentalists, oceanographers, and garden variety forecasters.

The meteorologist and author T. Morris Longstreth probably satirized the modern dilemma of precisely pigeonholing clouds when he wrote the following parody entitled the *Weather Bureau Hamlet:*

HAMLET: Do you see yonder cloud that's almost in shape of a stratocumulus castellatus translucidus?
POLONIUS: By the mass, and 'tis stratocumulus though there's a tinge of lenticularis opacus to it.
HAMLET: Methinks it verges on stratisformis undulatus.
POLONIUS: Undulatus like a sea serpent, but not stratiformis.
Floccus radiatus?
HAMLET: Floccus then, would you say? Floccus radiatus?
POLONIUS: Very likely a floccus, my lord, but rather cumulus humilis.
HAMLET: Ay, mighty humilis, as a forecaster needs be.

The argument goes on among the pundits, but for the sportsman it is enough to be familiar with Howard's basic classifications, updated to the present technology and amplified with short notes. As a practical guide, these 10 cloudforms, matched up to the existing clouds in your own locality, should give you a batting average in short term forecasting of about 75 percent.

In a later chapter, low and high pressure systems will be analyzed, but in order to understand thoroughly the machinery of clouds, it is necessary to know about atmospheric pressure.

Atmospheric pressure—the weight of air at any given altitude of measurement—is often difficult to comprehend because the term *pressure* is used rather than *weight,* which is easier to visualize. In *Figure 1-1,* a scale holds two imaginary containers filled with wet and dry air. Notice that the container of dry air is the heavier.

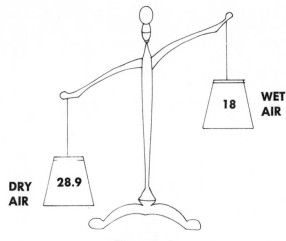

Figure 1—1

How can this be? I must admit this fact worried me briefly even after I made the elemental discovery that the molecular weight of dry air is approximately 28.9, up to certain altitudes, while the molecular weight of water vapor, or wet air, is only 18.

The reason dry air is heavier is that at any given atmospheric pressure it has more density because it is normally colder. Since it is colder and denser, it has more weight and sinks. For example, the air in a Polar Front is denser because its molecules have been packed together—compressed by lower temperatures. The weight difference between wet and dry air is so important to an understanding of cloud formation that it is now necessary to consider moisture in the air generally.

While it may seem to be an elementary observation (one we learned in grade school and probably haven't thought much about since), water is present in the atmosphere in three forms, and only one of them is wet: Ice is cold, perfectly dry until heat begins to melt it and turn it into water. The same is true of cold snow: It's dry until it melts. Similarly, water vapor, a gas, is another form of dry water. There is nothing damp, foggy, or wet about it until it begins to condense, changing into clouds of tiny droplets or beads of dew.

At first reading, "dry water," like dry air being heavier than wet, seems to pose an insoluble paradox. Water is wet, how can it be called dry? The answer is that moisture is present in the air at all times, but in its vaporous or gaseous state it cannot be seen, so it is considered to be *dry water* until cooling changes it. This is worth repeating a different way: Water vapor, always present in the atmosphere, remains dry until it becomes cool enough to condense.

Parcel of air

This is an invisible drop of cold, dry air which has a certain capacity to hold water vapor at a given temperature and atmospheric pressure.

This is the amount of water vapor present.

This represents its total capacity to hold water.

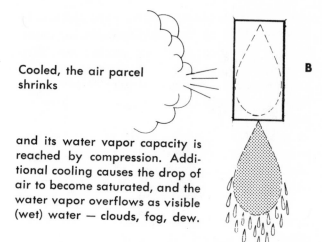

Cooled, the air parcel shrinks

and its water vapor capacity is reached by compression. Additional cooling causes the drop of air to become saturated, and the water vapor overflows as visible (wet) water — clouds, fog, dew.

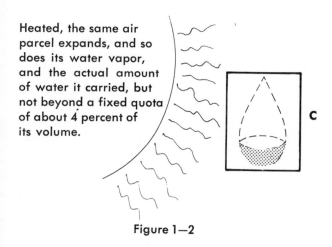

Heated, the same air parcel expands, and so does its water vapor, and the actual amount of water it carried, but not beyond a fixed quota of about 4 percent of its volume.

Figure 1—2

By referring to *Figure 1-2*, the dry air–dry water concept becomes clearer. A practical example taken from *Figure 1-2* is the fogging of the mirror in the bathroom after a morning shower. What has happened is that water vapor in the room has been changed from its dry, gaseous state to visible moisture. The hot stream of water

from the shower added more moisture to that already present in the room in an invisible state, thus raising the *dewpoint* until, at the temperature of the mirror over the basin, condensation took place and the mirror started "sweating." By past experience you know that you can clear the foggy mirror quickly by simply opening the door, allowing the bathroom air to mix with the air outside. As a result, you dry the room sufficiently to "raise" the mirror's temperature above the air's dewpoint. Yet all the moisture which you felt as dampness, or saw as fog on the mirror, is still present but has returned to a gaseous state.

Two definitions are now in order: *Dewpoint* and *humidity*.

Dewpoint: There is a limit to the amount of water vapor that can exist in any volume of air for each degree of temperature in the atmosphere. But as noted in *Figure 1-3*, vapor never

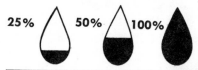

Drops pictured in the table express the percent of capacity for water vapor, up to saturation at 100%.

TEMPERATURE	RELATIVE HUMIDITY						
86° F.	16%	24%	31%	45%	57%	100%	
50° F.	52%	77%	100%	saturation			
	4.85	7.57	9.41	13.65	17.31	30.4	

(Grams of water per cubic meter)

Figure 1—3

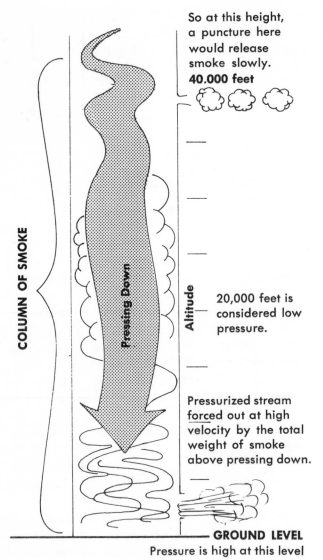

So at this height, a puncture here would release smoke slowly. **40.000 feet**

COLUMN OF SMOKE

Pressing Down

Altitude

20,000 feet is considered low pressure.

Pressurized stream forced out at high velocity by the total weight of smoke above pressing down.

GROUND LEVEL

Pressure is high at this level

Figure 1—4

reached its dewpoint, when it has acquired 30.4 grams of water vapor per cubic meter; conditions being right, it should rain. Notice though, that air at 50 degrees F. is saturated when it takes in only 9.41 grams of water vapor. This difference means that saturated air of 86 degrees F.— cooled to 50 degrees F.—would still have a relative humidity of 100 percent at the lower temperature, and also would release 20.99 grams of water—the difference between 9.41 and 30.4— as visible moisture in the form of rain or fog.

This brings us to the critical relationship of pressure to dry and wet air and temperature. Air pressure can be understood more easily if you think of a tower of smoke entrapped in a vertical column which extends high into the atmosphere. Air pressure, or weight, is lowest at the top of the column, as illustrated in *Figure 1-4*. At this elevation, a puncture would release smoke in dribbly puffs. Due to the pressure of all the smoke pressing down on the bottom layer, however, a hole jabbed in the column at ground level would cause the smoke to jet out in a high velocity stream.

The meteorologists express the relationship of pressure to water vapor changes in a series of complicated mathematical formulas. While the one following is not a mind-boggling equation, I am not going to attempt to reduce it fully here because one of its values (R) relates to a concept called the Universal Gas Constant, a discussion of which properly belongs in theoretical meteorology. However, if you understand that air is a mechanical mixture of several gases, but is treated as if it were composed of one gas only, then you've got the gist of the Universal gas Constant theory. Still, the equation itself is quite useful, if only as a reminder that there are physical laws which clearly tell us how a change in pressure, temperature, or density (any one of the three) produces the atmospheric circulation of the earth and the character of local skies.

If you have the tenacity to dig further into meteorological texts, the formula will tell you why, for example, a falling barometer indicates an approaching "low," accompanied by winds and rain—an event which reliably can be predicted by any weather-wise sportsman who takes the trouble to look at the sky and make a few simple surface observations.

In the equation $Pv = Rt$,
    P stands for pressure
    v is the volume of any unit of air

exceeds a maximum of about four percent. Thus, when a parcel of warm air is cooled to a temperature where its capacity to hold any more water vapor is zero, condensation occurs. The temperature at which this saturation happens is the dewpoint. And when the dewpoint and temperature are the same, clouds or fog will form.

Humidity is simply an expression of the amount of water vapor in the air. The term *relative humidity* has more meaning, since it expresses measurable quantities. It is defined as the ratio between the amount of water vapor the air actually contains at a given temperature and the amount it could hold if it were saturated at the same temperature. The brief table in *Figure 1-3* shows relative humidity at two temperatures and explains how measurable quantities are arrived at.

You will see in the upper column that air at a temperature of 86 degrees F. is saturated, or has

Figure 1—5

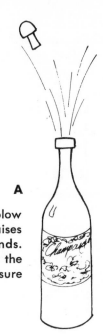

A

Heat champagne and it will blow its cork — because as heat raises the temperature, air expands. Since the volume of wine in the bottle remains the same, pressure goes up.

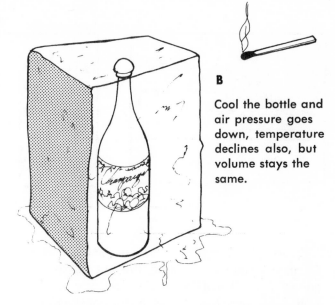

B

Cool the bottle and air pressure goes down, temperature declines also, but volume stays the same.

A

So the weather inside bottle A could be said to be in a state of high pressure.

B

while the weather in here could be described as low pressure.

The trouble with these simpified drawings is that weather changes: The volume of air is never conveniently fixed. By manipulating the temperature of wine in a sealed bottle, we know exactly what will happen. The equation $Pv = Rt$ told us that. Ideally, high pressure could be drawn as a mountain of air, while low pressure could be pictured as a valley. Please examine *Figure 1-6*. The contours tell you that in high pressure there is a mountain of density overhead pressing down. But in low pressure there is a valley of density making its lesser weight felt.

R is that Universal Gas Constant left to the meteorologists, and
t is temperature.

What it boils down to is that if air temperature is cooled, then to keep the equation balanced, it follows that pressure lowers. On the other hand, if temperature remains constant and volume lowers, pressure rises. Or if the pressure drops and volume doesn't change, then temperature will fall. The equation, then, actually reports that these values are vital, interchangeable parts in the odyssey of cloud formation and wind patterns. To better visualize this relationship, look at the champagne bottles in *Figure 1-5*.

But in low pressure there are rising air currents, turbulence and cloud formation.

High pressure: characterized by little or no rising air.

Fair skies and suntan weather

I must get out of these wet clothes and into a dry martini.

Figure 1—6

15

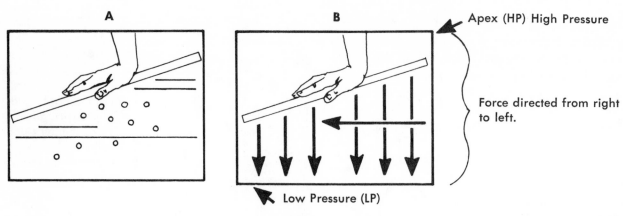

A

B

Apex (HP) High Pressure

Force directed from right to left.

Low Pressure (LP)

Figure 1—7

Years ago I saw a movie in which James Cagney played the role of an itinerant newspaper editor. I recall that he would "feel" the air by rolling his thumb and first finger together. Of course, nobody can measure the thickness of the air in this fashion. However, you can feel, see, and hear low pressure: Undoubtedly, if you own a boat or have spent any time around boat basins or harbors, you've heard on certain days a hollowness in the bleat of boat horns, as if their sounds were amplified in an echo chamber. This is an acoustical sign of low pressure. The cloud ceiling is lower and sounds reverberate back to earth with greater clarity, rather than radiating out to dissipate into the clear space of fair weather high pressure. Also, your sinuses can be an infallible barometer when the pressure is lowering.

Another way to visualize low and high pressure is to imagine that with the flattened palm of your hand you tilt water in a tank by pressing down upon it with a flat board. The pressure exerted by your hand on the board is equal to the force times the area of the board. So in meteorology this force is the MG—the force of gravity times the mass of air. The pressure exerted on the sloping water in Drawing B of *Figure 1-7* is greater to the right than to the left. Thus, the hand force pressing down directs the pressure from high to low.

In other words, the pressure at any depth in the tank is proportional to the depth—and since air is a fluid, the same is true of the atmosphere. If we were to draw horizontal lines of equal pressure through the water, we would be doing what the weatherman does when he inserts isobars on a weather map, expressing the variation of pressure with horizontal distance. The spacing of isobars indicates the *pressure gradient,* a term to be discussed more fully in a later chapter.

But viewing *Figure 1-7* may create a confusion because it seems to express a contradiction. There is actually more pressure being exerted at point LP, but it is called low pressure. To add to the confusion, the arrow pointing to the apex of high pressure indicates that at that point air pressure is lowest. How can this be? To clear it up once and for all, please remember that as altitude increases, atmospheric pressure decreases. With a normal distribution of temperature, the pressure on a mountain top is always less than at the bottom of an adjacent valley. A cubic foot of air at sea level weighs more than a cubic foot of air at any higher level. It is being compressed by the weight of all the air above it pressing down. Now, however, the weight of air also changes with temperature. So when a high pressure system moves in over Kansas, say, from Canada, it is always characterized as a mass of cold, dense, dry air which bears down on warm, humid air, plowing under and lifting the warm air up, much in the same fashion as a snow plow scoops up its load of snow.

Everybody knows that warm air rises. It does so because as its molecules are warmed by sunlight, by contact with the warm earth, it expands, and as it expands the population of its molecules decreases per cubic foot. The reverse is true of cold air whose molecules have been compressed, and so increased in number per cubic foot. Because of its lesser density, a column of hot air weighs less than an equally tall column of cold air, exerting less pressure. Thus, as warm air expands, the cooler, heavier air, under great pressure next to it, pushes sideways, forcing the warm air in the only direction it can go—up. This process is called *convection,* one of the cloud-making processes and the manipulator of local winds and breezes. If I were asked to pose a rule, it would be that there is little or no rising motion in clouds of high pressure—cold, dense air masses. Because of weight, these clouds descend and produce a settling effect. On the other hand, clouds of low pressure are always accompanied by rising warm air. *Figure 1-8* graphically illustrates how this vital role of heat exchange results in cloud formation. The accompanying cloud

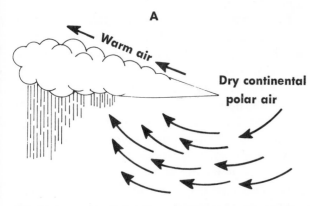

A

Warm air

Dry continental polar air

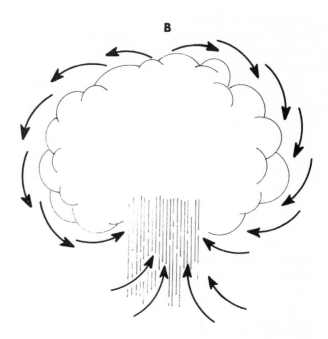

B

Warm air is forced to expand and rise to a level where dewpoint and temperature are the same, creating a relative humidity of 100 percent, and rainfall.

The full-grown cumulus is formed, and grows as the downdraft arrows of cooled air descend to lift more warm air from the bottom to feed the cloud.

Figure 1—8

photo, *Figure 1-9*, is a good example of convection current building a thunderhead.

The same process on a larger scale explains the circulation of air around the earth. Air at the equator receives much more heat than air at the poles. As a consequence, equatorial air rises and is replaced (in the northern hemisphere) by colder air flowing in from north to south. The

warm, light air ascends and moves poleward at high altitudes. As it cools, it sinks and replaces the cool surface air which has moved toward the equator. So, convection is the process that transfers heat from the tropics to the icecaps, and the thousands of places it touches in between. It is the manipulator of the sea breeze that blows in toward the hot land by day, and it is the welcome

Figure 1—9

This is cumulus congestus. At the right hand side of this photograph, notice the tower of cloudform building. If the process continues, the giant cumulonimbus would mature with a strong storm possibility in the offing. (Photo: Courtesy National Center for Atmospheric Research.)

land breeze that surges out to sea at night, after the earth has lost much of its heat by radiation. Understanding convection not only permits an understanding of why temperature is so interrelated with pressure, but clears the way to a brief explanation of how raindrops are formed in clouds.

For many years meteorologists theorized about raindrops, but couldn't back up their ideas with facts. And while there is still disagreement on the exact method by which raindrops are formed, the meteorologists now generally agree that cloud precipitation is created in two ways:

Warm rain that falls in large, splashy drops is believed to be caused by *coalescence*—the adherence of smaller drops to larger ones, much in the same way that a snowball rolling down a hill gathers more snow around it and grows bigger. This may be an electro-magnetic process, but so far the idea of electro-magnetic attraction has not been proved conclusively. Convection currents in the hot latitudes of the tropics are especially strong, forcing cloud droplets upward at a great rate. But as they drift downward, from the topmost regions of an updraft, the chances of collision with salt crystals evaporated from the seas are great. So, droplets forming around salt nuclei increase rapidly in size as they descend, gathering more droplets, and the snowball effect matures them into drops heavy enough to fall out of the clouds.

In the temperature zones, rainfall rests on the fact that most rainclouds have some ice crystals in their upper altitudes (in cumulonimbus clouds, near the middle). Water droplets present in the clouds evaporate, then condense on the crystals. These crystals grow until they drop as snow or ice pellets, but as they fall through the warmer air below, the higher temperatures change them into raindrops.

Pressure is measured by two types of barometers. The mercury barometer is in use by all stations of the United States Weather Service, and it is simply a glass tube sealed at the top and filled with mercury. The column of mercury is supported by the pressure of air upon a reservoir of mercury at the bottom of the tube. Mercury level in the tube itself is high, when the pressure is high outside, and low when the pressure decreases.

Figure 1-10 relates the mercury barometer to the mountain (high) and valley (low) comparisons of pressure. The mercurial barometer is

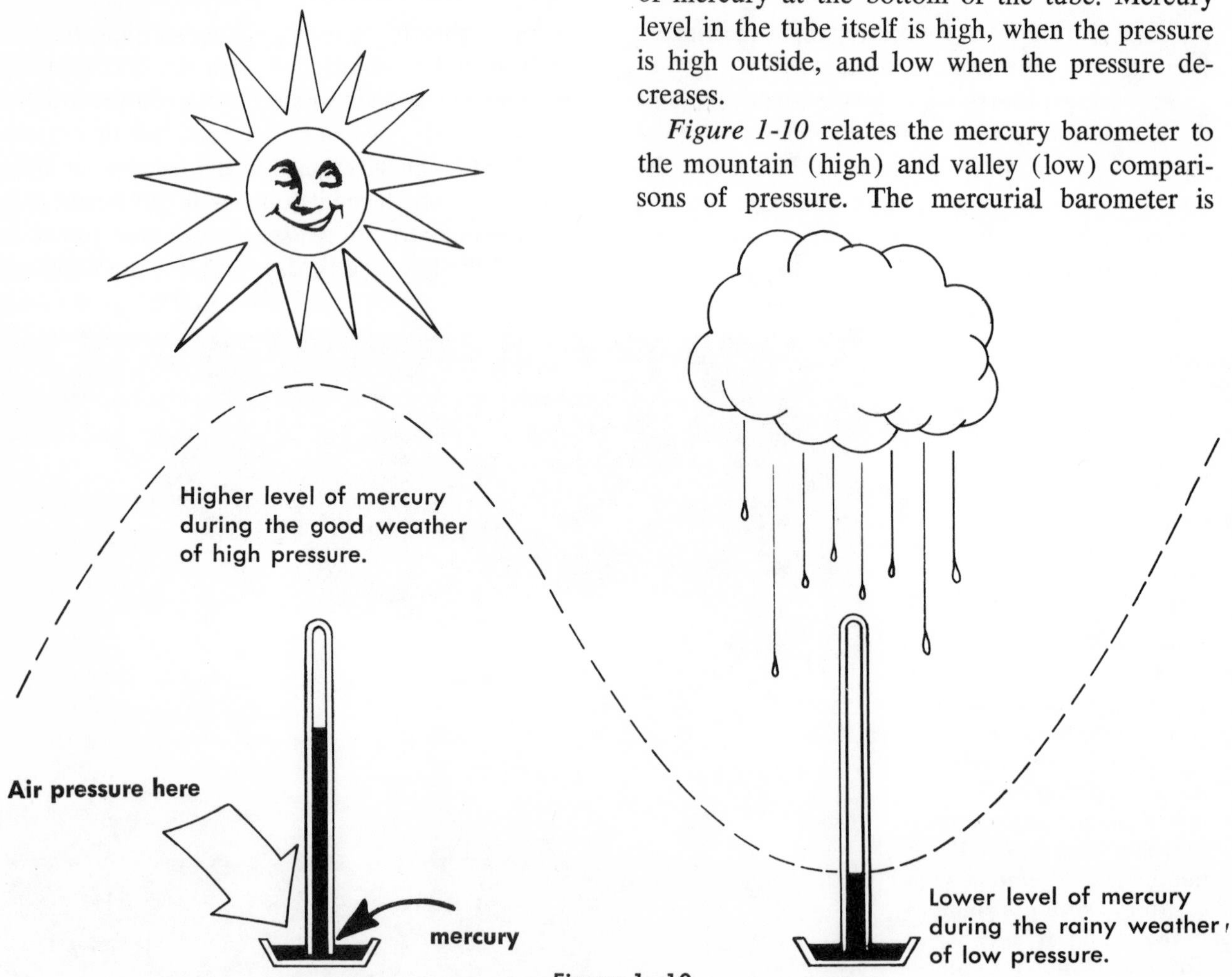

Higher level of mercury during the good weather of high pressure.

Air pressure here

mercury

Lower level of mercury during the rainy weather of low pressure.

Figure 1—10

18

simply a scale to measure weight, which makes it more efficient than the imaginary scale in *Figure 1-1* used to illustrate the difference between dry and wet air.

Physically, the barometer is a glass tube, slightly more than 30 inches long, closed at one end and partially filled with mercury. We are used to hearing weather reports which give the pressure in, say, New Orleans, at so many inches. What *inches* really means is that the barometer is counterbalancing a column of wet or dry air which is the same size as the mercury tube. The average sea-level height of mercury in a barometer is between 29 and 30 inches. Wet or dry air is the atmosphere the barometer measures—informing us of what to expect in the way of new weather.

Using. New Orleans as an example, we say cold, dry air has moved in. As "A" in *Figure 1-11* shows, it is heavier and exerts a strong push on the open side of the instrument, "B," forcing the mercury higher in the tube. In terms of contour lines, the high would represent a mountain of air flowing in, as in *Figure 1-10,* from left to right, from mountain into valley. We would say the barometer is rising.

The low in the valley is composed of warmer, lighter air and would not press down as hard. The mercury level would drop, and we would say that the barometer is falling. What the barometer is really saying, in this case, is that it will rain or storm soon, because as the cold air flows down into the valley it snowplows the warm air up, and the convection process leads to cloud formation and then to rain.

The barometer, therefore, simply indicates the relative weight of constantly changing air of different densities above the instrument. The most common barometer in use today is the aneroid barometer, which is based upon the action of a small, corrugated metal cell from which the air has been evacuated. (The altimeter on the instrument panel of an airplane is just another aneroid barometer.) The aneroid barometer works on the principle that as air pressure over the barometer changes, the sylphon cell (an accordian-like apparatus) compresses or expands. This change is reflected to a clock face dial through a system of links and levers.

The dial is calibrated to register atmospheric pressure as inches of mercury, or as millibars, or both. Novice barometer readers often get a bit fidgety when they notice slight changes on a dial reading scale. This is understandable because few people take into consideration the natural effect of diurnal or daily temperature changes which are fairly strong in southern latitudes, but disappear in latitudes above 60 degrees. These diurnal temperature changes are a result of heat exchange: The earth loses much of its heat by radiation after end of day, and the night ushers in a dense, heavier atmosphere, producing slight fluctuations in barometer readings; about .15 inches in the tropics and about .04 inches in the temperate zones. A slight fall in the barometer is not a signal for you to button up and batten down the hatches.

Since the barometer is quite sensitive to the atmospheric tide of diurnal variation, readings

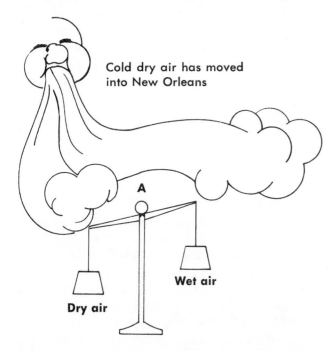

Cold dry air has moved into New Orleans

A

Dry air

Wet air

If we were to weigh it on a scale, it would be heavier than the warm air it displaces.

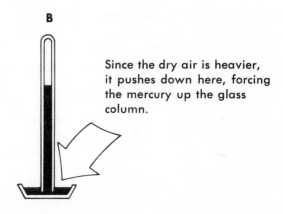

B

Since the dry air is heavier, it pushes down here, forcing the mercury up the glass column.

Figure 1—11

TABLE 1-1

WIND DIRECTION-WEATHER INDICATION CHART

Wind Direction	Barometric Pressure	Character of Weather to Expect
SW to NW	30.10 to 30.20—barometer steady	Fair, with little temperature change for 1 to 2 days
SW to NW	30.10 to 30.20—rising rapidly	Fair, with warmer weather and rain within 2 days
SW to NW	30.20 or above—barometer steady	Remaining fair with little temperature change
SW to NW	30.20 or above—falling slowly	Fair and slowly rising temperatures for about 2 days
S to SE	30.10 to 30.20—falling slowly	Rain without 24 hours
S to SE	30.10 to 30.20—falling rapidly	Rain within 12 to 14 hours. Wind will rise
SE to NE	30.10 to 30.20—falling slowly	Rain within 12 to 18 hours. Wind will rise
SE to NE	30.10 to 30.20—falling rapidly	Rain within 12 hours. Wind will rise
SE to NE	30.00 or below—falling slowly	Rain will continue 1 or more days
SE to NE	30.00 or below—falling rapidly	Rain with high winds in few hours. Clearing within 36 hours—colder in winter
E to NE	30.10 or above—falling slowly	Summer, with light winds: rain in 2 to 4 days. Winter, rain or snow within 24 hours
E to NE	30.10 or above—falling rapidly	Summer: probably rain in 12 to 24 hours. Winter: rain or snow within 12 hours
S to SW	30.00 or below—rising slowly	Clearing within a few hours. Then fair for several days
S to E	29.80 or below—falling rapidly	Severe storm within a few hours. Then clearing within 24 hours—colder in winter
E to N	29.80 or below—falling rapidly	Severe storm (a "nor'easter" gale) in few hours. Heavy rains or snowstorm. Followed by cold wave in winter
Swinging to W	29.80 or below—rising rapidly	End of storm—clearing and colder

should be correlated with other information. A wind direction indications table, nephoscope (for measuring cloud movement), barometer, and cloud classification chart add up to a pretty fair combination of sources.

The *table,* Wind Direction–Weather Indication Chart, is adapted from a U.S. Weather Service table based on average conditions in the United States.

At the beginning of this chapter, I noted the fact that in 1803 the English weather enthusiast Luke Howard got around to doing what no one else had done, giving 10 basic classifications to cloud types. The cloud classifications following are Howard's, updated into modern terms. They are preceded by an explanation of the three general divisions of clouds by height. If you remember these divisions and become familiar with the 10 cloud forms, you'll find enjoyment in the accuracy of your cloud forecasting.

There are three distinct cloud shapes, and there are three levels of height in which these cloud forms appear. The three levels of height are: the *low cloud level*—clouds whose bases form between land and 7,000 feet; the *medium cloud region*—cloud bases between 7,000 and 25,000 feet; and the *high cloud region*—where cloud bases occur between 16,000 and 45,000 feet.

Cirrus (Ci)—Detached high clouds that show no shadowing. The cirri sweep near the top of the troposphere, varying in height in the middle latitudes from 10,000 to 30,000 feet, and like long, white banners, achieve speeds up to 200 miles per hour. For all their serene streaking (in parallel lines) against the blue of a high pressure sky, they are one of nature's most reliable indicators of a storm. The storm probability of their presence is confirmed by a thickening of their narrow bands into cirrostratus, characterized as whitish veils of fibrous clouds covering part or all of the sky. The high-flying cirri shower ice crystals into slower winds below, helping to form depressions.

Cirrocumulus (Cc)—Cirrocumulus clouds resembled unclipped woolly sheep in long trailing groups. These woolly balls indicate a general unstable tendency associated with air layers that are lifting. This convection, and compensating falling of air, pushes this cloud form to heights between 10,000 and 30,000 feet. They paint mackerel skies, which if wet will shortly dry. Cirrocumulus will not show shadows.

Cirrostratus (Cs)—With cirrostratus, expect rain within about 24 hours. This cloudform can be identified as a continuous sheet showing no relief and not thick enough to smudge the outline of the sun and the moon. Cirrostratus is the slightest diffusion of cloud, but it portends a lifting over wide areas and to great altitudes. Fallstreaks—showers of ice from clouds high aloft, all streaming in approximately one direction—are one of the major clues to cirrostratus identification, and are a strong indicator that rain will develop.

Altocumulus (Ac)—Ragged rafts, or islands of varying size, but seldom covering the whole sky, typify altocumulus. The larger islands, or heaps, will show shading. The alto (higher) forms are composed more often of water droplets than ice crystals, and their range is between 6,000 and 20,000 or more feet. Thin, translucent edges of altocumulus cloudlets take on iris hues. In certain positions, these ragged cloud sheets exhibit the miniature castellated effect, warning of a change to showers. Often altocumulus looks as small and fine as cirrocumulus, but unlike the higher cloud, its makeup includes larger cloudlets with a darker color in the same layer. Generally, altocumulus appear about eight hours before rain, and if spotted forecast precipitation about 45 times out of 100. One poetic tongue-twister describes altocumulus as "ragged rafts that roam the random sky."

Altostratus (As)—Through these organized, flat and often featureless grey or bluish clouds, the sun and moon appear as if they were being viewed through ground glass, but with no halos. A steadily deepening altostratus is an almost certain sign of a long rainy spell, generally occurring within six hours of first sighting. Darker clouds may form beneath the undersurface of altostratus, especially near the horizon.

Stratocumulus (Sc)—Quite likely to be a roll cloud in groups forming a continuous layer, and darker on the undersurface. Sometimes stratocumulus arrange themselves in sombre grey lines toward the horizon. In winter, the rolls are so close that their edges join, causing a wavy appearance. Basically, Sc is a cloud form of unchanging situations, with normally light winds which shift, but not radically. Actually, Sc is a warm, moist tropical air mass, which, with a relatively strong wind, makes its appearance as the rear echelon of an active warm front. If it is seen forming near end of day, you can expect total sky cover by nightfall. If Sc gives up any rain, it will fall as a drizzle, or heavy mist.

Stratus (St)—This is a fog cloud, found at any level from 1,000 to 6,000 feet, with Nimbostratus lowering as close to the earth as 100 feet. It is described as featureless since it resembles a misty, grey curtain, only 50 to 100 feet thick, that falls close to the ground.

Nimbostratus (Ns)—This cloudform can be counted on about 75 percent of the time to yield rain, with a warning of less than four hours on the average. In appearance it is composed of a nearly uniform layer of low-flying forms. Ns is the lowest type of stratus cloud, as altostratus is the highest reaching member of the stratus family. It is not unusual, if high winds come in, for this cloud to break into shreds. If this fracturing occurs, Ns earns a new name—fractonimbus, which describes high, thin clouds shooting out in all directions, and portending heavy and lasting rainfall. This is often called the "scud" cloud, owing to a rearguard action, typified by scudding rags of cloud rolling along behind the rain storm. If this rearguard increases in size and height, look out for gale winds and slashing rain.

Cumulus (Cu)—A convection cloud formed by vertical air movement, the cumulus at the beginning may merely sit in a summer sky as a harmless puff, resembling a kernel of fluffy popcorn. But each puff lazes at the top of a column of rising warm air, and its underside indicates

Symbol as shown on a weather map	Shape	Height	Classification	Name
?	Feathery	10,000–45,000 ft.	Cirroform	Cirrus
ω	High Heap	10,000–45,000 ft.	Cumuliform	Cirrocumulus
⌐	Layer	10,000–45,000 ft.	Stratiform	Cirrostratus
ω	Medium-Level Heap	6,000–25,000 ft.	Cumuliform	Altocumulus
⌐⌐	Layer	6,000–25,000 ft.	Stratiform	Altostratus
⊽	Low Heap	Above Land to 7,000 ft.	Cumuliform	Stratocumulus
- - -	Layer	Above Land to 7,000 ft.	Stratiform	Stratus
◿	Layered-Vertical	Above Land to 45,000 ft.	Stratiform	Nimbostratus
⌂	Heap	From Land to 7,000 ft.	Cumuliform	Cumulus
⋈	Heap-Vertical	Above Land to 45,000 ft.	Cumuliform	Cumulonumbus

when cooling has reached the dewpoint. If you notice these puffs forming early, and they keep growing, they soon become thunderheads. But this does not mean they all will mature into the towering Cumulonimbus stage. This requires a thrust upward into the ice-crystal zone. This cloudform is most fascinating to watch, for you can see the violent swelling and upwellings as it grows. One indication that Cumulus has achieved the transition to Cumulonimbus is a shearing of the upper cloud edges, as if they were being strung out. This is a sign of high winds aloft, which are associated with the ice-crystal zone.

Cumulonimbus (Cb)—Everyone is familiar with this most awesome and magnificent of rain clouds. At its fullest development, it rears a mushroom or anvil head high into the sky. Meteorologically, Cumulonimbus is a sign that ascending vapor has penetrated the instant icing domain of the cirri. Mothered by Cumulus, Cb does not become an active rainmaker until its "brow is iced."

The thing to watch for is the development in the Cumulonimbus of a sultry darkening presaging the development of a major storm area, which may be lying in the wings with the more obvious thunderheads performing the first act in the heavy drama to come. One feature of Cumulonimbus is well worth mentioning in concluding a description of this cloudform: If you note udder-shaped protuberances extending from the underside of the cloud, and perhaps a greenish cast to the sky, you are looking at cumulonimbus with mama. This rare cloudform may be the precursor of tornados or waterspouts.

The foregoing descriptions of major cloudforms and the picture classification guide to cloud identification are the basic tools for the sportsman who aspires to be weatherwise. There are, however, three important clues to cloud behavior which should be noted in any weather log. These clues will help you forecast whether or not the weather is likely to remain stable, or take a turn for the worse.

Speed—Leisurely moving clouds generally mean continued fair weather, but if they scud across the sky, be prepared for rain and winds.

Direction—If higher clouds are flying in a direction different from that of prevailing winds below, or lower cloud movement, you can be certain that a general change of wind direction corresponding with the drift of the higher clouds

is imminent. For example, if at the time this wind-switching is observed there is a frost on the ground or a cold snap, and change in direction of the higher clouds is from northeast to southwest, a warming thaw can be expected.

Height—Clouds will often begin forming at high altitudes near the end of a warm spell. These generally portend a gradual change from fair to rainy weather, and if it comes, it is likely to set in for a week or more.

—"I change but cannot die"—

Clouds are always doing something, but some seem to sit stolidly upon the throne of the sky and refuse to budge even with the wind. Such stationary clouds demand attention, if only for the reason that they are not at all what they seem to be. Early seafarers knew that stationary clouds served as distant reflectors of land and sea topography. In his fine book, *Nature Is Your Guide,* Harold Gatty, who with Wiley Post made the epic eight-day-around-the-world-flight in 1931, wrote briefly of the significance of standing clouds above the St. Lawrence River:

"When winter comes to the valley of the St. Lawrence River in eastern Canada, the waters of the river and its tributaries are warmer than the air, and a strip of mist columns is often formed which is intensified by the spray of the waterfalls. Near Quebec, for instance, stationary clouds are sometimes seen hovering over the cataracts—over the Chaudière and the Montmorency Falls. Later in the winter small, well-defined cumulus clouds can often be seen standing above the falls, at an elevation of three or four hundred feet. Higher up over the surrounding mountains, clouds form on the mountaintops and may descend some distance down their sides, or remain suspended and 'standing' at some height above their summits. Clouds of the first kind are often seen before or after heavy rain, of the last kind usually in fine weather."*

In weather science nomenclature, standing clouds such as Gatty described are called *lenticular*—so named because they resemble roughly the shape of a lens—and they do indeed seem to remain obstinately still. The obvious presumption by anyone viewing such a cloud is that the wind aloft must have gotten tired and gone home for the day. Of course, nothing could be further from the truth, for as altitude increases the less atmospheric friction there is to impede wind speed.

* *From the book,* Nature Is Your Guide, *by Harold Gatty. Copyright © 1958 by A. Fenna Gatty. Published by permission of the publishers, E. P. Dutton & Co., Inc.*

Figure 1—12

These are lenticular lee-wave clouds of the kind often associated with the lee side of mountains. In this case, these relatively high clouds, after having lifted over Rocky mountain peaks are moving in a generally southeasterly direction. (Photo: Courtesy National Center for Atmospheric Research.)

There is wind aplenty up there where that cloud is stubbornly maintaining its position, and it is playing an important role in keeping the cloud stabilized.

Figure 1-13 solves the mystery of the stationary cloud by showing that its windward edge is growing as fast as its leeward edge is melting away. As you can see, what is happening is that warm air ascending from the windward side of the island is being condensed in the warm updraft to feed the cloud, while evaporation disintegrates the leeward edge of the cloud and replaces with cooler air the rising thermals flowing upward. This energetic round-robin convective process was referred to by Matthew Fontaine Maury in his sailing directions when he wrote, "They (stationary clouds) are often seen to overhang the lowest islet of the tropics and even stand above the coral patches and hidden reefs, a 'cloud by day' to serve as a beacon to the lonely mariner out there at sea and to warn him of shoals and dangers which no lead nor seaman's eye has ever seen or sounded out."

This same principle, downdraft replacement air flowing in to fill the gap created by rising currents, can be a valuable sailing aid. When clouds disappear over the water but are lying thick over the land, you can be certain of a strong onshore breeze—replacement air is rushing from sea to low pressure areas caused by the warm land evacuating air to the clouds over it.

Not everyone has a sufficiently abiding interest in the weather to compile a daily weather log book, but for those who do, I offer a convenient form I have used, along with four typical entries for the month of November, 1971.

The problem confronting many amateur weather observers is to find the time to take regular daily readings.

Temperature is particularly important, so if you can't get home for a mid-day reading, perhaps you can have your spouse take it. There are several variations to this weather log, and some

THE MECHANICS OF A STATIONARY CLOUD

Wind blowing this direction.

Warm updrafts feed cloud.

Atoll in the Pacific

Condensation feeds the windward edge of the cloud, while evaporation eats away the leeward edge, creating the illusion that the cloud is standing still.

Figure 1—13

23

observers will make a monthly summary. If you do this, it would prove informative, and a check against your own accuracy, to compare your summary with the information contained in "Local Climatological Data," a monthly publication available from the National Climatic Center, Federal Building, Asheville, North Carolina. It contains daily summaries for approximately 300 cities and towns in the United States, including temperature, heating and cooling degree days, dewpoint, precipitation, pressure, wind, sunshine, and sky cover.

However, the greatest value of a personal weather log lies in the record you'll have of your own forecasting ability as compared with what actually occurred on a certain day. For me, such a log has not only been helpful in planning outings, but has improved my sensitivity to the panorama of weather, and my awareness that the daily drama of the sky should never be taken for granted.

Date Nov.	Barometer		Thermometer				Temp.		Wind
	8 a.m.	10 p.m.	8 a.m.	12 noon	5 p.m.	10 p.m.	Max.	Min.	
1									
2									
3									
4									
5	29.78	29.60	40	46	46	45	46	40	SW
6									
7									
8									
9									
10									
11	30.24	30.15	16	27	22	17	27	16	SE
12									
13									
14									
15									
16									
17	29.50	29.83	37	44	39	35	44	35	NW
18									
19									
20									
21									
22									
23									
24									
25									
26									
27	30.12	29.95	30	37	39	40	40	30	S
28									
29									
30									

November 1971

5 A dull, damp day; intermittent drizzle.
11 Fog so thick you could cut it with a knife.
17 A fine night, after intermittent showers send sunshine.
27 Fair, but turned misty, increasing clouds later; predictable rain in evening.

CHAPTER THREE

Wind and the Sailor's Global Weather

CLOUDS' are excellent forecasters of the weather, but often are too far away. The wind, however, is a pressure chart we can feel, a flowing barometer. Paradoxically, wind is the least stable element on earth, but the most reliable guide to what the weather will be.

Wind is simply air rushing from high pressure to low pressure. This is an oversimplification, but true enough, for men have guessed—and later knew—that the wind carried messages. Wind blowing out of one quarter was an indication of fair weather, scolding out of another, storms. Today, the methods of linking the actions of wind and clouds—the two main great actors of weather—are somewhat more complicated than the gauge the old timers used, holding up a wetted finger to learn from the cool side which way the wind was blowing.

So this chapter will concern itself with the fact that weather is a circular affair. If you can understand the whys of large scale weather movements, why warm and cold air masses move in predictable patterns, why the Coriolis force in the northern hemisphere causes ocean currents to swirl to the right and winds to veer clockwise, you will, hopefully, gain an insight into the reasons for the wind and climate belts of our world.

The meteorologists have simplified the explanation of the general circulation of the atmosphere by describing it as two hemispheric loops or "conveyor belts" of moving air. Warm equatorial air rises and flows generally toward the north pole, while frigid, polar air sinks and flows generally toward the equator—a large scale example of the low and high pressure principle of dense, cold air sinking. Like the smaller convective systems of local cloud formation where imbalances of temperatures produce rain, the exchange of air between the two poles is the result of differences in temperature—heat exchange produces the winds of the world.

However, several factors complicate the apparently simple concept of conveyor belts of moving air-wind. One is the drag of wind against the surface of the earth, and the other is the rotation of the earth itself. These two forces, friction and rotation, combine to throw the general circulation into a sort of witch's brew of currents out of which many windy devils and dervishes are spawned.

Let's first take up the problem of rotation as it affects the flow of winds. Some 100 years ago, a scientist, William Ferrel, made an observation which has become a meteorological law: "In whatever direction a body moves on the surface of the earth, there is a force arising from the right in the northern hemisphere and from the left in the southern." But it was a Frenchman, Gasparo Gustave de Coriolis, whose realization that the earth's own rotation shifts the winds that has come into more common usage as the Coriolis force. Actually, the earth's deflecting force is an illusion, a force without punch, so to speak because the earth rotates west to east and all solid things attached to it move with the earth.

One way to visualize the Coriolis force is to imagine that you are in a balloon floating in a parcel of air which is moving directly from north to south. But the earth rotates eastward under the air which keeps your balloon aloft, so that with respect to the earth's parallels and meridians, your stream of air gradually assumes a motion

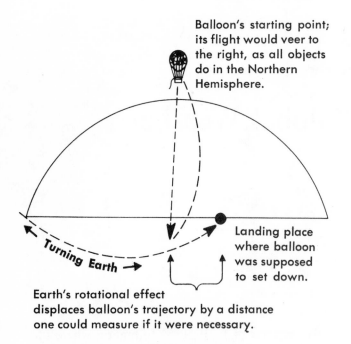

Balloon's starting point; its flight would veer to the right, as all objects do in the Northern Hemisphere.

Landing place where balloon was supposed to set down.

Turning Earth →

Earth's rotational effect displaces balloon's trajectory by a distance one could measure if it were necessary.

Figure 2—1

from the northeast to the southwest. *Figure 2-1* illustrates the concept. Supposing your balloon flight started at the north pole and your destination was a point on the equator. Were it not for the Coriolis force, your balloon would follow a straight course, but the destination you had chosen would have moved with rotating earth far to the right of your mark. If your theoretical balloon flight was in the opposite direction—from the equator toward a point near the north pole, your landing spot would have veered far to the left.

Now let's see how the Coriolis force and friction combine to disrupt those two hemispheric loops or conveyor belts of moving air. The logical place to begin is at the equator. There, a theoretical shifting line spans the globe through its torrid points. A region known since the days of sailing ships lies on both sides of this equatorial line—the doldrums. Meteorologists, however, call this the "zone of inter-tropical convergence." Air over the doldrums has a breathless quality because the sun's scorching heat lifts it almost straight up, with the result that there is little or no horizontal movement. At the high levels of the troposphere, this ascended air divides, portions spreading fountain-like north and south. One branch flowing toward the poles makes up the high level winds known as the anti-trade winds or upper westerlies. The other branch begins a descent back to earth in the area of the 25th parallel, creating a fair weather zone of little rain, calm air, and generally clear skies. A term for this area, the *horse latitudes,* was

probably originated by sailors of the windjammers when the calms and heat of the area killed cargoes of horses.

Once the descending air of the horse latitudes comes back to surface, it also splits into two streams, one which returns to the equator, the other heading toward the poles. The equatorial flow forms the persistent trade winds, which replace the air lifted from over the doldrums by the sun's blazing heat. Thus the gentle, persistent trade winds complete the equatorial convection system. Were it not for the Coriolis force, the trade winds would blow from north to south in the northern hemisphere, and from south to north in the southern hemisphere. This deflecting force also determines the direction of the air currents moving toward the poles from the horse latitudes: They veer eastward and merge into the prevailing westerlies—the second of the great wind systems of the general circulation.

As already stated, from the high-pressure zone of the horse latitudes, winds blow in a poleward direction and the earth's rotation causes these winds to veer to the right in the northern hemisphere and to the left in the southern. In the region between the 30th and 60th parallels, the westerlies circle the earth. In other words, in both hemispheres, belts of westerly winds prevail in these latitudes. In the southern hemisphere, where there is relatively more ocean and not too many surface obstructions to influence wind patterns, the winds are of higher velocities. They blow with awesome fury around the southern tip of South America, the region of the "Roaring Forties." But as they near the poles, the westerlies lose their speed and force, and at the 60th parallel they brush against the last of the bands of winds that make up the general circulation—the polar easterlies. It is important to realize that the westerlies dominate most of the temperate zone, and represent the battle ground of warm semi-tropical air from the horse latitudes and cold polar air from high latitudes. During the winter, this clashing of opposed air becomes intense and the westerly belt retreats southward. In the summer, the circulation is less intense and the westerly belt moves northward.

Just as there is a heat equator circling the earth through its hottest points, so there are poles of intense cold near the geographical north and south poles. These poles of frigid air send out far-spreading fingers of icy air that move toward the equator, causing a confrontation with the prevailing westerlies.

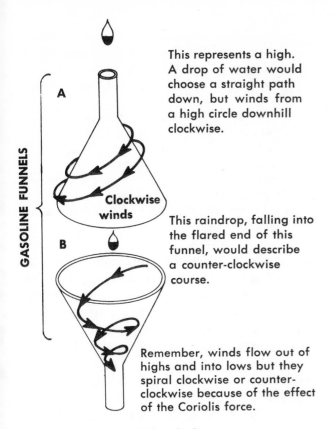

GASOLINE FUNNELS

A

This represents a high. A drop of water would choose a straight path down, but winds from a high circle downhill clockwise.

Clockwise winds

B

This raindrop, falling into the flared end of this funnel, would describe a counter-clockwise course.

Remember, winds flow out of highs and into lows but they spiral clockwise or counter-clockwise because of the effect of the Coriolis force.

Figure 2—2

and converge upon that center, rotating counterclockwise in the northern hemisphere, clockwise in the southern hemisphere. Anticyclonic winds rotate in a reverse direction—which may seem contradictory in view of the Coriolis force—around a high pressure center, and flow out from the center. In one respect, however, both systems are alike: They fan out over hundreds of thousands of square miles.

To the sportsman or amateur weather buff the business of rotation of wind systems must seem confusing when, as I stated earlier, that although objects are deflected to the right in the northern hemisphere and to the left in the southern hemisphere, low pressure winds move counterclockwise, and counterclockwise is certainly to the left. How can it be that highs and lows, both subject to the same deflecting action of the Coriolis force, move opposite to one another? *Figure 2-2* should help make the matter clear.

As noted in the previous chapter, high pressure is like a mountain of density overhead pressing down. But in low pressure weather there is a valley of density making its weight felt. So high pressure, since it represents colder and denser air, eventually slips down into the valley. Now suppose you upend a gasoline funnel, as illustrated in *Figure 2-2*. A drop of water would choose a straight path down if placed at the top of the funnel. But winds flow out of highs into lows, spiralling completely around clockwise, and they circle around because they veer from the Coriolis force. In the second half of the drawing, note that the funnel is sitting on its narrow end.

Wind veering into the flared end of the funnel, representing a low pressure area, flows inside counterclockwise. It is worth repeating, and the drawings worth remembering—winds of high pressure flow as if down the sides of a mountain. Winds of low pressure flow inside the hole or well of low pressure. This is important to remember for another reason, aside from making your weather-map reading easier: Because winds swirl counterclockwise around a low, you can face into the wind and point to your right to locate the direction of the nearest storm area. If the storm low is located to the west, then it should be approaching you. You can check this against a newspaper weather map, and estimate its time of arrival. A detailed explanation of how to locate highs and lows will be described later in this chapter.

No adequate explanation of the general circu-

So the polar easterlies represent some of the air which rises from the equator and moves at high altitudes all the way to the poles, where it blusters in, cold and dense, to form a dome of high pressure at each pole. This air breaks out irregularly in bulges and moves southward (or northward from the south pole) toward the prevailing westerlies. The earth's rotation causes these polar winds to veer somewhat to the right, causing winds that blow from a northeasterly direction in a zone from the north pole to about 60 degrees north (in the northern hemisphere). The winds in corresponding latitudes in the southern hemisphere generally come from the southeast.

Where the polar air meets the semi-tropical air at about 60 degrees latitude, a girdle of low pressure exists around the earth. This zone of clash between the polar easterlies and the prevailing westerlies is known as the polar front in the northern hemisphere, and it is the breeder of the changeable temperate zone weather.

Unlike the general circulation, however, these wind systems wax and wane. They are born and expire temperamentally. They are known to meteorologists as cyclones and anticyclones, and one is a mirror image of the other. Cyclonic wind systems swirl around a center of low pressure,

VERTICAL AND HORIZONTAL GENERAL CIRCULATION OF THE ATMOSPHERE

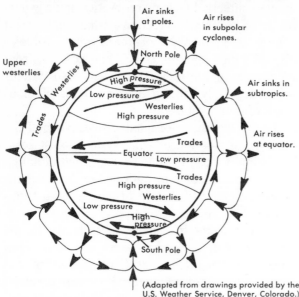

(Adapted from drawings provided by the U.S. Weather Service, Denver, Colorado.)

Figure 2—3

lation of winds would be complete without an illustration of primary wind circulation. *Figure 2-3* is a simple drawing showing how the interplay of temperature, centrifugal and frictional effects, and the Coriolis force produce vast movements of the winds previously discussed—the doldrums, the trades, the prevailing westerlies, and the polar easterlies.

What would be a better way to demonstrate the difference in temperatures produced by the wind-climate belts of the world than the actual log of the passage of a sailing ship from torrid to temperate latitudes, as reproduced in that fine old classic, *Weather and the Oceans of Air*.

March 11th: Latitude 10° N, off Panama coast, temperature 79° F, broken clouds, wind ENE moderate (trade wind), caught barracuda on trolling line.

12th: Lat. 12°, in Caribbean, temp 79°, scattered to broken clouds, wind NE X N fresh to strong (norther), sea rough, water temperature 78°.

13th: Lat 14½°, in Caribbean, temp 77°, scattered clouds, wind ENE fresh (intensified trade), water very rich blue.

14th: Lat 18°, just southwest of Haiti, temp 78°, scattered clouds to clear, wind easterly to light (in lee of Hispaniola).

15th: Lat 22°, near Bahamas and Tropic of Cancer, temp 77°, winds easterly to variable light (horse latitudes), scattered clouds to clear.

16th: Lat 26½°, in Atlantic, temp 73°, showers and thundershowers along a cold front, wind southwesterly moderate, shifting to NW with frontal passage.

17th: Lat 30½°, in Atlantic, temp 67°, scattered to broken clouds, wind NW moderate (prevailing westerlies), water dark steely blue, water temp 74°.

18th: Lat 35°, off Cape Hatteras in Gulf Stream, temp 60°, broken clouds, wind northerly fresh and increasing, water temp 60°, passed school of whales.

19th: Lat 38°, entering Delaware Bay, temp 35°, clear, calm to southerly light, water temp 50° after leaving Gulf Stream, 42° near coast, water dirty green.

Thus, as this log demonstrates, in the last few days of sailing, coursing a distance of about 235 miles per day, the vessel passed from a tropical climate of bland, blue skies to a temperate one—though in late March "temperate" is probably a poor euphemism for cold, driving showers, probable hail and thunderstorms. The cruise to the reader may seem to have been a slow 2,000 mile journey from "boredom to ennui" at a weary pace of about 10 knots, but the log does represent how the charted winds of the world do change the sailor's hemispheric weather.

It seems worthwhile to dispel, while the subject of the Coriolis force is still freshly with us, some of the myths attributed to the earth's rotational effect. There must be dozens of old superstitions still deeply rooted in the minds of many people. So, emphatically there is no truth to the sayings that drunks lose their balance, trains wear their right wheels first, snakes coil, sea shells convolute—all to the right in the northern hemisphere, and to the left in the southern hemisphere. Those drunks above and below the equator that I've observed pass out in whatever direction seems to be most convenient at the time.

I made the statement earlier that water, like air, is a fluid. To be absolutely precise, this could be amended to read: *Air acts like water which you can see and feel.* You can only feel air when it is stirred up by atmospheric condition which makes its weight or motion change. This leads to the subject of *air masses* and *fronts,* and a step toward understanding some of the hen scratchings and meteorological hieroglyphics you will observe on the weather map displayed on your television screen.

Returning to the subject of air as a fluid, several years ago, as a visitor, I witnessed an interesting demonstration in an elementary meteorology class at Florida State University, which trains many of our professional meteorologists. The instructor, an ingenious young fellow,

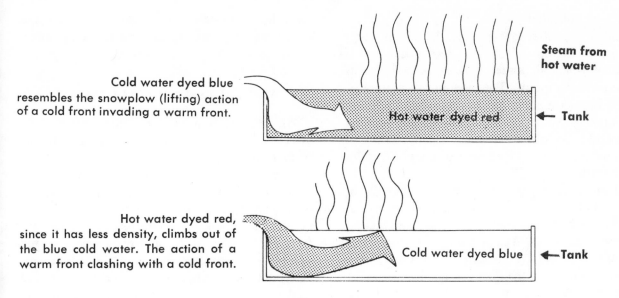

Cold water dyed blue resembles the snowplow (lifting) action of a cold front invading a warm front.

Steam from hot water

Hot water dyed red ← Tank

Hot water dyed red, since it has less density, climbs out of the blue cold water. The action of a warm front clashing with a cold front.

Cold water dyed blue ← Tank

Figure 2—4

had rigged up a large rectangular glass container attached to which at each end was a glass tube containing, in one, hot water colored red, and in the other, cold water dyed blue. The hot water inlet was opened first, creating a 6-inch steaming layer in the tank. Then he released the cold water, pointing out gleefully: "See, the cold water curls downward, moving under the hot water. The blue water plunging down represents a cold air mass. The forward portion invading the red is a cold front."

After draining the tank, the experiment was repeated in reverse, hot water invading a cold layer of blue. "And that," he said, "is a warm front, for the hot water climbs right over the cold."

It was an efficient demonstration of how our atmosphere acts when hot and cold air converge, and it is worth keeping in mind for it will help you to grasp the significance of a weather report which warns of an advancing warm or cold front. *Figure 2-4,* drawn from memory of the Florida demonstration, should help you visualize the action of cold and warm fronts.

I pointed out in the introduction to this book that its purpose is not to encumber the sportsman with such an abundance of weather facts that he will become disgusted and throw it away. If you want to be a meteorologist, you should go to school. Here, I want only to acquaint the reader with enough of the basic theory so that he may, with reasonable accuracy, anticipate what the weather will be.

This leads us to the question: Why should anyone want to be bothered about air masses and fronts? The answer is that like the choking grit and dust that gathers at the broad nose of a desert sand storm, a front is the prong of an advancing air mass. Therefore, a weather map plotter, who is a professional weather sleuth, charts the courses of new air masses by locating their fronts. In this way a determination of what the weather will be in a few days or weeks can be made with greater accuracy. You will be able to do this too, although with less sophistication.

Before getting into the business of describing air masses and fronts, it may be useful to define in a more detailed fashion how highs and lows are formed, and how to locate them in relationship to your own position.

Highs and lows are simply behavioral indicators of any kind of a front. The horizontal wavelike action between two highs of different temperature forms lows. The wave gets larger and finally breaks like a wave crest whose forward motion pushes it beyond gravitational stability. Whirling air creates the low pressure cell.

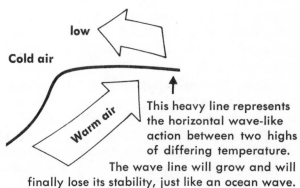

low

Cold air

Warm air

This heavy line represents the horizontal wave-like action between two highs of differing temperature. The wave line will grow and will finally lose its stability, just like an ocean wave.

Figure 2—5

It's a complicated process, but again, if you remember the valley low concept, the idea is easier to grasp. *Figure 2-5* shows how a local low is created when air under a large cumulonimbus cloud rises rapidly. This low-pressure area is filled by surrounding air moving in and twisting counterclockwise because of the earth's rotation (that old Coriolis force effect again). Lows of this nature form over an area of about 20 miles in diameter.

In a sense, highs are simply the opposites of lows, but that is an oversimplification. Local highs are born any place where air cools, compresses, and sinks. Again, remember a high is a mountain of density pressing down. One of the most important in the northern hemisphere is the large high-pressure region mentioned earlier: the horse latitudes. In this area air accumulates, becomes heavy, and settles to earth.

In terms of action, air flows from a high pressure area into the surrounding area of low pressure. Here again, that bugaboo, the Coriolis force, directs the way the air in a high shall behave, for as it pushes out, it is twisted to its right by the earth's rotation. Air sweeping north shifts to the east; air heading south shifts to the west. The result is the formation of a whirling high pressure cell. Such cells, forming north of the polar front, repeatedly move southward. Highs often extend to Mexico and the Gulf in winter. A large high pressure cell may cover the entire United States east of the Rockies.

You can locate a high or low coming your way by the simple application of one rule. Stand with your back to the wind, then turn about 45 degrees to your right. Your back should now be at an angle to the wind. The rule is that the high pressure center would be to your right, a low pressure center to your left. A word of caution: This rule will hold quite well for general or prevailing winds, but don't expect accuracy by this method for local breezes—land and sea breezes, for example, which are created by unequal shore-side heating, would not be infallible detectors of highs and lows.

It goes without saying that in the southern hemisphere you'd reverse your position to find the location of highs and lows. In the region of the prevailing westerlies, both highs and lows usually journey in an easterly direction, so a high or low to your west will most likely move over you. The uncertainty is that highs and lows may simply fade away, remain stationary, or change direction to north or south. But once you digest the following information about air masses and fronts, you'll be able to use this rule more effectively.

THE FACTS ABOUT AIR MASSES

An air mass, translated, is a high pressure cell. We already know that this cell is a thousand-mile-or-more parcel of air in which the conditions of temperature and moisture are much the same at all points in any horizontal direction. So an air mass (anticyclone or high) sucks up the temperature and moisture characteristics of the surface over which it forms. The sweeping and bumping of air masses across the North American continent—the confusion of warmer and colder air in conflict—causes rain, snow and other weather changes. You could characterize this action by saying opposites attract: When a hot, moist air mass meets a cold, dry one, a weather front is in the making. It's like a misunderstanding in your household; your wife may be cool and indifferent; you may be seething inside. A confrontation is bound to occur.

There is the danger at this point of misleading the reader into thinking that a cold front must be frigid air and a warm front steamy and vaporous with its load of heat. This isn't so. Summer cold fronts have been measured at air temperatures of 70 degrees. But supposing you reside in the hot southwest. An advancing cold front horns in where the diurnal temperatures have been averaging 103-105° F. This front would be characterized as cold by the forecasters, and as a great relief to southwesterners.

The difference in the definition between a cold or warm front is the singular fact that it is colder or warmer than the air it invades or displaces. The experiment I described earlier at Florida State University with the hot and cold water was an excellent demonstration of this displacement principle.

Now, as a final clarification, let's look at some front facts as they would appear on a weather map. First must come a definition of an *isobar*. Since the whole purpose of weighing the atmosphere is to construct weather maps, the meteorologists have necessarily had to develop symbols and a terminology of their own, the first adapted primarily from geographical contour maps. The word *iso*, from the Greek, translates as "equal," and *bar* refers to barometric pressure. Thus, as seen in the drawing *Figure 2-6a*, an *isobar* is shown as a line of equal pressure connecting

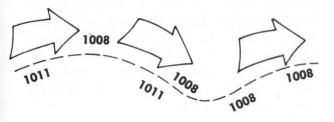

Figure 2—6A

The dotted line connects points of equal pressure. Thus the figures 1008 are points, or areas of equal pressure, called millibars.

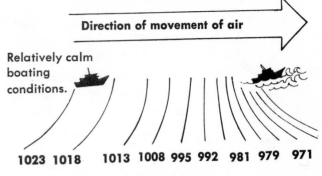

Direction of movement of air

Relatively calm boating conditions.

1023 1018 1013 1008 995 992 981 979 971

Figure 2—6B

points where the air pressures are the same. Isobars as seen on a weather map indicate how fast the air is moving. When they are spaced far apart, winds are light; when they are close together, air is moving fast, as seen in *Figure 2-6b*.

Once isobars were shown on weather maps only by numbers representing local barometric readings expressed in inches of mercury. With the increasing popularity of the metric system, however, meteorologists began using another

But over here where isobar lines would appear closer on the weather map, a boat would be subject to turbulence if it were in the water where the isobaric lines converge indicating low pressure for an area.

unit instead of inches of mercury as a barometric measure. This is the *millibar*. I would prefer to ignore a definition of this term, but in the interest of completeness, here it is: Millibars express barometric values in units of pressure, not height;

Figure 2—7

SECTION FROM A WEATHER MAP

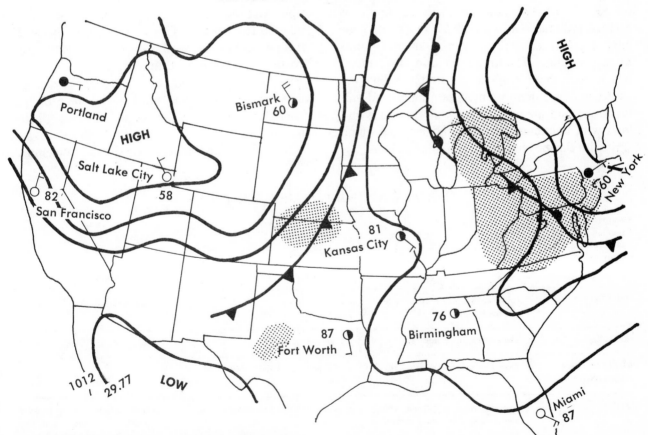

This map is not intended as a guide for the reader to follow the progression of lows and highs; rather to acquaint him with how weather symbols are employed by the professionals on an actual weather map. This one comes as a section from a larger map prepared for this book by the U.S. Weather Bureau, Denver, Colorado.

This is an advancing cold front.

Warm air mass
or front

But there is a dragging effect here, caused by the cold front's lifting invasion with the result that the bottom of the cloud form lags, while the top runs forward due to the wind effect at a higher altitude.

Figure 2—8

a millibar is 1/1000 of a bar, which is a force of 1,000,000 dynes per square centimeter.

"Normal" barometric pressure, at 15° Celsius or 59° F., at 45° latitude north or south, is 1013.2 millibars (mb) or 29.92 inches of mercury. I prefer isobar lines over numbered points in map reading. The important thing to remember is that these symbols all simply relate the contours of air density (mountain highs and valley lows) and are used to mark all the highs and lows with boundary lines—boundary lines which shift with the movement of the highs and lows.

As we discovered with the hot-cold experiment, cold fronts wedge their way under warm air as they advance. But the typical snowplow advancing edge of a cold front is blunted by the frictional drag against the ground of the bottom layer of the air mass. *Figure 2-8* illustrates the shape of this formation.

In the northern hemisphere, major cold fronts usually lie in a northeast to southwest direction and move toward the east or southwest, and cold fronts usually advance at speeds of about 20 to 30 mph—faster in winter than in summer, because in winter the air is colder and exerts greater pressure. The steep sloping edge of a cold front also produces fast lifting of warm air, so that storms along a cold front are generally abrupt and violent.

A warm front simply replaces cold air. In our northern hemisphere, warm fronts show up on the east side of low pressure cells and are usually followed by cold fronts as the prevailing westerlies move the low eastward—a fact you will remember from the discussion of wind belts.

The advance of warm fronts is usually at about half the speed of cold fronts, or about 15 mph. And the warm front does not have the typical cold-front bulge. This is, as we said, because ground friction drags the lower edge of the retreating cold air into a thin wedge.

Typical warm front cloud sequences can be detected at least 1,000 miles in advance of the front, and often 48 hours in advance of its arrival.

Now here are facts you should remember

TYPICAL COLD FRONT WEATHER SEQUENCE

Atmospheric Condition	In Advance	During Passage	Following
VISIBILITY	Generally poor.	Temporarily poor followed by marked improvement.	Usually very clear, except in scattered showers.
TEMPERATURE	Fairly steady; may drop prior to pre-frontal rain	Quick drop.	Continued slow drop.
PRESSURE	Moderate to rapid fall.	Sudden rise.	Rises, but more slowly.
WINDS (northern hemisphere)	Increasing and becoming squally.	Sudden clockwise shift; very squally.	Gusty.
CLOUDS	Altocumulus or altostratus and nimbostratus then heavy cumulonimbus.	Cumulonimbus with scudding action.	Lifting quickly, usually followed by altostratus, altocumulus, and cumulus, lagging behind.
WEATHER	Generally rain; often thunder.	Heavy rain; thunder and hail possible.	Heavy rain for short duration, then fair. Some scattered showers, 50% chance.

TYPICAL WARM FRONT WEATHER SEQUENCE

Atmospheric Condition	In Advance	During Passage	Following
VISIBILITY	Fairly good except when raining.	Poor; often mist or fog.	Mist or fog may persist to make visibility poor.
TEMPERATURE	Steady or slow rise.	Steady rise, sometimes sudden.	Little change or very slow rise.
PRESSURE	Falls steadily.	Stops falling.	Little change, possible slight rise followed by equal fall.
WINDS (northern hemisphere)	Increasing.	Clockwise shift, sometimes decreasing.	Direction steady.
CLOUDS	Almost always this order: cirrus, cirrostratus, altostratus, nimbostratus, occasionally cumulonimbus.	Low nimbostratus and flying scud.	Stratus, or stratocumulus; cumulonimbus may appear.
WEATHER	Continuous rain or snow.	Rain frequently stops.	Following drizzle or fog-like rain.

about all fronts: Fronts form at margins of high pressure cells. They form only between cells of different temperatures. Warm air always slopes upward over cold air. A front will be located along a low pressure trough, so pressure drops as the front approaches, then rises after it passes. Wind near the ground always shifts clockwise in the northern hemisphere—the Coriolis force—as the front passes. And finally, a front always rears upward over cold air either ahead of or to the rear of its direction of advance.

On the page at left and above are two tables which are handy tools for the weatherwise sportsman. They tell you what to expect in the weather sequences of fronts.

On our North American continent there are four types of air mass that influence our daily weather in one season or another. They are the Polar, Tropical, Continental, and Maritime air masses. The rule of thumb to remember is that any atmospheric condition of air is influenced by the characteristics of areas where it originates or over which it passes. So many of us ignore the fact that wet air comes from seas or lakes; dry air issues from deserts or dry lands; cold air emanates from cold areas, and warm air comes from warm regions. This may seem awfully rudimentary, but remember modern man is so used to having the weather spelled out for him that he tends to overlook some facts which should be apparent.

North America, unlike other parts of the world where weather is seasonally regular, is a region of constant aerial conflict. Here the four different types of air masses from six regions are

forever clashing. This vying of air masses is the reason for the changeability of U.S. weather.

Not only does each of these air masses usher in changes in temperature and humidity, but each exhibits its own pattern of wind as well. The exhilarating dry weather characteristic of continental polar air is usually accompanied by northwest winds. By contrast, maritime tropical air suggests warm, muggy conditions generally, and southerly winds. In this air, smoke fails to rise. The weather associated with maritime polar air, which is usually pushed by northerly winds, brings low clouds, fog and drizzle—the kind of weather that makes a lush garden of greenery in the Pacific northwest, fall through spring. Relatively light winds characterize the hot, dry continental tropical air mass, which is king of climate in the southwest during the warm months.

At least three different air-mass classification systems are used by U.S. meteorologists, but below are the principal air masses that affect our weather, and their typical paths. For our purposes as shown in *Figure 2-9*, P stands for polar (cold) air, T for tropical (warm, moist) air, M for maritime (wet) air, and C for continental (dry) air. Now, *Figure 2-9* shows two things: one, the sources and routes of major air masses that influence our weather, and two, six brief descriptions of what to expect from the weather patterns developed by these air masses in winter and summer. In conjunction with the two charts in this book that show typical cold and warm front weather sequences, plus the plotting instructions for frontal movements on a weather map contained in Chapter 3, you should be able

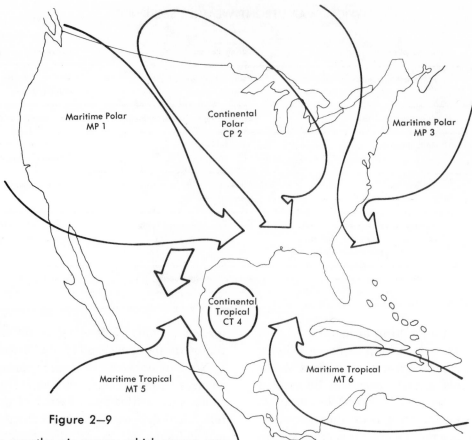

Maritime Polar
MP 1

Continental
Polar
CP 2

Maritime Polar
MP 3

Continental
Tropical
CT 4

Maritime Tropical
MT 5

Maritime Tropical
MT 6

Figure 2—9

As you can see, the air masses which sweep over North America are gigantic in scope. But it will be easier to understand what kind of weather they normally bring, season in and season out, if we refer to them in numerical order. Thus, MP 1 is characterized by cool, moist air the entire year. CP 2 brings in dry, cold air. MP 3 issues in cool, moist air during a

12-month cycle. CT 4 is a clear and dry air mass during summer, while MT 5 sends up moist warm air in winter, and MT 6 shoots up moist warm air during the whole year. The whole interplay of cold and warm air is what produces the weather in the continental United States.

to make some intelligent decisions regarding temperature, cloud cover, visibility, and rain from at least six hours ahead up to 48.

There are three other types of fronts which deserve brief mention here, but it is the active, moving fronts that concern the sportsman:

Stationary Fronts

These are fronts which are like parents who cannot decide whether to take the family on a picnic or stay home and let the kids go out and play by themselves. The conditions are very similar to a warm front, but are generally much milder. Stationary fronts with rain may hang around for days.

Weak Fronts

Except by the weather experts, weak fronts are hardly ever noticed. They occur when air masses

are almost the same in humidity and temperature, and are marked only by a wind shift as the front passes. The weather forecasters pay them attention only for the possibility that they may develop into strong fronts.

Occluded Fronts

An occluded front occurs when a cold front, winging closely behind a warm front, finally overtakes the former and snowplows the warm air mass off the ground. Either the warm or the cold front ascends.

Now that the reader has at least a brushing acquaintance with air masses and wind circulation systems, let's examine how wind influences sea currents, look at the principal methods for determining true and apparent wind, and suggest tactics in using thermals, wind blanketing effects, and onshore and offshore suction in sailing. We'll also examine some other wind factors.

Sailors have long known about how the rhythms

of the wind move the ocean currents, but generally have not realized that these movements are due to temperature plus wind. As the winds circle and recircle above, something very similar is happening in the oceans that surround us. You might say the ocean currents and the winds are partners, and they hold a worldwide power monopoly. The only trust-buster for this partnership can be the sun. The two absolutely control the circulation of water and air around the globe, but like shrewd investors, they grant permission to great inland lakes and seas to build smaller circulation systems of their own—but with the agreement that wind-water dividends on these systems shall be returned to the major partners.

In this partnership the winds generate the power and the currents do the work, circulating around the world, pushing warm water toward the poles and polar water toward the equator, feeding moderate temperatures to one coast and bitter cold to another.

Unlike the three-layer stratification of water in our northern inland lakes, discussed in a later chapter, the ocean is divided into four horizontal layers. Deepest is the very cold bottom water originating near the poles. Next is a deep stratum of warmer, lighter water; two top layers, the intermediate and surface, comprise the profile of the Pacific ocean.

The Atlantic, on the other hand, is perturbed by a current from the Mediterranean sea that flows between layers of deep and intermediate water, and makes a new design in its already complicated configuration. As would be expected from the earlier description of the Coriolis force's effect on winds, the movement of these layers is deflected to the right above the equator and to the left below it. It shouldn't be surprising for the reader to discover that the oceans have their highs and lows of pressure, too.

The profile of Atlantic ocean water movement proves this last statement. The bottom water of the Atlantic comes from the Antarctic. Its supply of deep water flows from Greenland or Iceland. Its intermediate layer comes from the Antarctic, and its surface water is developed from its own local supply.

At the Antarctic, water is made from melting ice. Warmed enough, this water rises and mixes with the Antarctic surface water.

Meanwhile, deep water from the North Atlantic is journeying south at a great depth. As it warms up on the way, it lifts toward the surface—remember the warm front-cold front experiment—and when it meets the warmer, lighter water, it is forced down again. At the equator the deep water slips into a trough five hundred or six hundred fathoms deep. Like the hot air above it, the cold deep water is swept along by the earth's rotation and skewed off to the north and south. At the edge of the doldrums the trade wind picks up the surface North Equatorial Current and blows it westward across the Atlantic to the Americas. This is upslope work because the level of the seas elevates about three inches every thousand miles or so. These winds, hot and dry from their origin across the far Sahara desert, soak up moisture on their Atlantic crossing and bring it to the coasts of the United States and South America. This is why the sand of Florida is partially made up of Sahara sand.

The North Equatorial Current, however, does not approach our Atlantic seaboard in a simple, straightforward manner. It turns and twists about like a leaf tossed by a vagrant wind. Blocked by the West Indies, it is forced to split, north and south. Excerpts from *Sailing Directions for the West Indies* indicates that its flow patterns are not as simple as north and south:

A branch of the North Equatorial Current flows westward into the Caribbean Sea, through the passages between the Windward Islands, at a rate of up to 2.0 knots. The general flow continues westward, through the Caribbean at about 1.0 knot. It is deflected northward by the coast of Central America, passes through Yucatan Channel, and spreads northward into the Gulf of Mexico and eastward through the Straits of Florida as the Florida Current. A second branch of the North Equatorial Current flows northwestward to the north of the Caribbean islands chain as the Antilles Current. This current is comparatively weak, flowing at about 0.5 knot. Branches of this current, setting in a northwesterly direction, pass between the Bahama Islands and between Cuba and the Bahamas. The major portion of the Antilles Current, however, stays northeastward of the islands, and joins the Gulf Stream northward of the Bahamas.

The Gulf Stream sets northward, paralleling the coast of the United States as far as Cape Hatteras. Near its axis it attains a rate at the surface of about 2.0 knots. Deflected by prevailing winds, it becomes a broad eastward flow across the Atlantic at between 0.5 knot and 1.0 knot, northward of Hatteras.

The part of the North Equatorial Current that

flows more directly north becomes the Bahamas Current, as can be deduced from the excerpts from *Sailing Directions,* but that portion of it which is driven south is blown by the trades through the Caribbean Sea until it runs smack into the coast of Brazil. One other excerpt from the *Sailing Directions* tells us what happens there:

> Caribbean Sea—Across the northern portion of the Caribbean Sea the mean rate of the prevailing westward-setting current ranges from 0.5 to 1.0 knot as far as 77° W. southward of Jamaica, where it begins to increase in strength. The axis of the current continues toward the Yucatan Peninsula, where it is deflected northward and passes between Cabo San Antonio and the Yucatan Peninsula at a rate of up to 3.0 knots.
>
> Just southward of Cabo San Antonio an offshoot from the main current is deflected eastward and continues along the south coast of Cuba as a countercurrent. This current is variable, but at times it may be quite strong, having been reported to be as much as 4.0 knots.

So we can see that wind-wave action, in partnership with temperature, makes up the mighty flow of the oceans. The part of the North Equatorial Current that has been forced to turn south parallels the coast of Brazil until it encounters the "Brazil Bulge" that points toward Africa. While the southern half of the current manages to maneuver around this Africa-directed thrust, the northern half is forced to the right and returns to the Caribbean from whence it came.

Prevented from going farther west by the landlocked Gulf of Mexico, as the excerpts from the *Sailing Directions* indicate, this meandering current bursts out into the Atlantic between Florida and Cuba, as though it were rushing downhill. Northward of Hatteras, it is bent northeast by the westerlies, where its flow is frustrated by the coast of Newfoundland. There it turns due east, and somewhere off of the Grand Banks, it mixes with the cold Labrador Current, with a resulting drop in its temperature.

The whole process is a demonstration of the same phenomenon of cold and warm fronts—water masses clashing in an ocean environment—highs and lows, twists and eddies, slow currents and fast ones. The only difference in behavior is that they perform their gyrations in two separate mediums—the atmosphere and the sea.

TRUE AND APPARENT WIND SPEED

The National Oceanic and Atmospheric Administration (NOAA) publishes a *Weather Service Observing Handbook on Marine Surface Observations*. The principal purpose of this booklet is to assist officers aboard merchant vessels to be more accurate in the weather observations they make at sea, and report to ocean station weather ships and other designated receivers. But portions of it, particularly wind observing techniques, contain some excellent information for the boating sportsman. If you will take the trouble to read each section carefully, digesting the pertinent information presented, you will be in a better position to gauge deteriorating weather conditions by wind signs, and thus head for shore before trouble develops. Some of the following remarks are based on information presented in the *Handbook*.

True wind direction is discovered by observing and estimating the direction from which ripples, small waves, and sea spray are coming, since they run with the wind. You can determine the direction from which waves are flowing by sighting along the crest of the waves, then turning your body 90° to face into the advancing waves. It stands to reason that you then will be looking in the direction from which the waves are emanating.

The following table, taken from the *Weather Observing Handbook,* is essentially a modification of the Beaufort Wind Scale. Its purpose is to provide a guide to true wind speed, defined as the average speed in knots of the wind blowing at, or close to the sea's surface. However, this table has been constructed to reflect two provisos that should be present for your wind-water surface observations to be accurate. They are:

1. The wind will have been blowing long enough in a specific direction to raise the existing wave conditions.

2. Your location is well removed from land.

Also, there are several factors that will modify or enhance your estimation of the true wind speed. If winds have just sprung up; if offshore winds are blowing within sight of land, or moderate to heavy rain is falling, smoothing the water's surface, the wind speeds reflected in the table will be lessened by these offsetting effects.

By the same token, two other factors must be considered in applying the table which would cause you to overestimate wind speed: Waves that run into shallow water and steepen, and a

DETERMINATION OF WIND SPEED BY SEA CONDITION

Knots	Descriptive term	Sea Conditions	Wind force (Beaufort)	Probable wave height in ft.
0–1	Calm	Sea smooth and mirror-like.	0	–
1–3	Light air	Scale-like ripples without foam crests.	1	¼
4–6	Light breeze	Small, short wavelets; crests have a glassy appearance and do not break.	2	½
7–10	Gentle breeze	Large wavelets; some crests begin to break; foam of glassy appearance. Occasional white foam crests.	3	2
11–16	Moderate breeze	Small waves, becoming longer; fairly frequent white foam crests.	4	4
17–21	Fresh breeze	Moderate waves, taking a more pronounced long form; many white foam crests; there may be some spray.	5	6
22–27	Strong breeze	Large waves begin to form; white foam crests are more extensive everywhere; there may be some spray.	6	10
28–33	Near gale	Sea heaps up and white foam from breaking waves begins to be blown in streaks along the direction of the wind; spindrift begins.	7	14
34–40	Gale	Moderately high waves of greater length; edges of crests break into spindrift; foam is blown in well-marked streaks along the direction of the wind.	8	18
41–47	Strong gale	High waves; dense streaks of foam along the direction of the wind; crests of waves begin to topple, tumble, and roll over; spray may reduce visibility.	9	23
48–55	Storm	Very high waves with long overhanging crests. The resulting foam in great patches is blown in dense white streaks along the direction of the wind. On the whole, the surface of the sea is white in appearance. The tumbling of the sea becomes heavy and shocklike. Visibility is reduced.	10	29
56–63	Violent storm	Exceptionally high waves that may obscure small and medium-sized ships. The sea is completely covered with long white patches of foam lying along the direction of the wind. Everywhere the edges of the wave crests are blown into froth. Visibility reduced.	11	37
64–71	Hurricane	The air is filled with foam and spray. Sea completely white with driving spray; visibility very much reduced.	12	45

wind speed that is noticeably decreasing. All in all, the table is most accurate. It certainly has worked well for me, not only on the open sea for which it is made up, but also when I've applied it while boating on large inland lakes which generate their own wind systems.

It takes a bit of practice to make full use of the information in the table, but you'll soon learn, by comparing actual conditions with those forecast in the table, when to modify the wind speeds given.

Now that we know how to estimate true wind speed, let's take a look at the basic differences between true and apparent wind. As you may have deduced, a true wind is one which blows relative to any fixed point on our globe, but an apparent wind is one which blows in relationship to a moving object. If for example your boat was chugging along in a northerly direction, say, at 10 knots in a dead calm, its motion would create an apparent wind from the north at 10 knots.

Assuming your boat were equipped with an anemometer, it would measure the 10 knots, and if it were equipped with a wind vane, the vane would point north.

However, if a wind were blowing from the north at 10 knots—in the same direction your boat is headed, and at the same speed, then the true wind would cause an additive force—the apparent wind of 10 knots would be reinforced by the true wind's speed of 10 knots. Your boat then would be subject to a total *resultant* wind force of 20 knots. This is made clear in the drawings of *Figure 2-10*.

In the absence of a wind vane, you can figure the apparent wind direction by standing in an exposed location on the windward side of your boat and facing directly into the wind. Unless you know how to convert apparent wind to true wind, a knowledge of the former has little value. Your boat's course and speed must be subtracted from the apparent wind to obtain the true wind.

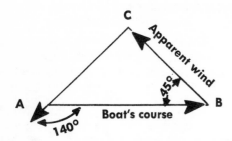

1. Your boat's course is 090 degrees, 15 kts. The apparent wind is 45 degrees off starboard bow, 10 kts. True wind 140 + 90 = 230 degrees. Length of vector line AC shows true wind speed of 11 kts.

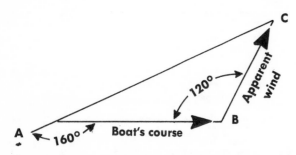

2. Your boat's course is 210 degrees, 15 kts. The apparent wind is 120 degrees off starboard bow, 10 kts. True wind 160 + 210 = 370 (−360) = 010, 22 kts.

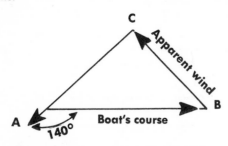

3. Your boat's course is 090 degrees, 15 kts. Apparent wind is 045 degrees off port bow, 10 kts. True wind 090 (+ 360) − 140 = 310, 11 kts.

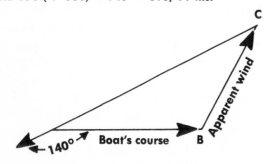

4. Your boat's course is 210 degrees, 15 kts. The apparent wind is 120 degrees off port bow, 10 kts. True wind 210 − 160 = 50, 22 kts.

Figure 2—10

(Adapted from vector diagram examples, Weather Service Observing Handbook, Marine Surface Observations.)

This is how it is done:

1. The true wind is always on the same side as the apparent, but farther aft than the apparent direction.

2. When the apparent direction is aft of the beam, the true wind speed is greater than the apparent wind speed.

3. When the apparent direction is forward of the beam, the true speed is less than the apparent wind.

Tactics in Using Thermals, Wind Blanketing Effects, Onshore and Offshore Suction in Sailing

The trouble with the vocabulary of weather is that one always has to return to definitions previously made in order to explain new concepts. So, to repeat, winds everywhere are fundamentally caused by differences in air temperature between two localities. These temperature differences always create differences in atmospheric pressure. In turn, atmospheric pressure conjures up the winds. When the resulting winds are confined to small areas, they blow directly from high pressure to low pressure.

The simplest sort of temperature-produced wind can be created by anyone in temperate latitudes in wintertime by just opening a porthole in the snug cabin of a boat. If the temperature in the boat is around 70° F. and the temperature outside is 20° or lower, you will notice a draft around your head. The cabin doorway might be a better example, for you would feel a draft of warm air flowing outward at the upper level of the cabin door, and a cold draft flowing inward at the sill level above the deck.

Now think of an ocean beach in midsummer, and you have an expansion of the cabin door boundary between cold and warm air—the sea breeze. Choose an arbitrary location where this heat-motivated breeze can be studied; let's say a long straight line of beach in about latitude 30° north, about level with Florida and southern California. During a 24 hour period here you might notice a surface breeze sequence similar to the following: early morning, calm; later morning, a breeze from seaward springs up and increases gradually until by midafternoon it is blowing at 10 to 15 miles an hour. By late afternoon it dies down to a flat calm. After midnight a fainter breeze begins to blow directly off the land, picks up speed to perhaps five to seven miles an hour during the wee hours, and finally dies to calm after sunrise, ready to begin the cycle anew.

What you have observed was first the sea breeze, and then the returning land breeze.

To the landlubber whose house may be close to the sea, the sea breeze is a refreshing breath of cool air, but the land breeze in most cases is a wind without punch, and because of its weakness, becomes a variable—the victim of stronger coast-line wind systems into which it is absorbed. There are some exceptions, but in general, the land breeze has little practical sailing application.

The sea breeze depends upon the sun's heating of the land: If the sun is blocked by clouds for a few hours, the breeze to shore will often give way to a calm or weak gradient wind. It stands to reason, then, that on a cloudy day the sea breeze will not be constant, and the boating sportsman will have to look forward to a diminished sea breeze when the sky begins to darken with truculent-looking clouds. The drawings in *Figure 2-11* demonstrate three effects of onshore and offshore winds that are important to the sailing man: the *cushion effect, blanket effect,* and the *wind shift line.*

In drawings A and B of *Figure 2-11,* the cushion and blanket effect are illustrated, and depict why sailors should avoid an immediate shoreline, aside from the obvious danger of breaking waves.

As you can see in both drawings, the wind is unreliable—generally slack or puffy.

This variability often extends as far out as 600 or 700 feet when the breeze is an onshore one. An offshore breeze can be unpredictable as far out as half a mile. In either case, onshore or offshore winds are recognizable by the change in the appearance of waves. There may be a distinct smoothness or a marked choppiness in the shoreline anatomy described.

Drawing C of *Figure 2-11* illustrates a phenomenon that surprisingly few sailors seem to be familiar with—the windshift line. This is a situation when the general prevailing wind is not blowing either directly on- or offshore, but at an angle. As you approach the shoreline, you will detect a change in the wind's direction so that it will be blowing at right angles to the shore. The strength of the wind, of course, will determine the position of the windshift line, but it can vary as much as half a mile from shores where the sea or land breeze is equal to a Beaufort wind force of about 4—which would be a moderate wind. A fact to keep in mind also is that where the shoreline—the topography of land meeting the sea—varies, the sea breeze and land breeze also will vary.

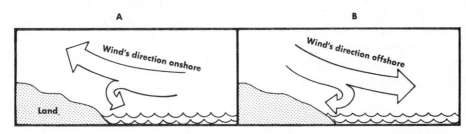

The curved arrows illustrate what is known as the "Cushion Effect." Now look at the "Blanket Effect" in the opposite panel.

The sailor will not get much help from an offshore breeze.

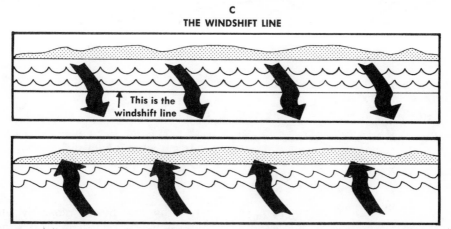

The arrows pointing up to the top of the bottom panel indicate an onshore breeze. An offshore breeze is indicated in the upper panel. A crafty sailor can make good use of this windshift line.

Figure 2—11

Quite often the wind aloft is puffing in several directions at once, contrary to sea-level breezes which may be so variable or light that your windvane is about as lifeless as an old sock. The sailor must learn to recognize that as winds tend to blow a few hundred feet upward from sea level, they slightly nudge the mass of atmospheric movement above, resulting in a slow downward tumbling of the movement. The process is analogous to a huge boulder perched precariously on a precipice, ready to fall at the slightest touch.

The seafarer can confidently expect that he and his boat will soon inherit any breezes moving from the direction of the nearest cloud form— assuming there is to be any change in the wind at all. Also, under conditions of cloudy sky, he can expect offshore or onshore breezes to lose their gusto, and what puffiness does exist will reach him from the direction from which the clouds are moving. Since we already know that the sun, producing heat exchange, is responsible for wind, a heavy cloud cover will simply blanket out the sun's local wind making. There will be wind, of course, associated with the moving clouds, but its direction will be the windshift. Some weathermen call it the storm windshift and the slackening of onshore or offshore breezes has come to be called the "lull before the storm" by laymen.

Figure 2-12 illustrates how the sailing man can utilize wind blanket effects and onshore suction to chart the shortest distance between two points in a sail race to reach a mark ahead of a competitor.

I would be remiss if I failed to report, as a matter of general interest, how fiendishly high winds can blow, and how in some areas howling winds arise with almost no warning.

Mount Washington in New Hampshire is the most singular example of high winds in the U.S. Though only a 6,000-foot peak, it sits squarely on a convergence of cyclone tracks which are followed by many storms leaving New England. This makes it climatically equal to a height greater than Pike's Peak. Winds have been recorded at Mount Washington's summit at a velocity of 231 miles an hour.

One of those winds of little warning is known as the "Tehuantepecer," a description of which was graphically presented in a book by William Wenstrom, *Weather and the Ocean of Air*. Nothing about the character of this wind has changed since Wenstrom profiled it in 1942.

"Tehuantepecers," . . . which occur in the Gulf of Tehuantepec are . . . little known to laymen but veritable bogies to intercoastal mariners; occur in winter and early spring when a great southward outbreak of polar air from Alaska or Canada sweeps southward across the United States, and across the Gulf of Mexico (as a howling "norther"), only to be partly dammed by the long mountain chain of the Central American Cordillera. But on the Isthmus of Tehuantepec is a wide low-level pass, through which the wind blows by a sort of funnel effect which, combined with a sort of remote airfall over the mountains, scours southward out over

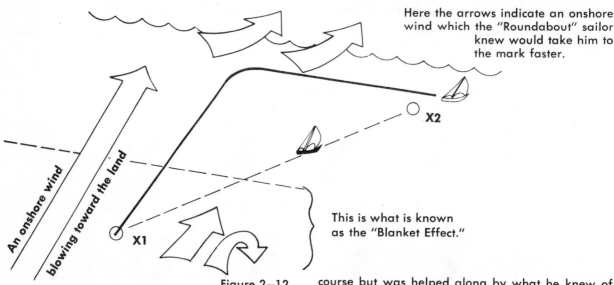

Here the arrows indicate an onshore wind which the "Roundabout" sailor knew would take him to the mark faster.

X2

An onshore wind

blowing toward the land

This is what is known as the "Blanket Effect."

X1

Figure 2—12

This is where you started in a race to a mark from X1 to X2. A competitor would have beat you to the mark, because he would have utilized a longer

course but was helped along by what he knew of land contours. He sailed briskly on a triangular course to take advantage of the onshore breeze. "As the crow flies" is not always the quickest distance from one point to another.

the Gulf of Tehuantepec at perhaps 60 miles an hour. These dangerous storms give little if any local warning, barometric or otherwise, of their approach. At one moment, the weather may be mild and pleasant, with only light winds or calms. Within an hour, a northerly gale may be blowing, kicking up a steep and high sea. Even a sturdy 5,000 ton freight steamer may lose a valuable deck load of lumber as the rising seas break of her bulwarks. Smaller vessels may be in actual danger of foundering.

The best Tehuantepecer warning for the weather-wise mariners, incidentally, is radio ship-weather reports from the Gulf of Mexico, north of the Isthmus—if there is no norther up there, no Tehuantepecer is possible.*

Most weather books seem to take it for granted that all laymen should know the difference between windward and leeward. But I have met many a boatman who not only doesn't know the difference between the two, but hasn't the vaguest idea of what a lee shore means.

Windward is the direction *from* which the wind is blowing. *Leeward* is the direction *toward* which the wind is blowing. Many mountains in the United States are heavily forested on the windward slope, but are almost barren on the leeward slope—a phenomenon we will explore more thoroughly in another chapter.

The table for determining wind speed by sea conditions on page 37 is an excellent guide to what the weather may be going to do, but *wind*

chill is a factor you certainly should know about as well.

Simply knowing the temperature will not tell you enough to dress sensibly for all cold weather conditions, since the speed of the wind also has a chilling effect. For example, if the temperature is 15° above zero and the wind is blowing at 15 miles per hour, the cooling effect on your body would be equivalent to a temperature of 25° below zero in still air; your exposed skin would freeze quickly. This is because the combined effect of wind and temperature determines the rate at which your body loses heat.

This combination is known as the "wind chill factor." The following table indicates that the wind chill factor increases with the wind speed up to 40 miles per hour. Above that velocity, any increase in wind speed will have little additional effect on your body's loss of heat. The wind chill table serves as a useful guide in determining the kind of protective clothing you should wear for cold conditions. However, the equivalent temperatures shown on the table are valid only if you are wearing dry clothing. Otherwise, evaporation of moisture from wet clothing will greatly increase the chill factor.

Locate the approximate temperature on the left side of the chart. Read across from the temperature reading, and down from the wind velocity reading. The number which appears at that intersection is the equivalent temperature determined by the wind chill factor.

WIND CHILL TABLE
Prepared by the National Center for Atmospheric Research
Boulder, Colorado

Little Danger		Increasing Danger		Great Danger That Exposed Flesh will Freeze						

Wind Velocity (MPH)

Temp. °F	0	5	10	15	20	25	30	35	40	45	50
−10	−10	−15	−31	−45	−52	−58	−63	−67	−69	−70	70
−5	−5	−11	−27	−40	−46	−52	−56	−60	−62	−63	−63
0	0	−6	−22	−33	−40	−45	−49	−52	−54	−54	−56
5	5	1	−15	−25	−32	−37	−41	−43	−45	−46	−47
10	10	7	−9	−18	−24	−29	−33	−35	−36	−38	−38
15	15	12	−2	−11	−17	−22	−26	−27	−29	−31	−31
20	20	16	2	−6	−9	−15	−18	−20	−22	−24	−24
25	25	21	9	1	−4	−7	−11	−13	−15	−17	−17
30	30	27	16	11	3	0	−2	−4	−4	−6	−7
35	35	33	21	16	12	7	5	3	1	1	0
40	40	37	28	22	18	16	13	11	10	9	8

* *From the book,* Weather and the Ocean of Air, *by Major William Wenstrom.* © *Houghton Mifflin Company.*

CHAPTER FOUR

Fundamentals of Forecasting
and Weather Information

IT MAY come as a surprise, but organized weather broadcasting in the United States did not begin in Washington, but in the Midwest, and was not sponsored by the government. One man, Cleveland Abbe, began issuing what he called "Probabilities" on September 1, 1869. In view of the vast network of weather reporting existing today, more than 105 years later, Abbe's declaration at the time was indeed prophetic. He said then: "I have started that which the country will not willingly let die."

From this absurdly humble beginning by one dedicated man, the National Weather Service, now a part of the National Oceanic and Atmospheric Administration (NOAA), has developed into a gigantic weather collecting and disseminating factory, with more than 350 surface reporting stations, over 100 radar surveillance posts, and in excess of 125 upper air sounding stations on land and sea. It has, counting all its weather and climatological research units, an annual budget in excess of $110,000,000. It employs one of the most sophisticated computers ever built, utilizes weather satellites, and sifts information collected by more than 100 other nations.

The task of NOAA is staggering beyond belief. But briefly, it is to observe, analyze, and report the atmospheric antics going on in about 2.5 billion miles of earth, air and sea throughout the northern hemisphere. Yet thousands of Americans, landlubbers and sailors alike, are discovering they can do an astonishingly accurate job of local weather prediction with only a few dollars worth of equipment.

Weather forecasting is a deductive process. The professional weatherman, like the medical diagnostician, looks for symptoms in present weather to arrive at a prognosis of what tomorrow's will be. The parlor meteorologist starts his diagnosis with four weather factors which were described in detail in the two previous chapters: temperature, relative humidity, barometric pressure and wind direction and strength. These four weather variables used in combination with the instruments explained here, and the reference tables illustrated, will enable you to make local or regional forecasts with reasonable accuracy. In addition to setting down some simple forecasting rules, we will expore briefly how to read a weather map, look at a simple method for determining the movement of fronts, and examine the sources of weather information available to anyone who wants to know what the weather will be.

As I pointed out earlier, temperature, in combination with relative humidity, is a key symptom of coming rain. Warm air, we know, holds more moisture than cold. If there is a sharp rise in the moisture in the air, but temperature remains the same, or conversely if there is a sharp drop in temperature while the humidity holds steady, we know that rain is probable.

So the first step in a weather diagnosis is to determine the temperature, and to test the air for its moisture or vapor content. Once the temperature is known, relative humidity must be measured. The instruments used for this are the standard thermometer, and the hair hygrometer or the psychrometer.

The hygrometer, *Figure 3-1*, utilizes a strand of human hair (long, fine blond hair seems to work best for some reason) to detect moisture in the air. As air becomes more humid, the hairs lengthen and the weights on the bar stretch them

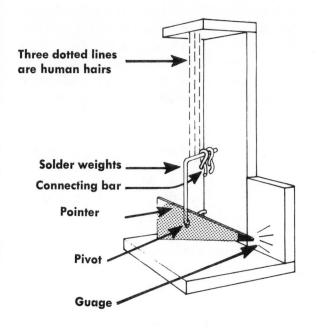

Three dotted lines are human hairs →

Solder weights →
Connecting bar —
Pointer →
Pivot —
Guage —

Figure 3—1

Drawing A records true air temperature. Its partner, Drawing B, has a thick string or wick attached to its bulb, with one end in a container of water. Because of evaporation from the wick, the wet-bulb temperature reading is less than that of the dry-bulb, unless the air is so humid that no water can be evaporated from the wick. The

The only difference between the two thermometers shown is that the left is called a wet bulb thermometer because temperature drops from evaporation from the string in the water.

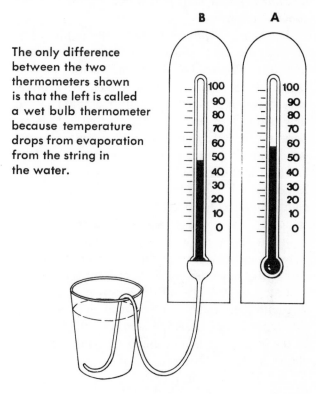

Figure 3—2

taut, and this causes the pointer to swivel on its pivot. Conversely, when less moisture is present in the air and the hairs dry, they pull the bar up, and the pointer moves down over the gauge.

While this hygrometer does provide indications of water vapor content in the air, it is rather crude in comparison with the psychrometer, or wet-and-dry bulb thermometer, illustrated in *Figure 3-2*.

As you can see, the dry-bulb thermometer in

Relative Humidity in Percent

Air temp., °F.	Depression of wet-bulb thermometer, °F.																								
	1	2	3	4	5	6	7	8	9	10	11	12	13	14	15	16	17	18	19	20	21	22	23	24	25
0	67	33	1																						
5	73	46	20																						
10	78	56	34	13																					
15	82	64	46	29	11																				
20	85	70	55	40	26	12																			
25	87	74	62	49	47	25	13	1																	
30	89	78	67	46	36	26	16	6																	
35	91	81	72	63	54	45	36	27	19	10	2														
40	92	83	75	68	60	52	45	37	29	22	15	7													
45	93	86	78	71	64	57	51	44	38	31	25	18	12	6											
50	93	87	80	74	67	61	55	49	43	38	32	27	21	16	10	5									
55	94	88	82	76	70	65	59	54	49	43	38	33	28	23	19	11	9	5							
60	94	89	83	78	73	68	63	58	53	48	43	39	34	30	26	21	17	13	9	5	1				
65	95	90	85	80	75	70	66	61	56	52	48	44	39	35	31	27	24	20	16	12	9	5	2		
70	95	90	86	81	77	72	68	64	59	55	51	48	44	40	36	33	29	25	22	19	15	12	9	6	3
75	96	91	86	82	78	74	70	66	62	58	54	51	47	44	40	37	34	30	27	24	21	18	15	12	9
80	96	91	87	83	79	75	72	68	64	61	57	54	50	47	44	41	38	35	32	29	26	23	20	18	15
85	96	92	88	84	81	77	73	70	66	63	59	57	53	50	47	44	41	38	36	33	30	27	25	22	20
90	96	92	89	85	81	78	74	71	68	65	61	58	55	52	49	47	44	41	39	36	34	31	29	26	24
95	96	93	89	86	82	79	76	73	69	66	63	61	58	55	52	50	47	44	42	39	37	34	32	30	28

Figure 3-3

greater the spread between the wet-bulb and dry-bulb readings, the lower the relative humidity.

It is worth repeating from Chapter 1 the definition of relative humidity: Relative humidity expresses measurable quantities. *It is the ratio between the amount of water vapor the air actually contains at a given temperature and the amount it could hold if it were saturated at the same temperature.*

The table, *Figure 3-3,* shows the relationship of dry-bulb and wet-bulb readings to relative humidity. *Figure 3-4* shows the relationship of the dry-bulb reading and the *spread* (the difference between dry- and wet-bulb readings) to the dew point. The dew point, of course, is the temperature at which air can hold no more water vapor, and the excess condenses as rain or fog. Locate the difference between the readings at the left of the table, and follow that line across to the right to the column closest to the temperature indicated by your dry-bulb thermometer. The figure at this point is the *spread,* the difference between air temperature and dew point temperature. If for example the air temperature is 60° as recorded on the dry-bulb thermometer, and the wet-bulb thermometer gives a reading of 50°, the difference is 10°. Reading across on the 10° line to the column of figures under 60°, the spread is shown as 20°. This means the temperature of the air would have to drop to 40° in order for fog or dew to form.

Generally, if the spread is less than six degrees at some point in the early evening, there's a good chance for fog to form during the night. This is indicated by the heavy line in *Figure 3-4.*

The barometer was described in Chapter 2. It indicates atmospheric pressure, expressed in inches of mercury or in millibars, and either designation or both may be shown on weather maps for your area.

Wind direction can be shown by any sort of simple weather vane, and strength can be estimated as indicated in Chapter 3. The professional instrument for this purpose is the anemometer (*Figure 3-5*), which links a windmill with cup-like vanes to a dial. There are anemometers available for home installation which record both wind direction and speed.

The next step in weather analysis is to relate local readings of temperature, humidity, pressure, and wind to those over a wide area which includes your local position. This is where the weather map comes in. A weather map must present a great deal of information in rather limited space, so symbols have been developed that provide a convenient shorthand. The com-

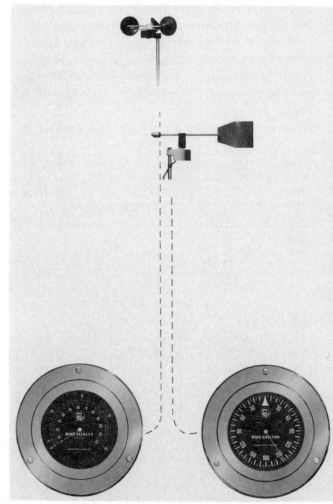

AIR TEMPERATURE—DEWPOINT SPREAD

(All figures are in degrees Fahrenheit at 30" pressure)

Difference Dry-Bulb Minus Wet-Bulb	Air Temperature Shown By Dry-Bulb Thermometer												
	35	40	45	50	55	60	65	70	75	80	85	90	95
1	2	2	2	2	2	2	2	1	1	1′	1	1	1
2	5	5	4	4	4	3	3	3	3	3	3	3	2
3	7	7	7	6	5	5	5	4	4	4	4	4	4
4	10	10	9	8	7	7	6	6	6	6	5	5	5
5	14	12	11	10	10	9	8	8	7	7	7	7	6
6	18	15	14	13	12	11	10	9	9	8	8	8	8
7	22	19	17	16	14	13	12	11	11	10	10	9	9
8	28	22	20	18	17	15	14	13	12	12	11	11	10
9	35	27	23	21	19	17	16	15	14	13	13	12	12
10	—	33	27	24	22	20	18	17	16	15	14	14	13
11	—	40	32	28	25	22	20	19	18	17	16	15	15
12	—	—	38	32	28	25	23	21	20	18	17	17	16
13	—	—	45	37	31	28	25	23	21	20	19	18	17
14	—	—	—	42	35	31	28	26	24	22	21	20	19
15	—	—	—	50	40	35	31	28	26	24	23	21	21

Opposite—Difference Dry-Bulb Minus Wet-Bulb and
Under —Air Temperature Shown By Dry-Bulb Thermometer
Read —Value of Spread: Air Temperature minus Dewpoint Temperature
Based on U.S. Weather Bureau Psychrometric Tables

Figure 3—4

COLD FRONT	WARM FRONT	STATIONARY	OCCLUDED
The line between cold and warm air masses generally moving southward and eastward issuing in brief storms and cooling weather	The line existing between a mass of warm air and retreating cold air, usually moving northward and eastward with a vanguard of rain and snow	The line between two air masses of similar temperature, moving only sluggishly. It often brings lengthy periods of precipitation.	The line on which a warm front has been overtaken by a cold front. It usually moves eastward, ushering in rain.

On a weather map, circles like those shown here are symbols of local weather

Clear ○	Rain ●●		Fog ≡
Partly Cloudy ◔	Cloudy ●	Thunderstorms ↳●	Snow ✳	Report Missing Ⓜ	Hurricane ⌇

Direction of Wind
Number of Tails Indicates Wind Speed

West Wind   East Wind

○ Calm	1–4	5–8	9–14	15–20
21–25	26–31	32–37	38–43	44–49
50–54	55–60	61–66	67–71	72–77

Prepared from Information Provided By U.S. Weather Service Denver, Colorado

mon symbols and their meanings are detailed in the table, *Figure 3-6.*

Having familarized yourself with the symbols in Table 3-6 used by professional weathermen in constructing a weathermap, let's look at the one below that follows the Weather Service's pattern.

The most outstanding features of a weather map are the curved lines which connect areas of equal pressure—called *isobars*—and the symbols that appear as *half circles* or pyramids attached to lines denoting frontal systems. In this map, *Figure 3-7,* isobars are marked at one end with

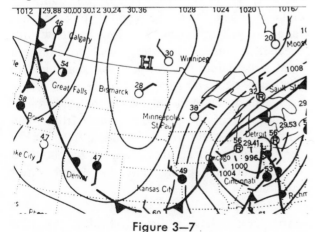

Figure 3—7

barometric pressure in inches and at the other end in millibars. You can see where high pressure systems are centered because they are so labled. Shaded areas indicate rain, and the circles and tails show local cloud cover and wind speed and direction. Single numbers near the circles are temperature readings. A second number underneath gives inches of precipitation, if any.

With this information, it now should be easier for you to make your own short-term analysis, using only one of two methods. Most sportsmen who have not had any formal training in the logistics of weather movements will use the "persistence" method of forecasting, and as they become more weatherwise supplement this method by intuition, which is, after all, promptings based on experience in watching for and listening to the signs of weather behavior.

Persistence forecasting imposes certain limitations because it involves predicting the weather from a single map, and you can only count on reasonable accuracy for about a 6 to 12 hour period. Nevertheless, even trained meteorologists use this approach to forecast short-range periods.

The trouble with the persistence method lies in

SIMPLIFIED WEATHER MAP USING THE CONTINUITY METHOD TO FOLLOW A COLD FRONT'S PROGRESSION OF LOWS

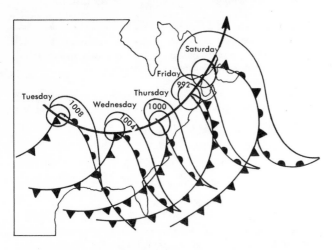

The heavy circles are the lows of the cold front in its progression Tuesday through Saturday. The line (East to West) through the lows connect them up, and by the time you have been able to make a forecast of the cold front's position, since its speed was decelerating each day.

Figure 3—8

the nature of a weather pattern. So many things can happen to change it.

The "continuity" method of forecasting is basically the persistence method enlarged upon by using a series of weather maps. In the example, following, I have simplified the continuity method. The movement of the storm front described can be plotted by the use of one single overlay on a series of separate maps.

Thus, while you won't qualify as a meteorological cartographer, you will be able to track the rate of speed and direction of a storm front's passage with better than average accuracy for periods extending much longer than 12 hours.

Let's try plotting by using as a model the action of a low pressure system centered over Colorado, employing the "modified continuity" method on one map, showing the progression of this cold front. The model is not theoretical. It is one of a legacy of actual low pressure systems whose movements have been forecast by the Denver Weather station of the National Weather Service.

Figure 3-8 illustrates a 1008-millibar low pressure system, about 60 miles from Denver, near Colorado Springs. It is a Tuesday, and a cold front has spread out and deepened southwest of the low. A warm front, on the other hand, seems not to have made up its mind what to do, but on

the same day has reached out to the southeast. In both cases, cold and warm fronts are located on what Coloradans call the Western Slope of the Rockies. Rain showers have been noted behind the cold front, while, as expected, a steady precipitation is soaking the ground ahead of the warm front.

By Wednesday, however, the low has become more depressed—by about 4 millibars. The central pressure area has deepened, in other words, from 1008 millibars to 1004. But in the process, the low has moved to a position near the edge of Western Illinois. In a roughly 24-hour period, it has moved leisurely eastward at about 35 miles an hour, or about 920 miles. What has happened then is that the cold front has begun to catch up with the indecisive warm front, developing a warm area between the two, south of the low center, and the cold front has begun to become squeezed by the rear confrontation (it has narrowed, while the rainfall in the vanguard of the warm front has broadened).

By Thursday, the low, still ugly, has depressed another 4 millibars, and the central pressure is now 1,000 millibars. The low has now traveled as far east as the southwestern portion of New York State, having almost overtaken the warm front whose early aimlessness has turned into a more flighty, but still slow, passage. In other words, the cold front has extended eastward at a rate of about 28 MPH in a round-the-clock period between Wednesday and Thursday. The low's frontal wave is in the process of forming an occlusion, which, if you'll remember, occurs when a cold front tailgating a warm front finally overtakes the latter and snowplows the warm air mass off the ground. Steady rain could be expected to reach out further in advance of the warm front.

As seen in *Figure 3-8,* by Friday the low-pressure system has deepened by an additional eight millibars, and the central pressure has fallen to 992 millibars. The low has now proceeded as far northeasterly as the northern border of Maine; but its speed has continued to drop, now reduced to about 23 MPH.

The next step in the odyssey of the cold front is its takeover of the preceding warm front. You now have a well-formed occluded front whose center low lies in an area bounded by about 75 degrees north latitude and 43 degrees west longitude.

Having patiently traced the cold front's eastward perambulations through Friday, you now wish to make a prediction of its position on a weather map as of Saturday.

At this point you are on your own, with the exception of reminding you of facts you should already have figured out.

1. The low's travel eastward has slowed each 24-hour day an average deceleration of about 6 MPH per day.
2. As a result, you should estimate that during the 24-hour period from Friday to Saturday, the average speed of the low would be about 17 MPH, or a distance covered of slightly more than 400 miles.
3. Note that after the cold front reached New York, it began to bend north and slightly northwesterly.

Okay, if you haven't figured out that the cold front should, by Saturday, have arrived at a position well above Montreal, Canada, then you made a forgivable mistake. Look at *Figure 3-8,* and you'll see what you should have done to forecast its likely position on Saturday.

Figure 3-8 illustrates the simplest and best method for predicting frontal movement: Take a blank map and overlay it on separate maps, following the front for at least three days, then trace the frontal positions and the lowest encircling isobar of each day's low onto the blank map. Next, draw arrows connecting the centers of the lows for each day. You will see that the connecting arrows usually become shorter each 24-hour period and that they point slightly more toward the north each day.

Having already spotted the cold front's anticipated position as of Saturday (above Montreal)

you could arrive at the same conclusion by drawing a curve which passes through the center of the front's positions Tuesday through Friday. Now, in similar fashion draw round-the-clock movement arrows for both the cold and the warm fronts and finally, connect the frontal arrow tips for each front to smooth in the progression of the low's position.

You have now plotted Saturday's position, and should be able to estimate that by Monday the cold front will have fizzled out.

It would be inexcusable to leave the reader at this point without some additional information on how to pinpoint the location of a front, for if you don't know what its approximate position is you can't very well predict its course and progress. Granted that from the foregoing information and tables you should probably be able to identify the nature of the front—cold, warm, occluded, etc.—but to simplify the process a step further, there are three sources from which you can get fairly reliable information: daily newspaper maps—though not as detailed as the official charts of the Weather Service—daily radio and television reports, and at sea, radio facsimile weather maps.

On Friday, April 5, 1974 the *Oregon Journal* published this forecast summary which was amplified by more thorough visual television analysis:

Gale warnings have been posted for the Oregon coast and heavy rain forecast for some parts of the state Friday as a storm front moves inland.

Rain is expected to diminish by late Friday night or Saturday. The freezing level will drop to 5,000 feet Saturday.

Some clearing is expected, especially in Southern Oregon, by Saturday. Temperatures will remain mild, except for some points in the Cascades and Eastern Oregon.

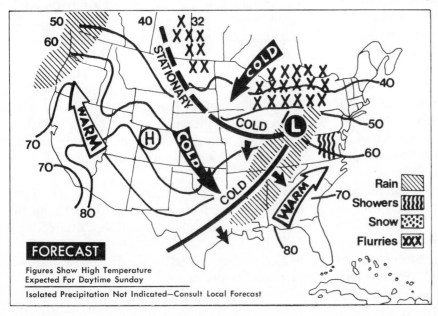

Figure 3—9

Daily Weather Map: The Sunday Oregonian, April 7, 1974.

Under the "forecast" heading, the *Journal* provided more explicit information on the same day:

Portland-Vancouver and Williamette Valley —Heavy rain Friday; decreasing Saturday with partial clearing. Highs 55–60, lows 40–45. Southerly winds 15–25 m.p.h. Chance of measurable rain decreasing to 80 per cent Saturday.

Oregon Coast—Gale warning posted for westerly winds 15–25 m.p.h. Friday night diminishing Saturday. Local seas 4–8 feet. Long ocean swells southwest 8–12 feet. Showers Friday night with partial clearing Saturday. Highs mostly in 50s, lows 40–45.

Thus, notice was given Friday of the storm front's coastal location, and its inland progress through southern Oregon by Saturday. The weather map published in the *Sunday Oregonian,* April 7, *Figure 3-9* graphically illustrated the position, at the time of publication, of the cold front—heading southeast and about to encounter another cold front low-pressure line extending west to northeast. Depending on the strength of the Pacific Northwest front by the time it had reached the west-northeast pressure line, one of two major changes could have occurred: the low pressure system heading northeast would have progressed far enough in that direction to have missed the driving reinforcement of the cold front coming down from Oregon. If that had happened, and the Oregon cold front still had power to spare, it reasonably could be expected to have plowed under the warm air wedge in Texas, dropping temperatures there and causing rain. Or, as in the case of the charted example of the Colorado front, simply may have pooped out.

Radio and television are major sources of weather information. Most broadcast stations give reports ranging from skimpy to thorough, based on information supplied at intervals by the National Weather Service. However, in most coastal areas, the National Weather Service has continuous broadcasts of conditions and forecasts, with emphasis on marine use. New tapes are prepared every few hours. The usual frequency is 162.55 MHz, and in locales where stations may be close together, a secondary frequency such as 164.00 MHz is used.

In addition to normal temperature, pressure, and wind information, the broadcasts include sea conditions and visibility at several coastal points. The broadcasts can be received on regular VHF sets, and on some newer AM-FM receivers. There are several makes of inexpensive transistorized receivers designed just for this service.

Many metropolitan TV stations today employ professional meteorologists as weathercasters— and the trend is toward hiring more of these professionally-trained people to improve the accuracy of wide local and regional weather analysis.

If you are served by two or three TV stations, be sure to ascertain which one utilizes meteorologists. The important reason for this is threefold:

1. The visual weather forecasts generally will be about three hours in advance of a complete weather forecast from your local weather station, if you could get all the facts you wanted.

2. TV weather professionals utilize three wire services provided by NOAA—NAFACX, FOFACX, and RAFACX. These are computerized weather facsimiles for a particular area and include in the first case several parameters of weather, except barometric pressure. The second and third services pertain to satellite photos and radar information. Additionally, a NOAA "weather wire" transmits other important information.

3. TV stations which do not employ professionals generally rely upon teletyped national wire service weather reports which are old before they are sent out—this also is one of the defects in daily newspaper weather maps—and upon data from the local Weather Service station. Thus, TV stations employing old-fashioned techniques televise information which is second and third hand before you get it.

The reason a TV station often reports more timely weather is due to Weather Service station makeup schedules. The TV weatherman must meet news deadlines which seldom coincide with the more routine assembling of weather reports compiled by Weather Service meteorologists. As a result his analysis is made independently, generally reaches the public sooner, and with few exceptions, coincides with the weather picture that his government colleagues come up with later.

His advantage lies in the resourceful use of the same basic methods and tools for patching together a forecast, plus the fact that a direct line from his TV studio to the weather station gives him immediate access to verification of his own professional forecast.

To summarize: By noting the position of a front as televised by a major metropolitan TV weathercaster, you then can extrapolate from this information how the front will progress, utilizing the modified "continuity" method, I've outlined in conjunction with the foregoing charts and tables which relate those four important variables—temperature, relative humidity, barometric pressure, and wind direction and strength.

One drawback with NOAA's service is a lack of planned integration of new weather sensing facilities with the Coast Guard.

In Galveston up to three years ago, the Coast Guard station personnel received teletyped weather reports for a wide Gulf Coast area, emanating from New Orleans. Regional teletyped reports cannot possibly relate to local wind-water conditions which spawn their own quick-to-rise line squalls and sudden hazardous weather disturbances. Yet the Galveston Weather Service station, which has one of the most modern weather sensing systems in the United States, arising out of research done at NASA in Houston, is not linked up to the Coast Guard station there.

Telemetered profiles of weather indices pouring into the Galveston weather station are due to NASA's work several years ago of studying wave propogation in the Gulf of Mexico. The research was aimed at developing safer splashdown techniques for astronauts returning to earth following moon shots. Consequently, the Galveston station has become a model for the Weather Service, since its weather sensing capabilities measure at least eight parameters of weather. A target date of 1976 has been established for the installation of refined models of Galveston's weather sensing devices in all principle Weather Service stations in the U.S. which serve all coastal and large inland lake areas.

Some idea of the value of Galveston's sensing devices can be appreciated by listening to FM broadcasts sent out over the air waves continuously during a 24-hour period on 4 and 6 minute tapes. These tapes are regularly updated every 2 to 4 hours, and the system is keyed to sudden weather changes in such a way that the tapes are interrupted for important or urgent weather advisories.

When I was there the Galveston USCG base was still seeking approval from its district headquarters in Houston for the purchase of a $200 VHF-FM receiver which could cue the Coast Guard station into the 4 to 6 minutes advisories from the Galveston weather station.

The situation is being improved, and no American citizen should denigrate the manner in which the mission of the Coast Guard is being carried out. It is exemplary. But until this vital link in communications between the Coast Guard and U.S. Weather stations which serve the same area can be remedied, the boating sportsman would be well advised to take advantage of the following publications listed, and to consult at the back of this book the addresses of Weather Service marine centers and port offices. At any of these offices, personnel will assist you to calibrate barometers, and aid you with problems regarding weather observations and forecasts.

NOAA publishes a booklet entitled *Marine Weather Services*. It is a worthy piece of information which has three headings of particular interest to the boating sportsman:

1. *Weather Warnings and Forecasts*
2. *NOAA VHF-FM Radio Weather*
3. *Marine Weather Service Charts,* 15 of which are available from the Superintendent of Documents, U.S. Government Printing Office, Washington, D.C. 20402, at 15¢ each. In *Weather Warnings and Forecasts* this statement is made:

Weather forecasts for boating areas in the United States and Puerto Rico are issued every six hours by the National Weather Service. Each forecast covers a specific coastal area, as, for example, "Eastport, Me., to Block Island, R.I." If strong winds or sea conditions hazardous to small-boat operations are expected, forecasts include a statement as to the type of warning issued and the areas where warnings are in effect. Similar forecasts and warnings are issued for numerous inland lakes, dams, reservoirs, and river waterways throughout the country. Daily advices indicating expected stream flow, river gage heights, and flood warnings as required are also issued by the National Weather Service. Latest forecasts are available over AM and FM radio, television, and marine radiotelephone broadcasts. Radio stations in cities along principal rivers include stream flow and river data in their weather messages. When storm and flood warnings are in effect, all stations make frequent broadcasts of these advices as a service to small-craft operators, the general public, and other interests.

CHAPTER FIVE

What You Should Know About Fog, Squally Weather and Swells

Too MANY novice boatmen ignore the danger of fog unless it is so thick they can't see beyond the boat. But an examination of U.S. Coast Guard Boating Statistics for any year, including the current one, will reveal that underestimation of the reduction in visibility due to foggy conditions is responsible for many accidents and fatalities. So, after defining the types of fog, how and why they occur, we'll examine two case histories of accidents investigated by the Coast Guard on Search and Rescue Missions, in which the boat operators failed to appreciate that hazardous form of cloud which is lowest to the sea or ground surface.

Fog is simply ground surface air cooled into aerial pools of water. It is composed of tiny droplets suspended in the atmosphere, with no visible downward motion, and is distinguished from haze by its dampness and gray color. Fog rarely forms when the difference between the temperature and the dewpoint (see Chapters 2 and 4) is more than 2.5° C. (6° F.) Also, fog by definition extends to a depth greater than 6 feet on land or 33 feet at sea, and reduces prevailing visibility to less than one-half nautical mile or about three-fifths of a statute mile. When the visibility is reduced, but not to this extent, three conditions can prevail:

1. *A Light Fog,* which extends above eye level but reduces visibility from less than 6 nautical miles to not less than about one-half nautical mile.
2. *A Shallow Fog,* which is not raised above eye level and does not reduce visibility at your height below one-half nautical mile. However, the density of the fog would reduce

your visibility to less than one-half nautical mile if you were in the fog.
3. *A Fog Bank,* not obscuring your boat, but lying at a depth below your eye level, also would reduce your visibility to less than one-half nautical mile.

Having described what fog is, let's examine the four basic types of fog and how they are typically formed. *Advection fog* is caused by warm air flowing over and being cooled by a cold surface. *Radiation fog* is generally formed when the earth begins losing heat into the night air. This results in a cooling of the air above. Since we know cold air is denser and heavier, it slides downhill—the "valley low" comparison—and settles in depressions as fog. Radiation fog can best be appreciated if you were in a tall building. From a high viewpoint, at sundown, eyeing through a wet, warm atmosphere, you would see dozens, or more, of white patches of radiation fog, resembling, for want of a better description, woolly sheep hugging the ground. To be sure, they would be big sheep.

There are two variations to advection fogs. These are steam fog and the upslope fog. Steam fog is formed when cold air flows over a warm surface. This also is called "frost smoke" or "arctic sea smoke." When the water is far warmer than the air, evaporation is so intense that steam forms on the water and fills the air with fog. While this fog is rare and rather shallow, its formation is analogous to a street cleaning machine spraying cold water on hot pavement in summer time. There is a hissing, and you can see the steam (fog) rise. Upslope fog is created when moist sea air blows against hills and is cooled by uplift into colder heights. A heavy wind would dissipate such a fog, which can occur along any coastal area. However, a slow and steady wind will feed fog, giving it persistence and staying power.

The Pacific Coast inherits more fogs than the Atlantic Coast due to the prevailing west-to-east wind. On the East Coast the prevailing wind swoops off the land and is less humid. However, great fog breeders are the moist winds of the Gulf Stream which frequently shear upward and east to greet the colder Labrador Current. This mixing makes Newfoundland almost as foggy as London Town at times.

Precipitation fog is the creation of rain or snow, relatively warm, dropping through cold air. A good example is when a storm chugs in to encounter cold, wet air. The result is that the storm rain falls into the chilled air, raising the dewpoint—fog occurs then in the same fashion that clouds form aloft.

The two fog-accident reports recorded here are from the files of the U.S. Coast Guard. Only the names of the persons involved and the boat identification have been changed; also non-pertinent facts have been omitted.

CASE 1
NO FOG HORN SOUNDING

From: Investigating Officer, MIO, Dubuque, Iowa
To: Commandant (BBA)
Via: (1) Officer in Charge, Marine Inspection, Dubuque, Iowa
      (2) Commander, Second Coast Guard District (bsb)
Subj: Ocean Spree and Motorboat MN 1600 BC; collision 30 August 1971 with loss of life

FINDINGS OF FACT

About 9:00 P.M. CDST 30 August 1971, the houseboat Ocean Spree and the unnamed Motorboat MN 1600 BC collided at Mile 11.5, St. Croix River, and Leslie Groves was drowned.

The vessels involved were:

Ocean Spree, a 40 foot steel houseboat, 14 feet wide and 3 feet deep; net tonnage of 18 and powered by two 120 horsepower gasoline engines.

MN 1600 BC was a 17 foot fiberglas open construction runabout, powered by a 60 horsepower gasoline inboard-outboard unit.

The drowning victim was:
Leslie Groves (M), age 16 years.

Visibility was poor due to fog and heavy intermittent rain and was 50 feet at the scene of the collision. The waves were 3 to 4 feet due to the 30 to 40 MPH wind which was blowing up the channel. The temperature was in the sixties.

The Ocean Spree, operated by the owner, Pat Pauley, was upbound at approximately 7 MPH. The running lights of the MN 1600 BC were noticed broad on the starboard bow prior to the collision. The MN 1600 BC, operated by Leslie Groves, was westbound at approximately 18 MPH. Neither of the vessels was sounding fog signals. As the MN 1600 BC passed ahead of the Ocean Spree's starboard pontoon, it struck the bow of the port pontoon on the inboard side. The Ocean Spree picked up Stephen Hess, a companion of Leslie Groves, from the capsized hull of the MN 1600 BC and searched the area for about twenty minutes with negative results. Hess was hospitalized at Hudson, Wisconsin. Sheriff's deputies recovered the capsized MN 1600 BC and searched for the body of Leslie Groves, which was recovered on 6 September 1971.

CONCLUSIONS

It is concluded that:
Neither vessel was sounding fog signals in fog and intermittent heavy rain. This is evidence of violation of 33 USC 331; and that the Ocean Spree, the burdened vessel, did not keep out of the way of the other vessel. This is evidence of violation of 33 US 344.

CASE II
RUNNING TOO FAST IN FOG

From: Investigating Officer
To: Commandant (BBA)
Via: (1) Officer in Charge, Marine Inspection, Boston, Mass.
      (2) Commander, First Coast Guard District
Subj: CC/Brown, collision and sinking resulting in the loss of two lives on 10 October 1971 in Nantucket Sound

FINDINGS OF FACT

On 10 October 1971 at approximately 11:15 A.M. (all times EDT) the CC/Brown struck Pollock Rip Channel Lighted Bell Buoy 5 and sunk resulting in the loss of two men's lives.

The CC/Brown was a 26′ McKenzie built, Cuttyhunk model boat which was constructed in 1963. It had a cabin and was built of wood with an inboard gasoline engine of 265 HP. The hull was green. As a result of the accident reported here, William Foley, died from exposure to cold water for a period of approximately 24 hours. Also, Richard Dory died from exposure to cold water for a period of approximately 24 hours. Both men were wearing life preservers.

The weather at the time of the accident was foggy, visibility was poor, the wind was very light with no sea running but a strong ebbing current was running toward Nantucket Sound.

Mr. Foley and Mr. Dory were returning to their home in Chatham from a morning fishing trip around Nantucket Island. They were running through thick fog when the boat struck, what was reported by them as a submerged object. They called for help on their radio; advising they were tied to buoy 5. Their call was picked up by the CC/MacIntosh and relayed to Brant Point Station. Buoy 5 was assumed to be McBlair Shoal Buoy 5, which is east of Great Point Light on Nantucket Island. When a boat from Brant Point Station arrived at the buoy, they found no boat. Later that day, another boat reported intercepting the call of the CC/Brown and proceeded to Pollock Rip Lighted Bell Buoy 5, which that boat assumed the call to mean. Arriving at the buoy, no boat was sighted. The visibility in the area was only 50 yards. It was noticed that the buoy had recently

been struck and there was still green paint on it. This was later confirmed by a boat from Chatham Station. After an unsuccessful night search by units of the Coast Guard, Chatham Station received a call that the wreck of a boat answering the CC/Brown's description, was sighted in the vicinity of Handkerchief Shoals. The CGC PT. BONITA proceeded to that area where they picked up the first body around noon on the 11th, and an hour later picked up the second body.

The wreck of the boat was later located and towed into Chatham where the damage was noted as that of two holes in the hull below the water line, the cabin was cracked at its supporting members and the engine was off its mounts.

CONCLUSIONS

Based on the preceding findings of fact, the following conclusions are made:

The boat collided with Pollock Rip Lighted Bell Buoy 5 and later sunk; the casualty was the result of operating at high speed in view of the existing weather conditions; a thick fog.

There was evidence of negligence on the part of the operator, and both men died as a result of being exposed to cold water for an excessive amount of time in relation to their ages and physical condition.

The above two SAR cases clearly demonstrate the degree to which fog can reduce visibility in

FIG. 4-1. TABLE OF HORIZON DISTANCES.

Height Feet	Nautical Miles	Height Feet	Nautical Miles	Height Feet	Nautical Miles	Height Feet	Nautical Miles
1	1.1	25	5.7	49	8.0	180	15.3
2	1.6	26	5.8	50	8.1	190	15.8
3	2.0	27	5.9	55	8.5	200	16.2
4	2.3	28	6.1	60	8.9	210	16.6
5	2.6	29	6.2	65	9.2	220	17.0
6	2.8	30	6.3	70	9.6	230	17.3
7	3.0	31	6.4	75	9.9	240	17.7
8	3.2	32	6.5	80	10.2	250	18.1
9	3.4	33	6.6	85	10.5	260	18.4
10	3.6	34	6.7	90	10.9	270	18.8
11	3.8	35	6.8	95	11.2	280	19.1
12	4.0	36	6.9	100	11.4	290	19.5
13	4.1	37	7.0	105	11.7	300	19.8
14	4.3	38	7.1	110	12.0	310	20.1
15	4.4	39	7.1	115	12.3	320	20.5
16	4.6	40	7.2	120	12.5	330	20.8
17	4.7	41	7.3	125	12.8	340	21.1
18	4.9	42	7.4	130	13.0	350	21.4
19	5.0	43	7.5	135	13.3	360	21.7
20	5.1	44	7.6	140	13.5	370	22.0
21	5.2	45	7.7	145	13.8	380	22.3
22	5.4	46	7.8	150	14.0	390	22.6
23	5.5	47	7.8	160	14.5	400	22.9
24	5.6	48	7.9	170	14.9	410	23.2

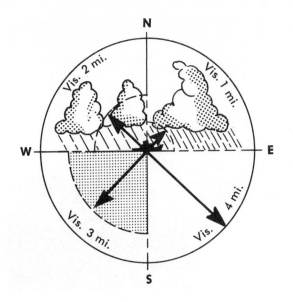

Figure 4—2

boating operations. It certainly seems worthwhile, in view of these and other tragedies, to report some observations made on visibility based on information from the Weather Service handbook, *Marine Observations.*

Visibility is a term that denotes the greatest distance from an observer that an object of known characteristics can be seen and identified. *Prevailing visibility,* on the other hand, is defined as the highest visibility that is equalled or exceeded over sectors of the horizon which, when combined, total one-half or more of the horizon circle. When the visibility is uniform in all directions "visibility" and "prevailing visibility" are the same.

Determining Visibility

Whenever possible, estimate visibility using objects whose distance is known. Estimating the distance to a boat may be based on its apparent size and the portion visible. The following table, *Figure 4-1,* is a guide for distance from an observer to the horizon and objects such as a boat whose height is known or can be reliably estimated. For example, the horizon from a height of 40 feet above sea level appears at a distance of 7.6 nautical miles.

Obviously, estimation of visibility is partially based on the sharpness of the object being observed. Sharp outlines, with little or no blurring of color, indicate that the visibility is much greater than the distance to the object. Blurred or indistinct objects indicate that the visibility is about equal to the distance to the objects. Now, when the visibility is not the same in all direc-

tions, the highest value common to one-half or more of a horizon circle should be determined. For example, if fog limits the visibility in the NE and SE quadrants of a horizon circle to one mile, while the visibility in the SW and NW quadrants is six miles, the maximum visibility common to one-half of the horizon circle is six miles.

Figure 4-2 illustrates non-uniform visibility which may be the result of squalls in one quadrant of the horizon circle, light showers and haze in another, and haze only in the third quadrant. The maximum visibility common to one-half of the circle is three miles.

In the summer of 1970, the Coast Guard Station at Galveston had every search and rescue vessel plus all the Coast Guard Auxiliary boats that could be mustered, to offer assistance to the more than 200 July 4th weekend boatmen who were caught totally unprepared by a sudden line squall that overturned sailboats like pins in a bowling alley.

Line squalls are violent, quixotic, and generally whisk through an area rapidly. If you will remember the earlier description of a cold front, you'll be able to understand a line squall, for it is really the front of a front. It resembles the effect of a cloudburst in the mountains that sends a roaring, racing torrent of water down a dry gulley. The front is a huge wave that picks up and carries with it anything in its path. When a cold front is fast, its downward snout roots up all the warm air in its path, sending it streaming aloft to form into a teeming mass of howling black-cloud fury. The winds are seldom less than sixty knots, often approaching eighty.

Figure 4-3 shows that the squall cloud is also the indicator of the direct wind shift line, diagrammed earlier. The drawings in *Figure 4-4* show how the winds in the vanguard of a cold front generally flow at right angles to the approaching storm line, causing the direct shift when the front passes.

If your face was presented to the pre-storm cloud, you can expect a wind shift to your right after the squall has passed. While it is true that in a violent line squall, the high and gusty surface wind may shift suddenly from southwesterly to northwesterly, fairly often there is a relatively calm zone along the front itself, so that its passage may be marked by a gradual dying away of the warm sector southwesterly or southerly winds. There will be a sort of stagnation of movement, an aimless milling about of the clouds and showers in almost calm air. Following this confused quiet, a wind will spring up, increasing gradually, out of the northwest or north.

There is no question but that the line squall is one of nature's most spectacular performances; a three-ring circus in the sky, combining awesome colors; turbulence, which has a voice that may be heard as a shrieking or whining, and lightning that fractures the black sky like the streaks of broken glass in a darkened mirror.

Wind waves and swell are two subjects the boating sportsman should become familiar with for the simple reason that the size of waves and swell, and the direction from which both may be coming are often forewarning of a storm approaching long before you see the sky darken.

Wind waves are systems raised by the local wind. If the wind increases, blowing steadily, wave steepness will increase—a sign to head toward port.

Swells, on the other hand, are waves not raised by the local wind but by a distant wind system, which may warn of an appoaching storm. Swells also may reach you after distant winds have ceased to blow. However, this last statement should be of little comfort to the boatman. Is a storm going to reach him, or will it have blown out, pushing swells ahead as a reminder that it had threatened to develop its fury? Continuous or periodic observations should establish a tendency fairly soon.

If you use the information presented here in conjunction with the table, Determination of Wind by Sea Conditions on page 37, you should have warning enough in advance to make your way to safety.

Having defined wind waves and swells, the boating sportsman needs to know how to determine three other facts: swell direction, wave period, and wave height.

Swell direction is the direction from which waves are coming, calculated in tens of degrees true; also wind wave direction, except in a confused sea, is assumed to be the same as the wind direction.

Wave period is the interval in seconds between the passage of two successive wave crests of well-formed waves past a fixed point.

Wave height is defined as the vertical distance between a crest and the troughs on either side of the crest.

To find out the period of wind waves or swell, locate a distinctive patch of foam or a small float-

Figure 4-3

ing object at some distance from your boat. Now, figure the elapsed time to the nearest second between the moments when the object is on the crest of the first and of the last well-formed wave in the group. Also record the number of crests that pass under the object during the interval. For best results, continue your observation until at least 12 waves have been timed. Add the elapsed times of the various groups together and divide the total by the number of waves to obtain the average period.

The wave height should be estimated from the best available point on your boat; one that permits the height of the waves to be compared to the height of your boat. Your eyeballing should be done at about amidships, where the pitching of your boat would be the least. Theoretically, wave height should be estimated when your boat is on an even keel. However, this often cannot be achieved, with the result that small wave heights

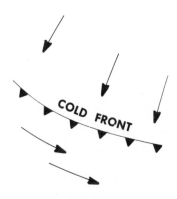

Figure 4—4

are underestimated, while large wave heights are overestimated. But don't let this bother you too much. Wave heights usually do not exceed wave lengths by more than 1/13, eyeballed from trough to trough.

Here are three ways to estimate wave heights:

1. Look over the side and compare the height of waves with points of known height on the side, cabin, or rigging of your boat.

2. When your boat is in the trough of a wave, move up and down until the wave crests appear momentarily on a horizontal plane with your eye. The wave height is then equal to eye-level height above the waterline.

3. When your boat is in the company of an-

other boat and your boat is on an even keel, the height from trough to crest of a wave against the other boat's side can be estimated as a part of some known vertical distance. For example, a wave height may be 1/4 of the other boat's height to cabin top of 16 feet, or four feet high.

To tie this information in with the table on page 37, let's suppose you estimate that the probable wave height is 10 feet. This would correspond to a wind force on the Beaufort Scale of 6. The wind would mean a strong breeze, and you would be noting large waves beginning to form, with extensive white foam crests. You would be in near gale conditions, and your judgment should tell you to head for home.

CHAPTER SIX

Storms and Lightning

HERE ARE DESCRIBED weather antics that bode no good—a fair warning about foul weather—storms and lightning whose great displays of atmospheric upheaval have been indelibly inked on the minds of men.

What is that storm? What makes it move so? What mysterious forces give it energy? The questions go on, for the exhilarating conquest and taming of bad weather against which men of all trades and professions, but sailors mostly, have tested themselves, is a contest older than memory.

William Pitt probably captured best the challenging spirit of seamen in *The Sailors Consolation:*

> *One night came on a hurricane,*
> *The sea was mountains rolling,*
> *When Barney Buntline turned his quid,*
> *And said to Billy Bowling:*
> *"A strong nor-wester's blowing, Bill;*
> *Hark! don't you hear it roar now?*
> *Lord help 'em, how I pities all*
> *Unhappy folks on shore now!"*

Even before Aristotle men were attempting to fashion laws for storms. The late 16th century scientist Robert Hooke, who was curator of the Royal Society in London drew up "the Form of a Scheme" for recording weather in an orderly way. His Scheme reproduced here in *Figure 5-1* is not so far removed from some of our modern tables of weather indications.

Yes, even today, more than 400 years after Hooke's Scheme, the question remains still not fully answered: What is that storm?

Another Englishman, Henry Piddington whose minutely detailed and carefully documented work, *The Sailor's Horn Book for the Law of Storms,* is a surviving classic of weather at sea, may not have envisioned the World Meteorological Organization that exists today, but that he recognized the need for assimilating and dispensing critical information on storm formation is evident in these remarks:

The Form of a Scheme. Which at one view reprefents to the Eye Obfervations of the Weather, for a whole Month, may be fuch, as follows.						
Days of the Month, and Place of the Sun	Remarkable hours	Age and Sign of the Moon at Noon.	The Quarters of the Wind, and its ftrength.	The Faces or vifible appearances of the Sky.	The Notableft Effects	General Deductions. Thefe are to be made after the fide is filled with Obfervations, as
June 14 ♊ 12.46'	4 8 12 4 8 12	27 . 9. 46 Perigeum	W - - - - 2 - - - - - 3 - - - - - - 3½ - - - - - - - WSW 1 - - - - - - - -	Clearblue, but yellowifh in the N E. Clouded toward the South. . Checkered blue.	A great Dew Thunder far to the S. A very great Tyde.	From the laft Quarter of the Moon to the Change, the weather was very temperate, but for the Seafon, cold ; the Wind pretty conftant between N. and W. &c.
15 ♊ 13.40'	8 4 6 12	28 24.51 N	N W 3 4 2 1	A clear sky all day, but a little checker'd about 4 P. M. At Sun-fet red and hazy.	Not by much fo big a Tyde as yefterday. A great Thunder-Showre from the N.	
16 ♊ 14.57 &c.	10	New Moon at 7. 25. A. M. ♊ 10.8 &c.	S 1 &c.	Overcaft and very lowring, &c.	No dew upon the ground, but very much upon Marble-ftones, &c.	

Figure 5—1

Hooke's weather report, as reprinted from Phil. Trans., 1667, in History of Science, Technology, and Philosophy, Vol. I. 1968.

". . . we may boldly say that merchants, ship-owners, underwriters and sailors themselves, must be willfully blind and deaf to their plainest interests when they do not encourage the researches relating to Storms; and not less so Governments, until they adopt some organized system for collecting, registering and digesting the vast masses of scattered information which already exist, and which are from the countless ships of England, America, and France alone, hourly accumulating and passing into oblivion. No single individual or association, without official authority and support, and adequate means can do this; but the nation and the ministry that accomplishes the great tasks which I have—sketched out—and truly gives to the mariner of all nations a Code of the Law of Storms . . . will fairly claim a share in the honours awarded to the Noblest Benefactors of the Human Race."

In Chapter 4, the weather reporting systems in the United States were discussed, and it was pointed out that on a worldwide scale, weather and oceanographic information, forecasts and warnings are readily available to the boating sportsman and to the professional seafarer. Additionally, when conditions of extreme weather develop, weather and sea observations are reported at more frequent intervals than the standard six-hour period and these reports are transmitted by landline or radio to those designated collection and control centers which relay this information on assigned frequencies to any recipient who can receive the broadcasts.

If an old salt like Piddington were able to revisit this earthly realm today, he would at least chortle with joy to express his enthusiasm over the globe-straddling network of meteorological forecasting—patchy though it still is. However, Piddington could pose some pertinent questions about the generation of storms to which he would still receive incomplete answers:

What is the force behind a tornado? A waterspout?

What makes a hurricane go?

Can a ship or boat trigger lightning?

Is St. Elmo's Fire a prelude to more dangerous electrical displays?

A necessary preliminary to exploring more thoroughly the nature of bad weather, and what you can do to avoid the worst of it, is an explanation of the thermal convection process that builds the cumulonimbus or thunderhead into a towering storm factory—the giant clouds, with the shape and the energy of the mushroom created by an atomic bomb explosion. Some idea of the fantastic air currents hurtling up in a thunderstorm—often they reach a speed of 350 MPH—can be comprehended from the experience of U.S. Marine jet pilot William Rankin, "The Man Who Rode the Thunder." Rankin's F8U-Crusader flamed out near Scotland Neck, North Carolina, July 26, 1959. He ejected at 47,000 feet into a violent thunderstorm. His pre-set parachute did not open until he had fallen to 10,000 feet. Normally, he should have reached ground in thirteen minutes. Instead, for forty-five minutes he was bounced up and down like a ping pong ball on a gushing fountain of air, rain and hail. Amid ear-splitting claps of thunder, he was tossed as much as 6,000 feet at a time. Once, when a violent blast of air blew him into his chute, collapsing the cold, wet nylon over him like a shroud, he was certain of death. But miraculously, the chute recovered its billow.

"I saw lightning around me in every shape imaginable. When very close, it appeared mostly as a huge bluish sheet several feet thick. It was raining so torrentially that I thought I would drown in mid air."

The concentrated fury in an average thunderstorm almost defies comprehension as physicist Dr. Marx Brook, of the New Mexico Institute of Mining and Technology, discovered when he measured the energy budget in a thunderstorm that spawned a tornado near the Tulsa, Oklahoma Geophysical Observatory of the Jersey Production Research Corporation on May 27, 1962.

Working from information supplied by a magnetometer—an instrument that measures the intensity and direction of magnetic forces—Brook calculated the tornado drained lightning power from a cloud storehouse towering more than six miles high and twenty miles long in a vertical current for about five minutes in an amount that exceeded one-third of the total electrical charge on the surface of the earth. This is roughly equivalent to exploding 10,000 one-megaton bombs simultaneously, or the power generated by the food consumed in one day by ten million people.

There are three distinct stages of development in the cumulonimbus. *Figure 5-2* shows these stages.

The cumulus stage of a youthful thunderhead might be compared to a giant chimney of furiously rising air, rapidly moulding building blocks out of water vapor present in the updraft. The

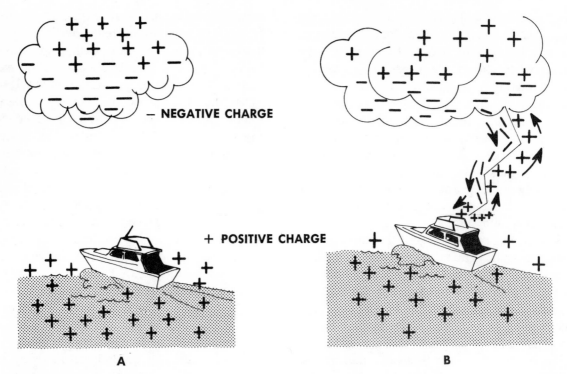

+ POSITIVE CHARGE

− NEGATIVE CHARGE

A

By friction or contact with rain, sleet, hail, snow or waves, boat builds up a positive charge.

B

By intensifying the electric field between cloud and sea, the boat, having built up a positive charge, triggers a lightning discharge.

Figure 5—2

taller the cloud grows, the faster the updraft and the more water vapor carried aloft. What happens is that the moisture condenses faster than the surrounding air can absorb it. As the moisture condenses, it releases heat that adds energy to the updraft, keeping the cloud growing in all directions.

In the mature stage the falling rain is said to be accompanied by lightning. Inherent in this statement is the old belief that rainfall makes lightning. Actually lighting is the rainmaker in a storm cloud.

The old idea was that storm clouds discharge lightning in order to release a buildup of electricity caused by the interaction of positive and negative charges in falling raindrops.

First in the Grand Bahama Islands, then later during the summers of 1961 and 1962 at Mt. Withington, New Mexico, a team of researchers, led by Drs. Bernard Vomegut of the State University of New York, and Charles Moore of The New Mexico Institute of Mining and Technology, photographed, radar scanned, and timed sequences of lightning and rain emanating from storms, and measured quantities of precipitation. From repeated observations, they figured out that somehow lightning accelerates the process

through which raindrops combine in a storm cloud.

One explanation is that electrical forces drive highly charged positive droplets at a furious pace through a cloud. These droplets attract, and collide with, negative ones. The collisions neutralize the positive droplets which, by their union with the negative ones, grow so big they fall quickly and add to their size by repeated collisions.

The size of raindrops in a thunderhead is what makes this storm cloud so reflectible on a radarscope. As we know, radar operates on the principle of electrical echo-feedback. It can only bounce back off something solid, and unlike other clouds which are composed of tiny drops of water, the huge storm cloud contains large drops and heavy reflecting layers of rain, snow and ice.

Another method by which lightning can make gushes of rain—one that the bell ringers of the Middle Ages may have figured out—is the acoustical shock effect of a lightning stroke. Dr. Duncan Blanchard of the Woods Hole Oceanographic Institution has learned that by firing explosives in a wind tunnel, with shock waves comparable to lightning bolts, he can jolt or fracture single water drops into five to twenty droplets.

The final, or dissipating stage of a thunderstorm occurs when you see the familiar anvil top. Too, you can almost see the high speed winds slicing the cap off the mushroom-shaped mature stage. Generally, within 30 minutes after the thunderhead has divested itself of its heavy burden of rain, the building process of the updraft chimney has been reversed, and, with less water to fall down, the downdraft slows. Ground winds lose their strength as the draft weakens, and finally the temperature in the storm cell approaches that of the clear ground around it. Finis the storm.

Lightning not only makes rainfall, but it is the primary electrification process which has been linked to the formation of weather situations that bode both ill and good. Therefore, it is only natural that this phenomenon is being studied on a variety of fronts—some of which are already providing valuable knowledge to the sportsman.

More times each year than the records ever reveal, a wandering bolt of lightning strikes the mast, radio, whip antenna or some other projection on a boat. Powerful enough to capsize the largest ship afloat, sink telephone poles in the ground, and toss a skiff hundreds of feet into the air, lightning accounts for well over two percent of all boat fires, and this is an unrealistic statistic because it is based on only those authenticated lightning fires.

In just the last year or so, science has pointed a finger at lightning as being the agent responsible for many missing boats and ships. Investigations into the sudden, baffling disappearances of craft ranging in size from Star Class sloops to 20,000 ton tankers have revealed exasperatingly little, but enough has been learned about the behavior of lightning to put it at the top of the list of major suspects in the mysterious sinkings of boats.

When lightning makes a strike on a boat the results, if not deadly, are always scary, as Wilmot Voliva, the captain of a shrimp trawler learned during a thunderstorm in Pamlico Sound, North Carolina, in 1961. Voliva was beating his way toward the calm of the Bay River in heavy seas when a lightning bolt struck through a cabin window, coursed up his left leg after burning his shoe, came out near his right shoulder, entered the backrest of his metal seat, then rammed on through the hull, shearing bolts, metal bunk hangers, and finally partially disabling the rudder in the stern of the boat. Physicians who examined Voliva later thought he escaped death because his shoulder was resting against the metal seat.

This is just one incident among many which demonstrates why today investigators around the world are pressing harder than ever before to learn the fundamental secrets of lightning's capricious behavior. As a result, some new facts about the nature of lightning hazards to boats have been revealed—facts that may at the least prevent damage to your boat if you are caught in stormy weather.

If you are inclined to underrate the hazards of lightning, the annual damage and death toll caused by lightning should give you pause for thought. Every year in the United States lightning kills more people than any other natural disaster, and this holds true all over the world. The U.S. Census Bureau reports an average of 500 dead and 1,500 injured each year. In the same period, lightning strikes every square mile of the U.S. 30 to 40 times, destroying more than $60 million worth of property, exclusive of losses from some 7,000 forest fires started by lightning.

Lightning behaves basically in a scientifically understood fashion: It acts to make an electrical circuit between a cloud and an object on the ground. Warm, humid air rushes upward in a vertical stream, cools and condenses as mist. This low-grade steam gradually assumes the familiar mushroom shape of the towering cumulonimbus cloud. Moisture in the top of the thundercloud collects a positive charge, and raindrops in the bottom accumulate negative electrical charges. Meanwhile, a corresponding positive charge builds up on the water below the cloud. It actually forms a mirror image and like a shadow follows the drift of the cloud. On land it climbs towers, poles, TV aerials, church steeples, lightning rods—anything with height that can bring it closer to the cloud. But on water, the most likely jumping off point will be a mast, antenna or the highest projection on a boat or even the high crest of a wave.

Eventually, the enormous differences in electrical potential between the cloud and its water image reach a critical point. When this happens, a leader—a gaseous arc path as seen in *Figure 5-3* which reacts to electricity like gas in a neon tube—reaches down from the base of the cloud, brightening, and strengthening as electrons swarm to it from the cloud. From the water a streamer—the opposite of the leader—suddenly snakes up to the cloud through the rip in the atmosphere made by the leader. The great sky-splitting spear of light observed when streamer meets leader is actually streaking up, not down,

A
Gaseous arc path reaches down ionizing air particles. This is the pilot leader.

B
Up the arc path burned in the air by the pilot leader, the return stroke, or streamer, ascends —through this channel lightning may restrike many times.

Figure 5—3

at a speed too fast for the eye to follow—about 87,000 miles per second.

Lightning can and does frequently strike the same place twice. If your boat is struck by lightning and you think the worst is over, you may be fooled. Chances are excellent that your boat may be struck again. Since an ionized path has already been completed, lightning is likely to choose this track to repeat because it offers the least resistance. And as a general rule, lightning is more likely to strike a wet mast on water than a similar object on land because of the relative flatness of water and the height of the projecting mast which acts as a beckoning finger coaxing the lightning on.

While no two lightning strokes are identical, lightning has been divided into two general categories.

The first is "hot" lightning, which has low currents of long duration and is more apt to burn or scorch the objects it strikes. Hot lightning is often mistaken for "heat" lightning, but heat lightning is simply an ordinary lightning stroke

which occurs too far away for the observer to hear the thunderclap. It can be of either the hot or cold variety. In *Figure 5-4*, you can see the difference between hot and cold lightning.

Figure 5—4
Inflammatory or explosive, lightning is powerful.

Figure 5—5

This is how a view of the launch ship Thunderbolt would look when it has loosed a rocket. When the rocket has gained an altitude of about 350 feet, trail-ing a length of steel wire, a lightning stroke rushes down and vaporizes the wire, clearing a path for the streamer — represented by the solid line — to climb.

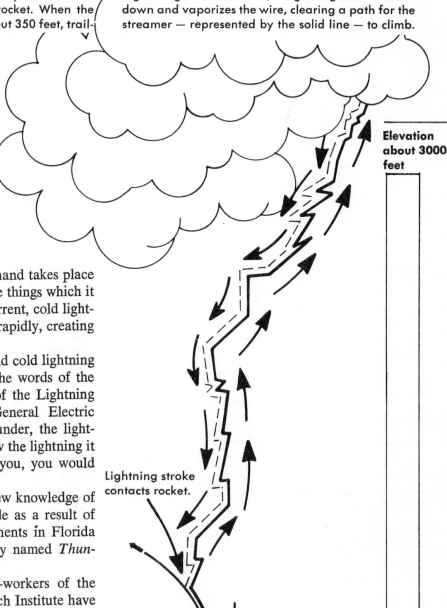

Elevation about 3000 feet

Lightning stroke contacts rocket.

"Cold" lightning on the other hand takes place in shorter strokes and can explode things which it hits. With its faster buildup of current, cold lightning heats and expands air more rapidly, creating stronger sound waves.

The distinction between hot and cold lightning is not an important one for, in the words of the late Karl McEachron, director of the Lightning Research Laboratory of the General Electric Company. "If you heard the thunder, the lightning did not strike you. If you saw the lightning it missed you; and if it did strike you, you would not have known it."

A major contribution to the new knowledge of lightning behavior has been made as a result of what may seem perilous experiments in Florida waters on a research vessel aptly named *Thunderbolt*.

Dr. M. M. Newman and co-workers of the Lightning and Transients Research Institute have deliberately triggered fantastic streams of lightning in order to learn more about currents, blast waves, and channel characteristics of bolts. Instead of a kite, such as Franklin used, they fire a rocket carrying some 300 feet of fine, stainless steel wire 500 to 1,000 feet high, directly under a thundercloud. The rocket disturbs the electrical equilibrium beneath the cloud and a lightning stroke comes ripping down, destroys the rocket and vaporizes the wire (*Figure 5-5*). As the wire is melted a path is cleared for the lightning and a streamer jumps up from the ship's deck to join a leader moving down from the cloud. In *Figure 5-6* a schematic diagram shows the lightning measurement platform used aboard *Thunderbolt*.

In a single day's work in August 1966, seventeen lightning strokes from a cloud 3,000 feet overhead were triggered by 23 rocket firings. The magnitude of the lightning which zeroed in on the instrumented impact point on the ship's deck was so great as to stagger the imagination. As many as 30 restrikes ripped down the air path in a matter of seconds, any one of which had sufficient power to lift a pocket battleship 500 feet out of the water.

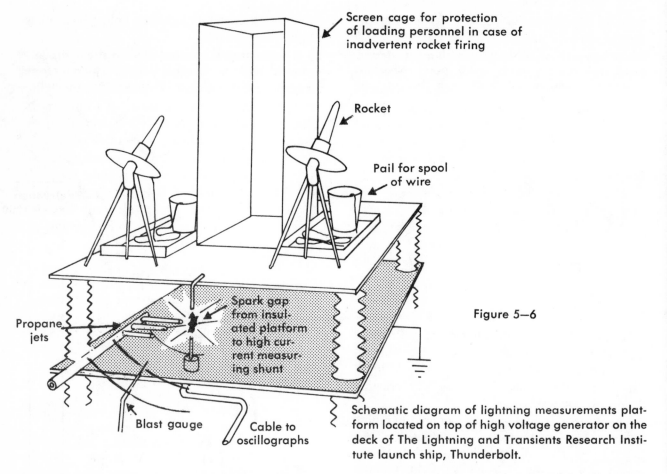

Screen cage for protection of loading personnel in case of inadvertent rocket firing

Rocket

Pail for spool of wire

Figure 5—6

Spark gap from insulated platform to high current measuring shunt

Propane jets

Blast gauge

Cable to oscillographs

Schematic diagram of lightning measurements platform located on top of high voltage generator on the deck of The Lightning and Transients Research Institute launch ship, Thunderbolt.

The primary purpose behind the lightning studies on *Thunderbolt* is to provide better protection against lightning for aircraft, computerized missile systems, and power transmission lines. But as a result of this research, present electronic circuitry in aircraft and aircraft metals and plastics, susceptible to lightning impulses, are being redesigned, substituted, or reinforced. However, these findings have great implications for boat owners and for the future of ships which ply the seas. One of the implications is that fuel vent outlets in many water craft may require modification because vapors are targets for plasma balls, or blast pressure waves and spark showers caused by lightning. Another is that even with adequate grounding, as described later in this chapter, lightning can and does do damage to power systems and semi-conductors in any radio electronic equipment.

While I cannot absolutely vouch for it, I believe lightning impulses were the cause of the failure of the alternators in the engines aboard a Coast Guard search and rescue vessel, upon which I was a guest observer during the summer of 1971. As a result we lost both batteries, and had to pass through the heavy traffic of Galveston Ship Channel at night with emergency-

rigged hand flashlights. Though no visible lightning struck the boat, we were in weather displaying strong signs of electrical behavior. Radio reception was poor, characterized by the "bacon frying" sound of electrical disturbance. The manner in which a boat may attract lightning or a corona discharge can be seen in *Figure 5-3*. Since this is an important concept, we will have to take a look again at electrical distribution in a thundercloud.

It was pointed out earlier in this chapter that collisions between positive and negative droplets in a thunderhead cause the growth of large raindrops, and that a lightning shock wave can fracture a single water drop into many smaller droplets. In other words, negative and positive electricity is separated—air currents rushing up in the cloud are loaded with a positive charge, while the raindrops these currents cause to be broken up are, in the main, negatively charged. It stands to reason, then, that since the updrafts rise more quickly than the raindrops, they will accumulate for the thunderhead a large reservoir of positive electricity in the upper half of the cloud. The lower half remains negatively charged, or neutral. Between the bottom of the cloud and the water below (as seen in *Figure 5-3*) an uneasy state of equilibrium exists. For example, if surface winds pick up and generate larger waves—which, due to wind friction and other factors, create their own process of electrical separation—these charged waves may increase the electrical potential between them and the cloud above, triggering a discharge from the overloaded cloud. Or the cloud, without the benefit of any attraction below, reaches a critical point and randomly discharges part of its powerhouse of energy.

When a boat comes upon the scene, it may pick up a positive charge by friction or contact with such particles as sleet, hail, snowflakes, or even water moisture. The effect is the same as rubbing a piece of glass with silk. Usually, such a charge will interfere with AM radio reception and is characterized by loud hissing or sizzling noises—the bacon frying sound—on the speaker. This is the signal that the boat has intensified the electric field existing between cloud and water. The manner in which this intensification becomes manifested depends upon the potential of the electrical field. But generally one of three forms of lightning may strike, or a combination of them: a lightning stroke, St. Elmo's Fire, or a plasma ball.

The following incident should serve to illustrate how devious a course a lightning bolt can take. On one cabin cruiser, a thunderbolt struck an unprotected radio antenna, streaked from the antenna to a metal handrail on the cabin roof, jumped from there to a bronze window screen, coursed down to a clamshell ventilator on deck and the metal duct to the bilge, then, whipped across the bilge to the engine block. It then flashed back along its original path and surfaced in a mooring bitt, blowing the bitt and an attached hawser to shreds, as it streaked toward the clouds. Obviously, if there had been any fuel vapor fumes in the bilge, nobody could have traced the path of the bolt. There wouldn't have been any boat left.

If not the weirdest manifestation of uninvited electricity any boatman is ever likely to see, St. Elmo's Fire runs a close second to lightning balls. It usually makes its appearance as a halo or corona of blue fire attaching itself to wet ropes, steering wheels, antennas and other protruding extremities on a boat.

St. Elmo's Fire was first so named by ancient sailors in the Mediterranean who interpreted static electricity on the masts and yardarms of their ships as the visual sign of their patron St. Elmo's guardianship. They believed the fire was a warning of a pending lightning bolt, which often turned out to be true.

A sailor with Columbus described a visitation from St. Elmo as "a ghostly flame which danced among our sails and later stayed like candlelights to burn brightly from the mast." We know now that St. Elmo's Fire is an effect which comes about when extraordinary quantities of ions—charged particles—bombard air molecules, causing them to glow like a neon sign. Luke Howard, in his book, *Climate of London,* quoted a Mr. M. Smith of Antiqua, whose encounter with St. Elmo's Fire, judging by his description, part of which is given here, was terrifying:.

"Towards the East the face of the Heavens presented to our view a number of fiery rods (electrical brushes) which were through the whole night shooting and darting in all directions; likewise fiery balls which flew up and down here and there, and burst into a number of small pieces, and flew to and fro like torches of straw, and came very near where we lay in the road. This was over the town. In other parts another sort of fiery balls flew through the air with great rapidity; and notwithstanding all those phenomena common thunder and lightning were abundantly great."

Even after centuries of authenticated reports of ball lightning, especially by mariners, this lightning phenomenon continues to irritate scientists—mainly because they don't thoroughly understand it and can't satisfactorily explain it. Thus, despite the fact that ball lightning is very intensively studied at such places as Los Almos, where the atom bomb was manufactured, many still adopt the kind of attitude a doctor friend of mine displayed, much to my surprise one night, when I asked him what he thought about supernatural happenings. Frostily, he said, "I will not discuss them since they are not subject to empirical investigation."

You can find as many people who condone this kind of attitude toward lightning balls as you can defenders for them. I, personally, have never seen one, but I'd like to, and I believe they are not figments of overactive imagination, for there is too much evidence to support their existence, and too many reliable survivors of ships that have been dismasted or sunk have testified to their powerful destructiveness. The following are just two documented cases out of hundreds:

On March 7, 1840, the English revenue cruiser Chichester was making its way up the coast of Galway in a thunderstorm. A lightning ball apparently descended from a cloud over the masthead—for it was first spotted on the masthead—and smashed through the deck, knocking down several crew members as it passed through into the captain's cabin. In addition to shattering dishes on Captain Stuart's table, the fireball produced this list of damages: the whole width of the deck in the center of the cruiser was raised off the beam, the patent lights were extinguished, the compasses aboard were destroyed, and those hands on board who had watches in their pockets discovered they had stopped. Despite a heavy pall of smoke, there was no fire and the Chichester put into port for repair.

The now famous case of the Iona May, a small fishing boat operating in South Atlantic waters in the late spring of 1961, illustrates what can happen in modern times when a plasma ball makes an eerie visit.

Skipper Harry Dillard said the strange visitation occurred seconds after he heard a screeching static on his radio. A fiery orange globe about the size of a basketball suddenly floated into the small wheel house, apparently having traveled down the fuel vapor vent—the diameter of which was much smaller than the ball—shattered the radio, incinerated charts on the shelf above the wheel, burned to ashes a paper sack lunch, then disappeared up the vent pipe with a loud bang after singeing Dillard's eyebrows. The fact the glowing sphere did not ignite gasoline fuel vapors in the vent was a mystery Dillard could only explain as Providence.

While no one theory has been accepted, it is strongly suspected that lightning balls are composed of air particles so superheated by lightning they become gases trapped in a magnetic field. Surface tension of these gas pockets reflect light, creating the illusion of a metallic object. What is known of their behavior indicates they always appear during stormy weather. They vary in size from an inch to forty feet, glow vividly for periods of from one second to three minutes, and are attracted to closed spaces—boats, houses, airplanes—which they enter through an open window, a vent, small crack, or through a chimney. Fireballs come in two varieties, one which fizzles out harmlessly, and a blueish-white ball that can incinerate any object it touches and explodes devastatingly with blast pressures up to 45 tons per square inch.

One of the most awesome sights at sea, and until recently one of the most misunderstood, is a waterspout. There is still a difference of opinion as to whether the funnel of a waterspout is composed of a huge column of water, or condensed water vapor. Most sailors who have seen them swear they are vertical columns of solid water. Actually, they are neither; they are simply tornadoes that pass over water. The fact that a violent tornado can pick up a railway engine effortlessly and drop it four or five miles away, argues well for the proposition that a waterspout can certainly suck a river dry. And there are verified reports of rainfalls of live fish, frogs, and crabs—the most notable in the U.S. being a deluge of fresh water perch and bullpout (a catfish) on the outskirts of Providence, Rhode Island, on May 15, 1900. Torrential rains and a strong wind pelted the area, and as a dividend strewed thousands of the fish in streets and gardens.

Proof of the fact that a waterspout is simply a tornado that goes to sea was the one that formed near Norfolk, Virginia on September 5, 1935. Starting as a tornado, it roared across a creek, becoming a waterspout that breathed in water like a vacuum cleaner, then gouged a long ditch in the exposed creekbed. After that, again a tornado, it destroyed several buildings, then changed back into a waterspout, it crossed Hampton Roads, switched to a tornado and upended some freight cars in a railroad yard. As a waterspout once again, it sucked up another creek along its path, changed again into a tornado when it touched land, and when last seen was thrashing up Chesapeake Bay as a waterspout.

That singular energy in nature that splits raindrops and conjures up plasma balls is the force thought to power tornadoes and waterspouts, alike. Repeated lightning strokes from cloud to ground in a thunderstorm (see *Figure 5-7*) form a chimney with a racing flow of super-hot air that stirs an eggbeater at the bottom. Bolts, streaking down the chimney, cause a drastic drop in the inside air pressure. Air outside rushes in at the bottom to replace hot air being drawn upward and a terrible rotating low pressure area is formed at ground level. Then, the whirling vortex of the twister compresses threads of lightning into a brilliant stream of energy which gives the tornado the fantastic power to maintain its agonizing contortions. At sea, or over any body of water, the waterspout is a tornado, which creates a whirlpool beneath a thunderhead or line squall, as it elongates and touches the surface.

Figure 5—7

Lightning in sheets, as a luminescent glow, as balls of fire, as blue, green, yellow and red flashes — all these forms of electricity have been seen by observers in the whirling vortex of a tornado. Lightning is the energy that gives a twister its twist.

Tornadoes and waterspouts generally move on a fairly straight track, usually not more than 12 to 15 MPH, and parallel with a squall line—east or northeast. So, unless you find yourself in the thick of a thunderstorm, they are not too difficult to outrun. The best rule is not to take any chances, and follow the rules suggested at the end of this chapter to protect yourself.

It would be wrong to imagine that a waterspout is more than a very minor hazard at sea, but at the same time thousands occur every year, and I would be remiss if I failed to relate at least one more case by which the destructiveness of a spout can be judged:

When the White Star liner *Pittsburgh* was struck at night by a huge waterspout in the Mid-atlantic on March 30, 1923, her electrical connections fused, the bridge was destroyed, the chart room was badly damaged, the crow's nest filled with water, and many cabins were flooded. It was estimated that tons of water had dropped

on her superstructure from the unexpected waterspout.

It should be pretty obvious by now that lightning, in its various manifestations, is the one most disruptive force in nature that you have to protect yourself against. Following, then, are tested rules for the installation of lightning protection devices on boats, based on recommendations by the Lightning and Transients Research Institute and the marine division of Underwriters Laboratories. Also in this section, you'll find some important advice which will enhance your chances of survival if you are unlucky enough to be caught in a hurricane, tornado or waterspout.

The problem of lightning protection is to conduct a lightning discharge through the boat into the water where it can be dissipated. In a letter to me suggesting some lightning precautions, J. D. Robb, of the Lightning and Transients Research Institute, made the following observation which should be of particular interest to sailboat owners:

"It is interesting to note that while I was on a visit to the south end of the South Bight of Andros Island, I learned that the Bahaman natives who make the Out-Island sailboats use only a single forestay on their vessels. And this is used primarily for lightning protection. They told me when I was there, that on the *Mystery J,* the Out-Island Regatta winner constructed the previous year, they had run the steel forestay only to the spreader, and this had resulted in severe lightning damage to the top of the masts. Therefore, they decided to go back to running the steel forestay from the tip of the mast to the bowsprit, and then down to the water. They prefer not to use steel shrouds, as they rust-stain the hull, and they use only a single steel stay for lightning protection."

SIZE OF WIRE

Other advice to the contrary, the size of wire that should be used to conduct an intense discharge safely to the surface, should never be less than that recommended in the National Lightning Prevention Code—No. 4 to No. 6. Some "expert" weather writers have advised that No. 13 gauge wire is sufficient as a conductor. Don't bank on it. You might wake up one morning after a line squall and find your whole power system shattered and electrical connections fused.

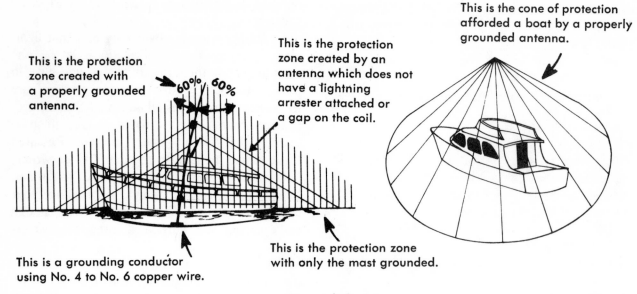

This is the protection zone created with a properly grounded antenna.

This is the protection zone created by an antenna which does not have a lightning arrester attached or a gap on the coil.

This is the cone of protection afforded a boat by a properly grounded antenna.

This is a grounding conductor using No. 4 to No. 6 copper wire.

This is the protection zone with only the mast grounded.

Figure 5—8

This illustration is for normal boats and is based on recommendations of the Lightning and Transients Research Institute.

HOW AN ELEVATED CONDUCTOR WORKS

As shown in *Figure 5-8*, an elevated conductor should protect a cone-shaped space underneath out to an angle of 60 degrees with a probability of 99% safety. But if the conductor is raised so the angle to the extremities of the boat is 45 degrees, the probability of protection increases to 99.9%. These are better odds than you can get sitting on the Empire State Building.

GENERAL RULES FOR PROTECTING YOUR BOAT

A perfect ground conductor is a metal mast, providing the bottom of the mast is grounded. On a wood or fiberglass mast, a pointed copper, brass or bronze rod about ¼-inch in diameter should be installed, projecting at least 10 inches above the tip. Attach this rod to the shrouds and stays with No. 4 to 6 copper wire, then connect the bottom of the rigging wires to ground. Bolts anchored through chain plates make a strong point of attachment inside a boat.

The hull of a metal boat is the best possible ground. On a wooden or plastic boat you can connect to the engine, or to a metal keel or rudder. If however, there is no metal in the water, you'll have to install a ground plate. This should have an outside dimensional area of at least one square foot.

RADIO-TELEPHONE ANTENNA AS A LIGHTNING CONDUCTOR

If you own a powerboat equipped with a MF radiotelephone, the antenna will work fine as a lightning conductor, but it must be high enough—at least six inches above the highest point on the boat—to provide the cone of protection. At the bottom of the antenna, a single-pole knife switch should be installed which has a rating of at least 60 amperes. The fixed contact should be connected to the antenna and the switch "arm" should be connected to the ground. When a storm approaches, simply close the switch. In order not to reduce the transmitting efficiency of your radiotelephone, the switch insulation should be plastic or glazed porcelain. Switches manufactured out of slate or other materials that absorb moisture will reduce the effectiveness of radiotelephone transmissions. It is important to remember to keep the grounding switch closed any time you approach bad weather, or when you leave your boat. Otherwise, you have an "open" invitation to trouble.

RIGGING AN ALL-STEEL BOAT FOR SAFETY

In order to provide the necessary continuous path from the top of the mast to the water, the mast should be connected by means of heavy wires, or "jumping," which span the insulating material used to separate the mast from the structure. The bolts or rivets which fasten the super-structure to the hull complete the conducting path.

DON'T USE
SPIRALLY-WRAPPED ANTENNAS

Lightning just doesn't take the time to twist its way through coils and turns. It will jump somewhere else instead, so the cone of protection around antennas that have loading coils aloft must be calculated from the bottom of the coil. Antennas consisting of a spirally-wrapped conductor can't be expected to give protection.

On a powerboat that is not radio-equipped, or on which the antenna is not adequate for protection, you can install a stub or "military" mast, equipped with an elevated pointed rod and grounding conductor. However, radio antennas are generally quite satisfactory if—to repeat—they are not spirally-wrapped, and if they are equipped with transmitting-type lightning arresters.

SMALL BOAT PROTECTION

A wire trailing in the water will provide protection but even better, buy a metal "whip" antenna such as the 9-foot metal citizens band antenna you see attached to car bumpers. It should be grounded directly to the engine to be effective. It is best to clamp the whip directly on the motor, but don't, if you purchase one of these whips, use a spring base mounting.

These measures should protect your boat against damage. But for the maximum safety of people who may be aboard, any extensive metal structure on top or inside the boat should also be grounded as a precaution against somebody being struck by high voltage which lightning might induce in these objects. Ground handrails, davits, window screens, windshield frames, ventilation ducts, flying-bridge controls, etc. All large bodies of metal in the engine room, likewise, should be grounded so that erratic side flashes cannot set off fuel fumes below decks.

Lightning conductors should be routed as straight to ground as possible. Sharp bends or loops encourage lightning to side flash.

TREATMENT FOR ELECTRIC SHOCK

The subject of lightning precautions should not be concluded without a few words on artifi-cial respiration. Electric shock can make a person stop breathing: A short pulse of direct current from lightning can cause temporary paralysis of the nerves that control the action of the lungs. So, if someone on your boat, or nearby, is knocked unconscious by lightning, check to see if he is breathing. But even if he is not, he may have a good chance if you act quickly. Start artificial respiration at once—the mouth-to-mouth technique is best. Don't waste time going for help. The human brain can be irreparably damaged by loss of oxygen in less than five minutes, unless artificial respiration is applied. Continue giving artificial respiration until the victim responds, or a doctor confirms he is dead. Keep the victim warm, and raise his feet slightly to stimulate flow of blood to the brain.

Hurricane safety rules below, adapted from instructions published by NOAA, are the result of many years of observation of the before and after effects of these dangerous storms. Most injuries are not the result of hurricane winds, but the debris these winds carry. If you heed these precautions you can quite confidently survive this one of nature's most spectacular displays.

Enter each hurricane season prepared. Every June through November, recheck your supply of boards, tools, batteries, nonperishable foods, and the other equipment you will need if a hurricane strikes your town.

When you hear the first tropical storm advisory, listen for future messages; this will prepare you for a hurricane emergency well in advance of the issuance of watches and warnings.

When your area is covered by a hurricane watch, continue normal activities, but stay tuned to radio or television for all Weather Service advisories. Remember, a hurricane watch means possible danger within 24 hours; if the danger materializes, a hurricane warning will be issued. Meanwhile, keep alert. Ignore rumors.

When your area receives a hurricane warning: Plan your time before the storm arrives and avoid the last-minute hurry which might leave you marooned or unprepared. Keep calm until the emergency has ended. Leave low-lying areas that may be swept by high tides or storm waves. Moor your boat securely before the storm arrives, or evacuate it to a designated safe area. When your boat is moored, leave it, and don't return once the wind and waves are up. Board up windows or protect them with storm shutters or tape. Danger to small windows is mainly from wind-driven debris. Larger windows may be broken by wind pressure. Secure outdoor objects that might be blown away or uprooted.

Garbage cans, garden tools, toys, signs, porch furniture, and a number of other harmless items become missiles of destruction in hurricane winds. Anchor them or store them inside before the storm strikes. Store drinking water in clean bathtubs, jugs, bottles, and cooking utensils; your town's supply may be contaminated by flooding or damaged by hurricane floods. Check your battery-powered equipment. Your radio may be your only link with the world outside the hurricane, and emergency cooking facilities, lights, and flashlights will be essential if utilities are interrupted. Galley stove, portable lights and radios from your boat may come in handy. Keep your car fueled. Service stations may be inoperable for several days after the storm strikes, due to flooding or interrupted electrical power. Stay at home, if it is sturdy and on high ground; if it is not, move to a designated shelter, and stay there until the storm is over. Remain indoors during the hurricane. Travel is extremely dangerous when winds and tides are whipping through your area. Monitor the storm's position through Weather Service advisories.

Beware the eye of the hurricane. If the calm storm center passes directly overhead, there will be a lull in the wind lasting from a few minutes to half an hour or more. Stay in a safe place unless emergency repairs are absolutely necessary. But remember, at the other side of the eye, the winds rise very rapidly to hurricane force, and come from the opposite direction.

When the hurricane has passed: Seek necessary medical care at Red Cross disaster stations or hospitals. Stay out of disaster areas. Unless you are qualified to help, your presence might hamper first-aid work. Drive carefully along debris-filled streets. Roads may be undermined and may collapse under the weight of a car. Slides along cuts are also a hazard. Avoid loose or dangling wires, and report them immediately to your power company or the nearest law enforcement officer. Report broken sewer or water mains to the water department. Prevent fires: Lowered water pressure may make fire fighting difficult. Check refrigerated food for spoilage if power has been off during the storm.

Remember that hurricanes moving inland can cause severe flooding. Stay away from river banks and streams.

Tornadoes spawned by hurricanes are among the storms' worst killers. When a hurricane approaches, listen for tornado watches and warnings. A tornado *watch* means that tornadoes are expected to develop. A tornado *warning* means a tornado has actually been sighted. When your area receives a tornado warning, seek inside shelter immediately, preferably below ground level. If a tornado catches you outside, move away from its path at a right angle. If there is no time to escape, lie flat in the nearest depression, such as a ditch or ravine.

CHAPTER SEVEN

How Game Fish React to Weather

IN THE INTRODUCTION to this book, I mentioned that I have been puzzled on many occasions as to why fish feed voraciously on certain days and pass up the best you can offer them on others. I pointed out that part of the explanation lies in the weather around us and that fish fail to rise on those luckless days because they are responding to some environmental clue that we have either failed to apprehend or have overlooked.

In a way it would be gratifying to be able to report that at last the fishery biologists of the world have sweepingly charted the behavioral symptoms of all game fish and are now ready to publish a piscatorial weather calendar listing the exact days of the year when fishing will be excellent—all you would have to do is to faithfully follow the printed instructions and you could be assured of bringing home a plentiful catch. What a dull prospect!

Nevertheless, the time will come, and soon, when science shall solve some of the elemental mysteries of fish behavior, making angling less of an art and more of a craft. Alas, when this happens, I think I shall be tempted to store away my fishing rods and look for another hobby. Unfortunately I can't think of a single other avocation that combines in one mood the mystique, joyful anticipation, and un-thinking contemplation that fishing does. When I recall some of the wilderness spots where with a companion I've dropped a line, my feelings join with a fragment from a poem, *The Fish,* which Rupert Brooke penned many years ago:

His bliss is older than the sun.
Silent and straight the waters run.
The lights, the cries, the willows dim,
And the dark tide are one with him.

I am sure this bliss, older than the sun, is an inherent feeling in the bones of every angler whose own combative instinct is a natural, primitive one to outsmart the cunning fish on its own terms. *The trouble is that most fishermen fish on their own terms, expecting the fish to comply.*

Clues to better fishing methods are what the fisherman requires, and to that end hundreds of books have been written purporting to advise the angler on proper casting techniques, rods, reels, baits, lures, etc. Weather is a factor often completely ignored, or only mentioned in passing usually in connection with how the ups and downs of barometric pressure affect fishing.

The truth is, as Al Sparks* told me, "There is an appalling paucity of research on marine game fish. What does exist is a hodgepodge of information, which has not been correlated and which leaks out incompletely in dribbles to fishermen who snatch up some tidbit of information, declaring it to be authoritative, with the result that a new fish-catching hypothesis is announced that has little basis in fact. The one thing we do know for sure is that atmospheric conditions are the single most controlling factor in the behavior of all fish.

"When marine biologists begin concentrating seriously on total weather factors affecting fish

---

Chief of the National Oceanic and Atmospheric Administration's Bureau of Commercial Fisheries, Galveston, Texas.

harvesting—salinity ratios, sun-compassing in fish migrations, the tidal pull of moon and sun, etc.—we will only then begin to chart major predictable behavioral patterns of fishes. The sportsman, however, wants to know *now,* how to improve his luck. His best bet is to look to and try to interpret how weather affects fish activity."

In his witty book, *Why Fish Bite and Why They Don't,* James Westman, who is Chairman, Department of Wildlife Conservation, Rutgers University, presents the current scientific dilemma of lack of accurate information on the relationship of atmospheric phenomena to fish catching:

"One of the great difficulties in measuring the effect of a natural factor—e.g., the full moon or atmospheric pressure—upon the catchability of fish, is that other factors are so often tied up with the one we seek to measure. The full moon, for example, may mean calm, cool weather with high pressure. If so, what is being tested? There is always something associated with a full moon, or for that matter with no moon, or a half moon. It is only the incomplete angler out to convince himself, or the bogus authority out to convince many others, who goes for the 'hocus pocus' stuff or who has the final answer about the moon and sun and gravity and pressure, etc. etc. The real pro looks to his lures, the species, the situation, and the presentation. And he knows, as the Good Book states, that 'to him that hath, more shall be given.' He keeps his lamp well oiled and leaves but little to hunch and guesswork."*

At first reading, it would seem as though Sparks and Westman were opposed in their beliefs, but this isn't so. Westman was expressing the exasperation of the scientists who look upon unproved laymen's hypothesis, no matter how well some of them may coincide with consistent fish catching, as untested and out of context with the whole array of atmospheric influences. As a matter of fact, if you were to consult all of the tables, calendars and almanacs that have been published for good fishing days and precise times to fish, you should be hauling them in by the basketful every day. Sparks was merely stating what a good many fishery biologists, climatologists and oceanographers are now just beginning to appreciate fully: Invisible atmospheric rhythms underlie most of what we assume to be constant in nature. The life of a fish is in a state of continual flux, but the changes are regulated adjustments, and not chaotic. The rhythmic nature of life on earth is perhaps its most ordinary but overlooked property. A fish, no less than a hu-

man, is surrounded by rhythms of gravity, light waves, air pressure, sound and electromagnetic fields—all of these influences are the components of weather. To suggest that fish are unaffected by these influences would be as foolish as to deny the existence of gravity.

But in order to make certain that the following observations cannot be classified in a "hocus pocus" category, this chapter will be confined to those known and proved atmospheric influences that can be reliably translated as clues to better fishing for the sportsman. Thus, we will consider weather factors affecting fish behavior under four major headings: temperature relations to fish feeding; location by marine topography of saltwater species; excerpts from the weather log of a fishing enthusiast; and finally, the fish's reaction to refraction and diffraction of light.

Before getting down to specifics, it may prove thought-provoking for the reader to learn how just two of those *invisible atmospheric rhythms* affect, first, the susceptibility of fish to electromagnetism, and second, how certain fish have worked out exact time cycle equations for spawning that are phased precisely with the movements of the sun and moon.

Fish react curiously to electricity. At low levels of power, an electrical field in fresh or brackish water frightens them, but at higher levels it lines them up toward a positive pole in the water, and as the power is gradually raised, they seem irresistibly forced to swim toward the positive pole, where eventually they may be killed. Russian commercial fishermen have already taken advantage of this phenomenon to attract fish to a pump intake aboard a huge collecting ship at sea.

You could say the grunion, a tiny smelt-like fish whose habitat ranges along the sandy California coast, is moonstruck, but this would be a gross untruth, for the spawning activities of this fish are but one striking example of the sense of environmental rhythm in living creatures.

The moon, as science has long shown us, is the prime mover of the tides of the sea, but the sun plays a complimentary part. In its orbiting around the earth, the moon in two positions is directly on a line with the earth and the sun. At one point it is between the earth and the sun; at the other point the earth is between it and the sun. In both positions the pull of the moon and the sun are combined to make the tides higher than average. These are called *spring tides,* no matter what season they occur. About seven days

* *From the book,* Why Fish Bite and Why They Don't, *by James Westman.* © *1961 by Prentice-Hall, Inc.*

later, when the moon has traveled one quarter-way around the earth, its position will be at right angles to the sun, and the two celestial bodies tug at right angles, resulting in tides lower than average, which are called *neaps*. Every two weeks from March to July, eggs of mature grunion become ripe. With unfailing regularity at the time of a spring tide some cosmic signal trips a biological release, driving the grunion to lay and fertilize their eggs at the limit of the tide zone marked by the higher spring tides. At night, in great numbers, the fish rise and fall in the surf until just after high tide. At a precise moment a signal is received and they begin to ride on the crests of the waves until they land high up on the beach. There, the female drills a hole in the dripping sand with her tail. Into it she deposits her eggs, which are fertilized by the nearest male, and the fish then squirm their way back into the next wave and make their way out to sea. It takes less than sixty seconds for the whole mating act—selection of partners, drilling the nest and dropping the eggs—to be performed. The spawning complete, the spring tide recedes, and the next day, safely buried three or four inches deep in the warm, moist sand, the eggs develop under the sun. Two weeks later the next spring tide scours them from their nest, washes the grunion fry out of their egg-membranes, and sweeps them to sea.

The eggs take about nine days to develop, but the fry, which apparently possess at birth an inherent physiological time sense, do not emerge until the waves dig them out of the sand. They are thus ready for the appointment with the ocean world ahead of time, in case winds or sudden squalls should bring the releasing tide earlier than usual. Nevertheless, if they did not wait for the spring tide to set them free, they would emerge into the almost dry sand, and would die.

The whole process is a marvelous example of atmospheric rhythms which prescribe the unity and complexity of the life force. Is it any wonder that the scientists, never mind the happy-hearted fisherman, have a long way to go to reach an understanding of the strange influences that govern the behavior of fish?

As the foregoing illustrates, the timing of any event may literally tip the balance between health and illness, survival and death. Temperature and timing, for example, are now definite factors in fry plantings by many state fisheries. Fishery biologists have come to realize that fingerlings, as

well as adult fish, register size, their ability to resist the shock and changes in temperature, a to resist is greater or smaller at the day.

TEMPERATURE RELATIONSHIPS TO FISH FEEDING

Temperature as one weather factor has been scientifically demonstrated repeatedly to be a critical influence on fish feeding habits, and on fish behavior generally. It can be direct influence, as in the rate that a fish digests food or on its food preference. There is also no question but that fish have definite preferences for certain ranges of temperature. As a matter of fact, with many species if the temperature climbs beyond a certain range the fish will die out. This has happened in many many U.S. streams where heated effluents from industrial manufacturing plants pour into lakes or rivers to be recirculated back through the plant. The effects of temperature are particularly noticeable in northern lakes during ice-out at spring and serve well to illustrate how a variety of fresh water denizens react to the thawing process as the waters warm and stratification begins. This knowledge can be invaluable for the angler, who while he may appreciate the yet unsolved mysteries of circadian rhythms (from Circa Dies; around a day) is obviously more interested in results. But if you will appreciate that these rhythms do indeed govern how fish react, become agitated, become dormant and where they lie, eat and rest, then you can be assured of far better results in the same waters you may have been fishing for years.

If you can't find fish you can't catch them. This is a truism every angler knows. And I don't think that there is a dedicated fisherman alive who under oath would fail to admit that on occasions as a youngster he fervently prayed to land a whopping big fish, solemnly promising in exchange that he would mow the lawn faithfully every Saturday. But prayer, luck, or a random successful cast have little to do with consistent good fishing. Temperature, depth and water movement are the three factors which largely determine what fish will be present where and when.

Earlier I explained that the functions of bodies of water properly belong in the category of weather because water like air is a fluid. But it is the dynamic, changing state of this fluid in lakes and ponds that concerns us here. When nature or

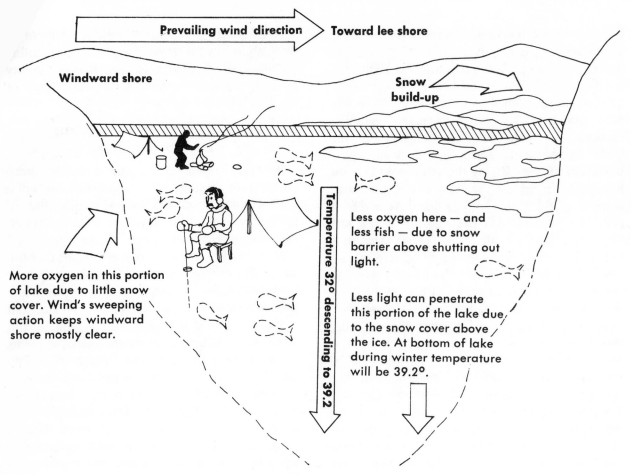

Prevailing wind direction ▷ **Toward lee shore**

Windward shore

Snow build-up

Less oxygen here — and less fish — due to snow barrier above shutting out light.

Less light can penetrate this portion of the lake due to the snow cover above the ice. At bottom of lake during winter temperature will be 39.2°.

Temperature 32° descending to 39.2

More oxygen in this portion of lake due to little snow cover. Wind's sweeping action keeps windward shore mostly clear.

Figure 7—1

man impounds water, some interesting things happen to fish which are important to fishermen. So let's examine these impoundments, in relationship to temperature, by looking at the deep lakes of the northern United States and Canada.

There are hundreds of northern-region lakes which are called oligotrophic (a term describing bodies of water with abundant dissolved oxygen). These northern latitude lakes are exposed to biting winter temperatures that fall well below the freezing point. The angle at which the sun's rays strike them is more oblique than in more southerly latitudes, accounting for the fact that the quantity of plant nutrients in the water is less than in warmer or more shallow lakes. With less dissolved plant nutrients to exert pressure on biological oxygen demand, the result is more oxygen in the deeper parts of the water.

Now, how do these deep, cool lakes appear at different seasons of the year, and what is the effect of seasonal changes upon the catchability of fish? The winter season is a good place to begin an explanation.

Say the lake we are studying is in eastern Oregon or deep in Maine. Its surface will be frozen in the dead of winter with up to three feet

of ice. The surface temperature can range from 32° F. to many degrees below zero. As winter locks the lake in a colder grip, the ice temperature may drop further, but water in the depths will probably be 39.2° F. Remember, water like air sinks when it is dense and heavy and at this temperature sinks to the bottom.

Figure 7-1 illustrates an interesting weather fact that works to the advantage of the ice fisherman. *Snow generally piles up higher on the lee shore of a lake toward which the prevailing wind is blowing.* The exception to this rule are lakes surrounded by high mountains which block off wind action. Most experienced ice anglers know how the prevailing wind on open lakes snowplows for them. What is not apparent is that the windward side will produce better fishing results. Why should this be? It is simple when you think about it, and consult *Figure 7-1*.

In the drawing heavy snow cover on the leeward shore permits less light to penetrate the ice sheet below the snow. The windward shore, relatively free of snow, is exposed to greater amounts of light, and allows more oxygen to be formed, even though the temperature at the surface below the ice is the same as the snow-covered portion.

This is where you'll find the greatest concentration of fish.

When "ice out" comes in spring or early summer, a great change takes place. As the surface water warms and reaches the temperature of the depths, convection currents, present throughout the lake, homogenize the water. This is the time anglers have anticipated, because it is then that hungry lake trout, landlocked salmon and rainbow can be caught close to shore and at the surface.

When true summer makes its appearance, another great change occurs in these lakes. Warmed slowly but steadily by the sun, the water begins to stratify in layers of different temperature. At the surface, obviously, a warm layer forms. It is called the *epilimnion*. From only a few inches deep, this surface layer descends as the summer weather warms to a depth of as much as 30 feet or so. Beneath this first layer is a horizontal stratum which is typified as an area of rapidly descending temperatures. It is called the *thermocline*—and is of paramount importance to the lake angler. The term thermocline defines that layer of water where the drop in temperature falls at least two degrees F. for each 3.5 vertical feet of water. The depth of the thermocline will range on an average between 4 and 20 feet.

The remainder of the lake—the cold water zone—is called the *hypolimnion* and will register little change in temperature all the way to the bottom. Assuming the lake is over 75 feet deep, the temperature at the bottom will be what it was in the winter, about 39.2 F. See *Figure 7-2*.

The end result of this summer stratification is the three layers mentioned above. In effect, temperature stratification forms three separate lakes, one lying on top of the other.

The epilimnion is usually too warm for game fish and is inhabited, as a rule, only by small fish and non-game-fish species, except during the night and early morning hours when the water is cooler.

The lower portion of the lake, the hypolimnion, composed of cold water, is almost devoid of forage fish, and generally has a low oxygen content.

So it is in the thermocline where game fish, during the heat of summer, will be found, because here is the most favorable combination of water temperature, food, and oxygen.

The division or stratification of lakes by temperature and season not only concentrates some of the larger game fish in the thermocline, but also has a decided effect upon distribution of all the fishes present in the lake. The lake trout moves into the cold depths and will be accompanied by whitefish, smelt, deep water sticklebacks, ciscos, and other species which prefer cold temperatures. Landlocked salmon, rainbow, brook and brown trout usually prefer the temperatures in or just below the thermocline.

The final stage in the cycle of water stratification takes place in the late summer or fall when the lake turns over again—when the surface temperature descends to that of the depths. The lake has again become homogenized. The fish too, are homogeneous, in that they are mingled

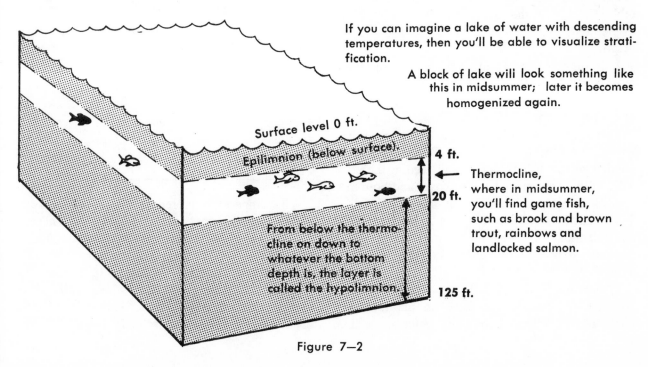

If you can imagine a lake of water with descending temperatures, then you'll be able to visualize stratification.

A block of lake will look something like this in midsummer; later it becomes homogenized again.

Surface level 0 ft.

Epilimnion (below surface) 4 ft.

Thermocline, where in midsummer, you'll find game fish, such as brook and brown trout, rainbows and landlocked salmon. 20 ft.

From below the thermocline on down to whatever the bottom depth is, the layer is called the hypolimnion. 125 ft.

Figure 7—2

together; the perch, the landlocked salmon, the bass, the rainbows all share a common temperature environment, until winter sets in in earnest to complete the cycle.

All this may prove interesting information, but how does the angler benefit specifically by it? For any given lake, how can he determine the depth of the thermocline where the fishing will be consistently better?

You can always attempt by trial and error to drop your lure, or live bait, foot by foot until you get a strike, but this method will not guarantee you limit catches, because your bait may be struck by a random fish. For best results, purchase an electronic thermometer. The probe is lowered slowly into the water, while the angler observes the dial face of the instrument. When the dial registers the area of rapidly descending colder temperatures, the thermocline has been located. Since the cable to which the probe is attached is marked in foot intervals, depth can be read instantly.

It would be grossly misleading to suggest that locating the thermocline will, without some other information, guarantee you a fishing experience you've only dreamed about. You should know the temperature preferred by the fish you are after, and then do your fishing in water of that temperature. If you cannot find water of exactly the right degree, then the next closest reading above or below the optimum preference would be your best bet. At the end of this section there is a brief table listing temperature preference ranges for a variety of fresh water fish. But if you're going after species not contained in the table, check with the local fish and game people in the area you've elected. You'll find them very helpful.

Important as temperature is in determining the most probable location of any species of fish in a particular body of water at a given time of the year, it is not the whole story. Even when water temperature seems to be just right, if the cover is wrong, the fish won't be there. But almost any good book on fish behavior and feeding habits will outline the various types of cover and bottom conditions favored by different species of fish. This knowledge, when it's combined with an understanding of temperature preferences, will markedly improve your chances of lugging home a full creel.

One example should suffice to prove the importance of water temperature on the feeding habits of fish. When surrounding water tempera-

tures goes too far above a preference level of a species, the fish tend to go off their feed, becoming sluggish. Salmon fishermen in Lake Michigan found this out during the fall of 1968 when the water temperature rose to 66 degrees down to a depth of about 120 feet and ranging out as far as 8 to 12 miles from shore. The inverse has proven to be true also. When water temperature drops below the preferred range, the metabolism of the fish is retarded. Fish won't feed or react as actively as normal.

Not all lakes develop a thermocline. But it is a proven fact, one that can be of inestimable value to the angler, that if you fish any oligotrophic (northern latitude) lake, the seasonal behavior of water and water temperatures will be the same, and the behavior patterns of the fish present in such lakes is predictable. Southern lakes, which are not exposed to the northern extremes of temperature, do not develop thermoclines as definable as those farther north. But stratification does exist, especially in the deeper southern lakes.

TEMPERATURE PREFERENCES OF SELECTED FRESH WATER SPECIES

NAME OF SPECIES	TEMPERATURE PREFERENCE	TOLERATION ZONE
Brook Trout	58	48–68
Brown Trout	61	48–68
Rainbow Trout	61	48–68
Lake Trout	41	40–50
Largemouth Bass	70–72	65–75
Smallmouth Bass	67	60–70
Chinook Salmon	54	50–63
Coho Salmon	53–56	45–60
Muskellunge	65	60–80
Northern Pike	65	60–80
Walleyes	60	55–70
Crappies	68	60–75
Yellow Perch	68	60–75
Bluegills & Sunfish	·72	65–80

The temperature preferences listed above are a guide, but this does not mean they will necessarily always hold true for the same species identified in all waters. Barometric pressure, turbidity of the water, seasonal variations in heating or cooling, the fishing pressure—these and other factors affect the final result. However, despite these variables you can reliably expect consistently better catches using the thermocline method. It is one of the benefits that our fledgling fishery science has brought to the angler.

LOCATION OF SALT WATER SPECIES BY MARINE TOPOGRAPHY

A couple of years ago, I overheard an envious fisherman make a remark about a late friend of mine, Judd Hill, with whom you will become more thoroughly acquainted later in this chapter: "Boy, that guy must think like a fish. Look at that catch he's got." Judd and I, at the time, were surf casting in the waters of North Carolina's Pamlico Sound.

Judd, having heard the comment, said quietly to me, "That sums up the trouble with most fishermen. They feel in order to catch fish, you've got to think like one. I'm no expert," (so he said) "but I've learned a thing or two in 25 years of angling all over this country. Fish don't act like humans, but most of them have memory, and they are predictable critters of instinct. That fellow was upset because his luck turned sour, but if he'd bought some maps, and used a little common sense and water savvy, he'd probably have done as well as us."

The situation Judd was referring to was our own earlier failure to do any good with surface lures. So, rather than pack up our gear, Judd had reached into an oilskin packet and had consulted a U.S. Coast and Geodetic Survey chart covering a wide stretch of the area where we were located. "We'll go bottom fishing," he announced equably, and we moved about a quarter of a mile up the sand beach. The result in about a half hour's time were two 12-pound blues, and three good-sized flounders.

Not every surfman turns to bottom fishing because of disappointment with the often unrewarding and tiresome business of continuous casting with metal squids, feathered jigs, or plugs. They seem to take the viewpoint that the weather, luck and the fish have conspired against them, and they go home for the day. But quite often bottom fishing is the only practical way to fish. Frequently game fish turn obstinate and refuse to feed on top, where artificial lures work best. The weather is often a factor in the fish's decision to sound, but there are other factors too which determine where these top feeders have gone. And this goes back to Judd's statement— "Fish are predictable critters of instinct." Sometimes stiff onshore winds, seaweed-fouled waves,

or other adverse conditions make it necessary to anchor a tempting morsel of live bait on the bottom where the fish have descended. This gets us to the other point Judd made: the use of charts.

Bottom fishing, especially in strange waters, is more rewarding if you see a chart of the area to locate the likely spots. These moderately priced charts are now published by the National Ocean Survey, successors to the Coast and Geodetic Survey. Most marine-supply outlets carry them. Make certain, however, that you select one that covers the beaches, not the offshore grounds. All these charts are carefully detailed.

With these charts, you can locate deep holes, sandbars, cuts through bars, sloughs alongside sandbars, rock piles, shellfish beds, and likely places for worm beds. It is a good idea to obtain a tide table for the area too, if available. Plan to arrive on the beach you select at low tide or just before it. That's the best time to study the water and make your plans for the incoming tide and the following ebb.

Large-scale NOS charts show depths in feet along the beach at low water. If shallows—two to eight feet—show up within casting distance of offshore, adjacent to a hole 15 to 20 feet deep, the indication would be that you've found a likely spot. Too, the water over such holes will generally appear darker than water covering shallows except on overcast days, or on clear days when puffy clouds make deceptive reflections. During the flood or first half of the ebb tide, fishing in these holes will produce better results. There is a good reason for this, and it has to do with the way fish adapt to the variations of sunlight. Smaller, shallow-water fish, whose reflective coloring is more light-adapted, and upon whom larger predators feed, often land in these holes during these crucial tide times. Science has demonstrated that predators will attack light-adapted fish more readily than those whose coloring is darker. This should also serve as a clue to type of bait to use in such holes: Bright artificial "distress" lures, anchored to the bottom in the manner you would attach live bait, often work wonders in deep holes.

Sandbars are indicated on NOS charts in much the same way deep holes are. Look for shoal markings of two to four feet with deeper, channel-like runs alongside. Some sandbars are exposed at low water. Those with cuts or outlets which permit tidal water to flow in and out are best. Gamefish prowl in these outlets in search of food as the tides flood and ebb. Open-ended cuts are often easy to spot because of the turbulent water swirling over the entrances and exits. Even if you can't reach a cut with your best cast, remember that gamefish are active and often prowl beyond these rip-type openings.

A slough is frequently found near the long sandy beaches such as those found in Virginia and the Carolinas. Sloughs are simply ditch-like hollows found at the ends of sandbars. Sloughs, located at the outer ends of slanting bars are often difficult, if not impossible, to reach with heavy sinkers and slabs of cut bait such as mullet, spot, or butterfish. The shoreside ends of slanting bars certainly are easier to reach and often serve as a collecting point for channel bass and other gamefish on a par with the seaward end of the slough. Unlike deep holes in hard bottom, sloughs are seldom stable. Shifting winds and currents can fill a good slough with sand and detritus in only a few days, so sandy areas must be watched closely.

As would be expected, the water covering sloughs is darker in color, but with practice, and heeding the play of shadows, you can soon detect location of a slough that has shifted. Learning how to do this pays off because sloughs yield the largest channel bass (redfish) every season.

Shellfish and worm beds are located along many beaches of the Northeast. On the NOS charts shellfish beds are designated *sh* (shells), *hrd* (hard) or *rky* (rocky). Holes in such areas are excellent spots for many kinds of fish, especially blackfish (tautog).

Some spots on the charts are labeled *sft* (soft). Holes and depressions in such places are often productive, but they are always filling with sand and shifting, and cannot be relied on day in and day out. Except in channel bass territory, it is usually better to rely on firmer and more stable bottoms.

WEATHER LOG OF A FISHING ENTHUSIAST

Judd Hill, whom I introduced earlier, was a dedicated fisherman who passed on not too long before this book was completed. He made to me a gift of a fishing weather log of his which he started about 15 years before his death. Judd's consuming passion was fishing. He was a bachelor (probably a good thing in view of the demands of his absorbing avocation) and he earned his living as a master mechanic. Judd was so adept at his trade that employers hired him with the implicit understanding that if his idiosyncrasy might leave them short-handed on occasion, he could always return in good graces. His pursuit of fish was so genially fanatical that he bought an old airplane, rebuilt it, took flying lessons—all so that he could fly into fishing areas not ordinarily accessible to the weekend angler. He said once about his preoccupation with fish: "I have tried to work out their personalities and resistance to different baits to a fine mathematical point. My aim is to know the fish better than they know themselves. As a person I am not complicated, and I have a brain. So, over and over, I've analysed every possible instinctive reaction of a fish in a given fishing situation—all the factors of the weather that were present; I've read almanacs, studied books, lain on my stomach for hours observing fish movements through a scope, and I've watched fish react to hatches of insects— these are just a few of the things I've done. I probably sound like a nut, but I guess I'm like the compulsive gambler who can't stay away from the gambling tables, and is always trying to figure out a way to beat the system."

When Judd gave me his log he apologized that it wasn't "written in style," but was composed of longhand notes. I've amplified and paraphrased those excerpts from Judd's notes used here, and for the purpose of clarity, have added some explanations where needed. Except to provide separate headings for his remakrs, I have not tried to categorize his observations. Not all of the comments are strictly weather-related, but the majority are. Those others I've included for the simple reason that they provide some darned good fishing information that I haven't seen presented before. Judd and I fished many streams, lakes, estuaries, ponds and ocean shores together, so I feel I have an investment in his remarks. More importantly his mind reflected a mixture of the true man of nature and the curious man of science. He also had a sense of humor. His definition of relative humidity went like this: "Relative humidity is when a relative wants to borrow some money and you say pee on you." Anyway, we never competed for the biggest fish; we participated in joyful experiences. I think that if we could all achieve this eager but restful participation, perhaps we would not vie so remorselessly with one another; we could keep from worrying about dunking our ego-chins in the water—but then isn't that what the real spirit of fishing is all about?

FISH AND COLOR VISION

No fish is known not to have color vision. Thus, a lure or dry fly floating on the surface is seen from below as a silhouette, without much color except on bright days. But a cloudy day means that the silhouette will be less distinct, and the color more difficult to discern. But fish still eat on cloudy days. Try a wetting agent on the same dry fly you would ordinarily select for the stream on a sunny day: The trout will at least be able to see the shape, if not the colors, of a wetted dry fly. Works fine.

THE LUNKERS LIE ON THE LEFT SIDE OF THE CURRENT FACING DOWNSTREAM

Judd's observation here is one I've never heard or seen printed in a book on fishing, but it makes great sense. In the discussion earlier of the phenomenon known as the Coriolis force, it was pointed out that in the northern hemisphere winds, ocean currents, projectiles are deflected to the right due to the earth's rotation. Thus, in northern latitudes, the cold, high-density water will lie to the left of the current if you are facing downstream. However, there is another factor that tends to modify the effect of the Coriolis force: the slope of the stream or river due to the force of gravity. In small streams the gravity effect would tend to almost completely neutralize the Coriolis force. But in larger streams and rivers the cold, high-density water will more frequently be found on the left side of the current as you face downstream. Larger fish lie in deeper water—an elementary conclusion—except when foraging or in case of the species that swim upstream to spawn, during this period. It makes sense to utilize the existence of the Coriolis force in your fishcatching strategy.

WATCH WHERE THE WIND BLOWS WILD EDIBLE FRUITS

Terrestial foods, tiny animals and insects and fruit, are blown by winds into lakes, streams and ponds, and form a most important source of food supply for fish. While most fish are not vegetarians, they do vary their diet and they seem to know instinctively when wild berries and grapes are ripe enough to fall from bush or vine.

If the bush or vine happens to extend over water, this is a lucky happenstance for the fish and the fisherman. For as one or two overripe berries fall, the fish will patrol the area leisurely waiting until a brisk wind comes along to shake the bush or vine, creating a shower of fruit. The importance of this apparent need for a variety in the diet of fish can be illustrated by a direct quote from Judd Hill's log:

> Fishing today on branch of the Umpquah (Central, Oregon), efforted two small brookies. Dressed them out. Noticed wild strawberries in their stomachs. Scouted the branch but couldn't locate strawberry bush. Got wise to myself. Checked direction of prevailing wind. Scouted back from bank into woods. Found tangle of berries. Tried one, size of marble on small hook. Got 4 good size browns this way.

Deducing from Judd's terse remarks, the prevailing wind, probably prior to a thunderstorm when it would be stronger, blew some of the overripe berries off the bush. The rain following washed them down into the stream. Judd mentions that he has fished for catfish with wild grapes, particularly in areas where vines overhang a stream—the result, excellent.

For those who may be skeptical about the above, it is true that few fish take vegetation as food, but fishery biologists interested in the possibility of rearing herbivorous fish for human food have already discovered some 15 different species which feed on bits of plants or scrapings of plant growth on the surface of submerged rocks. Most notable of these fish is the Tilapia of Africa and Asia. And fish generally are not gourmets, as the following partial list of undigested food taken from the stomachs of a great variety of fish attests: beans, laundry soap, cauliflower, cotton seed, chewing gum, peanuts, tobacco, hard candy balls, and toothpaste. (The fellow who swallowed this at least had clean teeth.)

HOW TO FIND ALL THE WORMS YOU WANT AFTER A RAIN

This is an Old South technique which is still used by commercial worm diggers in the southern states. The only equipment you need is a tire iron, a heavy metal stake and a tin can. Drive the stake into the ground far enough so that it is firmly secure, then hit it until it vibrates. Keep this up for two or three minutes, and, depending upon your location, anywhere from 15 to 150 hackles (worms) will pop out of the earth and head for the source of the vibration.

Why, exactly, the worms react to the vibrations of the metal stake is undetermined. Several mammologists have studied the phenomenon and have theories, too complicated to report here. But the fact is that the worms do surface, and they do so in greater number after a rain. If the method does not produce results on your first try, don't be discouraged. You may have selected an area where the worm population is sparse. Try again, selecting an area where humus and sod covering is fairly deep.

There is another way to find worms so simply that many fishermen may have forgotten all about it. It comes from a nature lesson most of us learned in the third or fourth grade. Watch for robins when they have migrated north in the spring. These cheerful songsters have supersensitive hearing. A robin can hear the rustling movements or sense the vibration of a worm—sounds of such diminished magnitude that a pin dropping upon a leaf of grass would sound loud by comparison.

Take time one day to watch a robin at work. He hops then stops, cocks his head in an intent listening attitude and plucks out a worm gnawing away in the top of the soil from which the grass is growing. This is your cue to dig where the robin has been hunting, for the robin doesn't have a spade to turn over worms that lie deeper down.

SURE-FIRE FISHING IN SMALL TRIBUTARIES AFTER A RAIN

Many fishermen ignore the tributaries which are formed from bubbling brooks which grow into small streams that feed full grown rivers. In these small tributaries, large fish generally do not abide. As a result they are mostly ignored by the anglers who often crowd the major streams shoulder to shoulder. But present in these tributaries and small streams are salamanders, sculpin, and a variety of aquatic insects (some anglers call them water babies) underneath smooth bottom stones—food aplenty for stubby brook and brown trout which are largely neglected by the majority of anglers. There are some colorful descriptions for the following fishing procedure. "Dickie bird fishing" is one; another is "dunk and pull," but the results if you follow the instructions carefully are almost always rewarding.

First of all remember that sound travels. Fish, like humans, have ears that detect certain sounds. They are internal hearing organs, however, located on each side of the head. A fish also has a lateral line system that runs along each side of its body. Little is known about it, except that it probably functions as a detector of low frequency sounds that may help fish in locating its prey. But getting back to your approach to the stream, if the weather ceiling is low all sounds will be amplified, and even if this is not the case, a fish can locate the angle from which a sound arrives with amazing accuracy.

If its head is turned slightly toward your direction, the ear closest to your angle can measure the probable distance from which the sound emanates. It may be hard to believe but fish have been tested and found to be able to detect time differences in the location from which a sound is made as small as six-millionths of a second. Also, remember that fish live in a medium which conducts vibrations more rapidly and efficiently than the airy envelope in which we humans live.

However, lest this information intimidates you into running out to buy a pair of rubber-soled cushioned sneakers, take into consideration the fact that in its fluid environment the fish lives amid a cacophony of sounds. But he is alert to foreign noises. Were you or I subject to the bubbling distortions of a fish's environment, we would either plug up our ears or check into the nearest sanatorium until our sense of sound balance was restored. Nevertheless, if you want to catch fish by the method following don't go bumbling around like a haymower cutting oats.

Another precaution to remember is that a strange shadow suddenly appearing across the stream can frighten the timid brookies and browns that lurk under the overhang of banks, or idle under brush or fallen trees lying in the water. Thus, a stealthy approach is a must. As you near the stream, with rod in hand baited with a garden variety worm, keep low until you spot an opening in the shrubbery lining the bank. Moving slowly (for a sudden movement will give away your presence) peer downstream until you detect a shadowed bank indentation or hole, which may be overhung with the same kind of growth that conceals you.

Now, work your rod tip through a part in the shrubbery and let your worm (or fly if you are a purist) drift with the current. Unless the hole is empty, a dark flash will whip out and take your worm. Don't jerk immediately, but wait a second or so, then yank straight up and you'll find that you've landed a stubborn brook or brown in a tangle of bushes within arms' reach. Once you've freed him and dropped him in your creel, proceed cautiously downstream until you spot the next hole. You may not go home with the biggest trout you've ever caught, but a tasty half dozen or so, captured in a solitude where few other anglers choose to go, is fine compensation for your efforts.

READING THE WEATHER TO DETERMINE WHICH FLIES, BAITS, OR LURES TO USE

Referring back to the business of "dunk and pull" fishing, it is obvious that an important factor in the presence of a good supply of fish in that stream is the amount or variety of natural food the fish can feed upon. If fly hatches are good (in a small stream or a large one) chances are that the fishing will be good, too. But if there is a dearth of natural food drifting in or on the water, the fishing generally will be poor.

The rule is that when there is an ample supply of food present, fish will inspect and quite often unhesitatingly strike at anything resembling food which happens to come their way. This being the case, it behooves the angler to look to the weather to see what samples it is presenting to fish, and where these samples are landing in a stream or lake.

Temperature, depth and water movement, as previously stated, largely determine what fish will be present, where, and when. But it is also true that fish have definite feeding grounds or stations in the current and they have resting stations where they take cover, digest food, or use them for protection and relaxation. But feeding stations of game fish vary according to the type of food which is present at a given time and according to the vagaries of weather. On a full hatch of stream insects the station will usually be on the edge of, or often directly in, the main current. If the food supply comes from the trees and bushes along shore, as in the case of willow flies, oak worms, beetles, flying ants, etc., then the feeding station is likely to be near the source of supply regardless of the current conditions. Another decision in the choice of feeding stations will depend on the abundance of bottom feed such as angleworms, hellgrammites, and stone fly larvae. During the day fish exercise a tendency to feed in the heavier water, while at dusk and at night the shallow flats and backwaters seem to enjoy top preference.

Having said this, I caution against interpreting these observations too literally. If the prevailing wind is strong enough to direct the flight of hatches to a different section of the stream, that's where the fish will congregate. Fresh water fish, too, it has been recently discovered, have an affinity for agitated water. This can be the washboard effect caused by the water rushing over ripples in the bottom, or a local wind-wave effect. In either case, it has been observed that where this frothy condition exists dead insects appear more lively due to the fussiness of the water, which apparently makes the bobbing insect's body appear to be struggling for release. It is a well established scientific fact that almost every species of fish has a competitive, bullying instinct. A fish will often disgorge and continue to feed at the sight of a competitor chasing a smaller fish.

The point of this section may seem somewhat elusive, but if you watch the wind, notice where rain-made gullies drain into streams, check carefully how the current is carrying detritus, and follow the path where this refuse (which almost always carries food items) is trapped in an eddy, you'll find the more likely spots where the fish will be feeding. A gully leading to water obviously is a runoff for land insects, grubs, small frogs, etc. The competitive instinct mentioned above leads to the next section, one of those which I warned has little to do with the weather, but, as a gleaning from Judd's log, I could not resist adding, for it is another aid to better fishing success.

PREY-PREDATOR RELATIONS AMONG FISH

In the excellent book Sports Fishing U.S.A., Warren J. Wisby wrote a section entitled "Understanding Fish Behavior." In scientific terms Wisby explained a phenomenon old Judd apparently figured out for himself some years ago: A fish that looks funny, acts peculiar, or attracts attention to itself by unusual behavior is sure to be chased and eaten in preference to a normally-acting fish.

Wisby's observation was this, making remarkably the same point as Judd's thought: "Other experiments . . . have shown that a minnow's chances of living increase with the length of time it remains in the tank. Newcomers are eaten while the old-timers survive—because they have adapted.

"The general principle of predator-prey relationships is this: An animal out of phase with, or not attuned to, its environment is more likely to be eaten than an individual adapted to its environment.

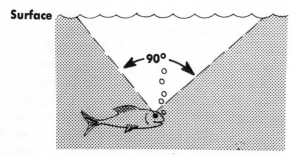

Surface

90°

Figure 7—3

"However, a blind minnow often has a better chance of surviving in a tank of bass than a normal minnow. But this is not so strange if you look closely at the circumstances. When a young bass approaches a normal minnow, the minnow responds in typical prey style by fleeing. This in turn usually results in a typical predator response from the bass. He chases the minnow, catches and eats it. When a bass approaches a newly introduced and therefore slightly confused, blinded minnow, however, the bass's seeming self-confidence vanishes. The minnow does not flee because it has seen nothing."

Judd made the discovery that if you dye the bellies of live minnows in colors that would be incompatible with their surroundings they were gulped up greedily by a variety of fish. In other words, the off-color minnows were definitely preferred by predators to ordinary run-of-the-mill minnows. It is gratifying to learn that Judd's shrewd non-scientific experiments have now been verified by researchers who have proved, as Wisby, for example, reported that largemouth bass confined in a tank prefer altered live minnows—those that have been dyed unnatural colors!

THE FISH'S REACTION TO REFRACTION AND DIFFRACTION OF LIGHT

As I have stated earlier, weather is a variety of things, some which seem to be totally unrelated to rain or sunshine, storms or calms. But it is the total atmospheric envelope in which we live. Refraction, then, as you will learn, is a vital part of the atmospheric story and a darned important factor to the angler.

Now, have you never wondered why, when you have approached with utmost caution a trout stream in which you can actually spot some lazing lunkers, they suddenly spook? They can't have seen you, you say. You didn't make a whisper of a sound in your approach, but in the wink of an eye they scattered.

Why?

Refraction or diffraction is probably the answer. The angles and distance at which a fish can spot objects above his watery domain depend entirely upon its distance from a bank that would obstruct its oblique angle of view. We all know that the principle of refraction is the deflection in a straight path undergone by a light ray when passing from one medium into another—the bending of light. To the angler, refraction makes a fish appear to be farther away than its actual position in the water. Secondly, refraction limits the fish's usual angle of sight to an inverted triangle of about 90°, with the point of the apex between its eyes. This means that the base of the triangle would be a looking glass through which the fish could peer up. To the fish the angler would appear higher up than he actually is. In other words, as in *Figure 7-4*, the fish, as seen from the viewpoint of the angler is not in the position where he is solidly outlined, but is actually swimming in the spot where his figure is dotted. For the angler to cast where the fish actually is, he must drop his lure at a point in front of the fish.

The size of the looking glass through which any fish can view objects above the water is apparently limited by (1) a fixed angle, and (2) the distance of the fish below the surface. Turbidity, available light and the condition of the

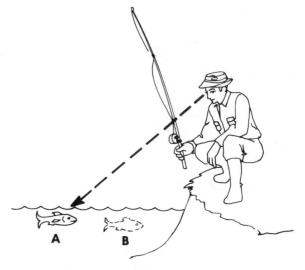

A   B

Figure 7—4

To the angler, refraction makes the fish he's going to try to tempt with a fly appear to be at position A. Actually the fish is in position B where he is shown as a dotted outline. Thus, the angler should cast in front of where he sees the fish to put the fly where it ought to go. By the same token, the fish, looking up, would view the angler at a higher distance than he actually is.

stream's surface are factors that may distort the fish's outlook.

There is another form of viewing apparatus a fish uses when the surface of a pond or lake appears to be motionless. This is the underside, or the thin layer of watery skin that separates the air above from the water below. I use the term "watery skin" because water in any container—from a small cup to a large lake—has surface tension. This refers to the cohesive physical forces in water that make it stick together. The membrane-like film (surface tension) that forms the skin or upper edge of water has stretchability up to a given point of physical force necessary to tear it apart. Unbroken, the surface tension supports objects much heavier than water; insects for example (water skimmers) skate across the surface of a pond as if it were solid.

The surface tension or film acts like a mirror to fish lurking below. How light or dark this mirror may be depends on the brightness of illumination penetrating the water from the atmosphere and being bent by refraction, which

we have already discussed. The important thing to remember is that the vision of a fish, as reflected by the mirror effect illustrated in *Figure 7-4*, is subject to change depending on cloud cover, shadows and the intensity of sunlight.

This drawing should be quite helpful if you are fishing in water which has a glassy smoothness. *Figure 7-5* indicates a depth of from four to eight feet. In relatively shallow, calm water, a fish can see reflected bottom areas that otherwise would be obscured to him. Thus, fish B far to the left in the drawing is heading for a cast plug. His decision to go after the plug rests on the fact that fish A is too big for him to swallow and he is too far removed from fish A's reflected line of vision to see what A is viewing—the small fry to the right of the log. A's probable attack, as the dotted outline of him shows, will be around to the log to the minnows—the most direct, and swiftest approach.

It should be obvious that when fishing in a water mirror, you are more than normally disadvantaged. Judd Hill with whom you have become

WATER MIRROR VISION

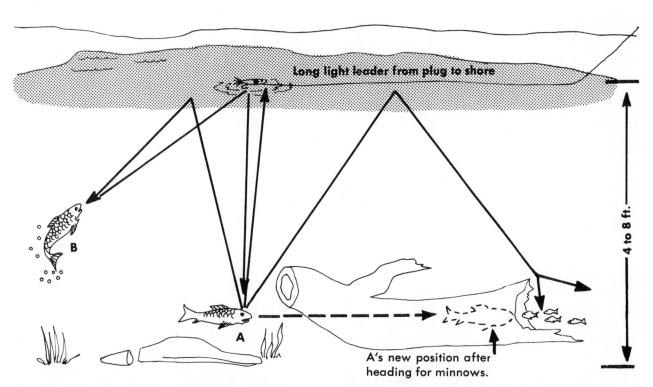

Though fish have binocular vision limited to a small area in front of them, their eyes are placed in such a way as to create monocular vision—an ability to see in an arc of 180 degrees. Thus, B can see A, but de- cides he is too big to eat. A also can see B heading for cast plug and will not attack B or go for plug because B is also too big and will reach plug first anyway. Thus, A takes most direct route to minnows, around the log.

Figure 7—5

acquainted earlier would cast to a water mirror using a thin, transparent leader 15 feet or longer. His strategy lay in the knowledge that once his lure or bait broke the surface tension, creating a shadow and splintering the mirror, fish, whose circle of vision encompassed the lure, would be spooked until their anxiety passed. When I have fished water mirrors with Judd, we unfailingly checked to determine the direction of our own shadows. A large, strange shadow suddenly falling on a mirrored pond will scare the fish and delay their feeding.

Mirages are a phenomenon that can play against the angler. A fish can occasionally spot an angler even if he is beyond the fish's horizon of sight. It usually occurs when the angler is standing against the sky or minus an obscuring background.

Many fishermen have been absolutely frustrated, ready to tear out their hair, when at near darkness trout are spooked at almost absurd distances. But this can be explained by the diffraction of light which sometimes occurs at sunset or during the afterglow when rays of light are broken into dark and light bands or into the colors of the spectrum when the rays are deflected or bent at the edge of an opaque object. The result of this curious effect is that a portion of light illuminates a normal shadow object (an angler) causing a colored or whitish radiance to outline it. A good example of the diffraction effect is illustrated in *Figure 7-6*. Here an angler is standing with the afterglow of sunset creating an aura of light around him. He seems momentarily to take on a silhouette which is outlined by the radiance. The deflected light under this, and other circumstances, may be intense if the angle of deviation is small, but lessens rapidly with larger angles. The effect is similar to the diffraction of light when water droplets in certain cloud formations, as we learned in Chapter 1, cause a radiance around the sun or moon called a corona.

If there is one moral in the above section it is *don't be refrangible to fish.* Refrangible simply means capable of being refracted—so for the sake of better fishing, watch your refrangibility.

CHAPTER EIGHT

Using Nature's Signs as a Guide to Better Camping and Boating

MAN KEEPS a record of time by calendars and clocks—bookkeeping conveniences—but nature's calendar is the great cycle we call the year. Within that span, natural signs cycle in and out: the way a tree bends before the wind, the habits of sea birds, the flow of the tides, the color of clouds, the distribution of snow on terrain, the rise and fall of temperature, the color and activity of insects and animals. The most dominant influence in this annual cycle is weather. It is the Master Builder of nature, but man, caught up in his own mechanical time keeping, has developed the habit of ignoring natural cycles.

Our past experience tells us that weather and time are inseparable and differ from space in a strange way, in that a time-weather sense seems to be instinctive, while a spatial sense has to be learned.

The primitives on our continent, the American Indians, had no word for distance, nor any regard for space. Time was not used as a monitor of work, recreation and sleep. But the primitive made use of time as an innate sense, *a weather co-equal* since time-weather was the framework upon which their hunting, fishing, seed gathering and planting depended.

I know a man, Ralph Thorson, who possesses this time-weather sense to a remarkable degree. He also has a sharp eye, for he spends his time as a wildlife photographer. On one or two occasions I've visited Ralph at a winter campsite in northern Idaho. Ralph is not a true pathfinder, in the sense that he grew up in the woods, but one day he demonstrated to me how nature's signs are infallible direction finders if you open your eyes to the visible signatures on a natural landscape.

The southwest wind blows in great force in this northern Idaho region as well as in the southeastern portion of Washington, in the Palouse area. As a result, over the centuries, the land topography has become dunelike from erosion and drift. In the winter, the southwest wind blows continuously and sweeps the windward slopes of the hilltop almost bare. Snowdrifts pile deep on the leeward slopes, immediately below the crests of hills. As a result, the windward slopes have been leveled, the inclines are more gradual, while the lee slopes are steeper and more rugged.

Thorson pointed out to me something fundamental about the weather-working of nature. Since the deepest snows are deposited on the leeward, or northeast, side of the hills, greater erosion has taken place, and the erosional effect has worn away the soil and rocks so that the lee slopes drop down at an angle of almost 50 degrees from a horizontal line. The windward slopes have a mild gradient of about 15 degrees.

This condition is so persistent throughout the entire Palouse region that any backpacker, or hiker, can infallibly determine his direction simply by observing the steepness of the hills.

The point of this chapter then, is to explain some of the visible signatures that weather has laid upon mountains, streams and deserts, and how, by observing the reactions of birds, animals, trees and plants to atmospheric changes, you can utilize nature's signs for your own benefit—as a certain guide to a more "at home" feeling when the only canopy over your head are the twinkling stars winking back the lights dancing from your campfire.

For easier reference, I have divided these visible signatures of weather into three general categories: 1, Using nature's signs to choose a campsite; 2, Forecasting persistence and judging the time of day for thunderstorm activity; and 3, Forecasting probabilities by watching the behavior of birds, animals, insects and plants.

Before we explore these categories, let's start with one simple drawing, a brief study of which will tell you something about the personality of the weather and by the signature it has left, what its character is likely to be for the locality it depicts. This sort of exercise is good practice, for if you get into the habit of examining carefully the mental picture your eyes photograph of a wild area, you will discover many things in the scene that would previously have eluded you.

In *Figure 8-1,* notice the birds in the pond,

facing toward the grazing cow. They are also facing into the wind: Like roof tiles or shingles, a bird's feathers overlap. As a result, birds avoid placing themselves in a position where the wind can drive rain or cold water under their feathers. So you know birds will always face into the wind.

The cow is another indicator of the wind's direction. And not just cows; all animals graze with their tails to the wind so that the scent of danger can reach them, while they watch for other danger in the opposite direction. Since an east wind is generally a rain wind and a west wind a fair wind, the direction of a cow's tail to the prevailing wind is a weather indicator. This is a sign experienced hunters have learned to rely on. In this case, however, the prevailing wind is from the north.

Figure 8—1

If you know certain facts, an analysis of this drawing can tell you at least four things: the time of the year, the direction of the prevailing wind, approximately what time it is without consulting a watch or compass, and what kind of weather to expect the next day.

Two other weather signatures give us the wind's direction; one is the large tree, the other is the smaller, unfoliaged sapling in the foreground. It is afternoon, and from the length of the shadow of the sapling, we can tell precisely where south is. Bear in mind for the moment that in the Northern Hemisphere from morning until noon the shadow of the sapling (or anything else) will keep shortening, but once past noon, the shadow will lengthen. The exact opposite holds true in the Southern Hemisphere.

If we know that the shadow of the sapling is pointing south, then the easy deduction follows that the large tree is almost bare of foliage on the side facing north because of a prevailing, chill north wind. There is another sign indicating the wind's normal direction—the bent reeds and willow catkins growing at the edge of the pond. Their attitude slants to the south. West then would be at the bottom of the picture and the sun would rise from the east over the far mountain.

As far as the time of the year is concerned, this is elemental; the budding sapling informs us that spring has just arrived. But what should be expected about tomorrow's weather? The mountains in the distance are hazy, a fair weather sign of the convection process. Additionally, those puffy cumulus clouds lazing in the sky are sure portents of continuing good weather, particularly if they grow smaller at sunset. The varied language of nature speaking through the visible signs of weather can provide anybody with a sense of self-confidence and comfort, even if he finds himself in an area completely alien to him—just so long as he exercises a little initiative and really opens his eyes and ears to what is going on around him. I am certain that most of us have encountered weather-wise outdoorsmen whom we awesomely credit with a sort of mysterious "sixth sense" about woodcraft, but I think through practice they've become alert to weather signs that seem unapparent and mystifying to most sportsmen, who, except for the weekends, have no more than two or three weeks in a year away from office routine.

Using Nature's Signs to Choose a Campsite

Food, warmth, shelter and clothing are the four necessities which the weather insists we plan for. Shelter, the choosing of a campsite, is probably the most logical place to start, with a survey of nature's signs.

Several years ago I was one of a party of four, including a guide, on a canoe trip to the Boundary Lakes region of Minnesota and Canada. We had canoed and portaged until late in the afternoon; it had been apparent for some time that our guide had been heading toward a particular campsite he had used before. When finally he signaled that we were to stop, the place was a rocky slab of landscape pointing out into the lake. We were surrounded by tall trees but no thick-growing underbrush. The tongue of land was scarcely 100 feet wide and on either side of it was open water. Here was a spot where the prevailing winds would sweep away any mosquitoes and nits. It had everything we could ask, wood for the fire, freedom from mosquitoes and flies, a good place to beach canoes up for the night, and a level space for the tents.

Too, there was no high land surrounding, where cold dense air would flow down into a valley low, making us uncomfortably chilly. I was particularly interested in the guide's choice of a site because I recalled a most disagreeable night a few years earlier when a float trip on rubber rafts in late February through Mariscal Canyon in Big Bend National Park turned out to be much longer than planned, with the result that in darkness, still an estimated two miles from camp, none of us had the spirit or the imprudence to tackle unknown obstacles in the river at night. As we discovered, once the canyons of the Rio Grande shut out the sun, the temperature may drop as much as 40 degrees.

Exhausted physically from hours of unplanned paddling, our food supplies soggy and inedible from lack of proper waterproofing, a rising wind flapping our miserably wet clothes against our chilled skins, we beached the rafts and walked uphill, carrying the two youngest children, until we were partially dry.

By some miracle my son-in-law's cigarette lighter, which had been immersed with our unprotected matches, finally gave a weak flame, enough to start a fire. We carried a flaming branch down to the shoreline and camped near the river. This was a mistake, for the remainder of the night, Barry and I alternated gathering scarce driftwood to keep the fire ablaze. We slept fitfully under the lee of the two rafts we turned on end, to partially block the wind whistling cold and damp across the river.

I relate this incident because at the time, neither of us had sense enough to choose a campsite up the side of the hill close by, where we would have been warm, although hungry. The rule I later learned, one that certainly applies in

Air flow direction

Figure 8—2

Cool air becomes more dense, thus colder, along the lower slopes of hills and mountains after night falls. It replaces the warm air, accumulated during the day, but which at night is radiated out into the atmosphere. On an average valley air will be 50 percent colder than the highest temperature of the day. These campers should have located a spot up the hill where it would be warmer and downflowing breezes would provide comfortable ventilation flowing over and around them. Here too, next to the river, which is always colder than the bordering shoreline, the mountain downflow has a natural alleyway where it can pick up speed and lower its temperature by conduction.

almost all mountain and desert regions in the Northern Hemisphere, is that temperature falls at night as a rule by half its highest degree of heat during the day.

This is a meteorological truism. As night falls, the earth loses heat by outward radiation and the air at ground level cools by conduction—as it comes into contact with the cold, dense air which replaces warm air radiated into the atmosphere. This cool air becomes colder and more dense along the slopes of hills and, referring again to the mountain/high, valley/low comparison of air pressure, flows down hills and fills up depressions, valleys, gullies, with cold air which on an average, is 50 percent cooler than the air on the hillsides. *Figure 8-2* demonstrates this principle. It is also important to remember that semi-arid regions are more reflective of heat; they have a lower specific heat generally and support less vegetation to retain the heat of sunlight.

Judging the Time of Day for Thunderstorm Activity and Forecast Persistence

Air is always doing something. That space of stillness a moment ago suddenly fills up with a small bluster and sends your hat spiraling off of your head to land on a bush on the far side of a creek. Winds blow, calms occur, currents rise, then the repertory changes, but at some place air is rising, falling or blowing at some angle—and it can be doing all of these at the same time in a single square mile. But upward nearly vertical motions of air are produced to a great extent by the influence of topography, by the convergence of horizontal air currents, by the upgliding of one air mass over another, and, of course, also by that old standby, convection. But no where do blowing winds create vertical currents, and sculpt the terrain, as dramatically as in the mountains.

The air blowing toward a mountain is forced to rise on the windward side as in *Figure 8-3,* but sinks on the leeward side. As a result of this adiabatic (since this book forswears technicalities, adiabatic simply means *without transfer of heat*) cooling, orographic (the mountainous effect, from the Greek *oros* mountain) clouds and rain form on the windward side, but sink on the leeward side. Dense forests populate the windward side of Western ranges, as seen in *Figure 8-3,* but the lack of transfer of heat produces desert conditions on the leeward side, and as the wind touches the valley floor, it arrives hot, eye-stinging, throat-parching and moisture-free. You don't have to climb over a high ridge into the adjacent valley to know this. For from the top, often without a pair of binoculars, you can spot lenticular (lens-shaped) clouds that form high to the leeward side of the mountain in crystalline air with extraordinary visibility. The unusual photo on page 00 is a lenticular leewave cloud.

The foregoing is important only as a point of information, for the average sportsman is not really concerned with the manner in which nature budgets energy, or stores heat. It is sufficient to know that as a scrupulous accountant, she keeps her books balanced. What may be lost as heat in one place is regained in another. But mountains do produce special wind and storm effects and the question that needs to be answered is how can the camper judge the time of day and frequency of thunderstorm activity.

It is important, however, to know generally the process which makes orographic (mountain) weather. *Upgliding* is the most common method of thunderstorm formation. This takes place when a mass of warm air encounters a wedge-shaped mass of cold air. The warm air, since it is lighter, flows up over the cold mass, setting up large cloud layers which release rain. The boundary between the two air masses is called—you guessed it—a front.

One other intrusion of fact needs explanation before describing the method of judging the time of thunderstorm activity in the mountains. On hot summer days, due to heat at the ground layer, heated air, or thermals, rise rapidly to

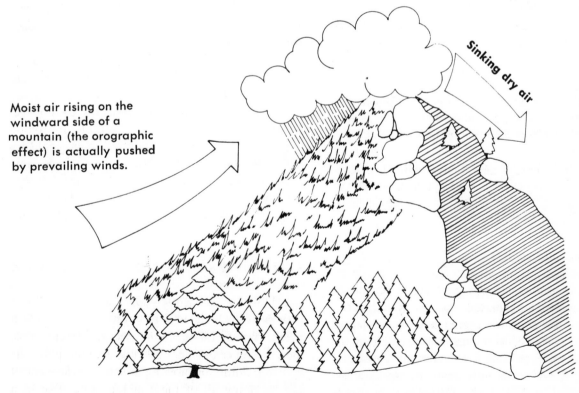

Moist air rising on the windward side of a mountain (the orographic effect) is actually pushed by prevailing winds.

Sinking dry air

Figure 8—3

Through the orographic effect, or in combination with the normal convection process, the moist air cools with altitude, dewpoint and temperature correspond and it rains. Since the leeward side represents a depression or low, the now moistureless cloudform sinks, leaving the lee side with little or no moisture. This leeward desert-like phenomenon can be seen on mountain ranges of the Pacific coast.

produce shower clouds by the cooling and condensing method. This ascending movement, which almost always leads to the growth of cumulus clouds and the subsequent release of rain from thunderstorms, is, as was noted, the thermal convection process, but convection may also occur at night, when the ground is not being heated by the sun. In this case, it is the result of cold air flowing in at upper levels overriding warmer air lying below. This process results in instability and overturning of air, producing the old, familiar convection process.

Now that we have some familiarity with orographic rainmaking, how is it possible to pinpoint, with a fair degree of accuracy, the time for mountain showers?

There is a general rule of thumb based on sound principles that thunderstorms occur at the maximum heating time of the day—usually about 11 A.M. in mountainous regions. I stress the word *usually,* because topographical factors may alter the time when maximum convection occurs. The topography of an area cannot be ignored if you expect to make an accurate reading of the weather signatures around you. For example, following are two excerpts on mountain weather taken from *Station Descriptions of Local Effects on Synoptic Weather Patterns,* an NOAA publication.

Mount Shasta, California

Mount Shasta, elevation 3,500 feet, is located in a narrow north-south valley with the rugged northern California coastal mountains rising to 10,000 feet on the west and Mount Shasta towering 14,000 feet to the northeast. The station is greatly influenced by topographic features, especially with regard to winds being channeled through the valley. Northerly drainage winds 5 to 15 miles per hour are prevalent during night and early morning hours.

A cinder cone rising 2,900 feet above the valley floor 4 miles north of the station has a pronounced small scale effect on the winds, caused by constricting the surface flow in the valley. Thus northwesterly wind speeds are two to three times as fast at the station than at locations either to the north of the cinder cone, or at locations two or three miles south of the station. Pacific storms accompanied by strong southerly winds blowing up the narrow Sacramento River Canyon produce a marked orographic increase in precipitation from valley stations 50 miles to the south up to the vicinity of Mount Shasta. The valley slopes gradually downward to the

north of Mount Shasta. Frontal systems moving across the mountains to the north or west frequently dissipate and produce only light amounts of precipitation at the station. Fog is a rare occurrence at the station. Nocturnal inversions are frequent and pronounced, but nearly always dissipate before noon.

Flagstaff, Arizona

Flagstaff airport lies at an elevation of 7,000 feet on the backbone of the Coconino Plateau. The 12,000-foot San Francisco Peaks are 14 miles to the north. The terrain drops sharply about 10 miles south of the station. South-to-west flow is markedly upslope. A strong cold front will shift the wind to northwesterly, but the wind will not persist from this direction. A northerly flow is deflected to northeasterly by the San Francisco Peaks. Strong solar heating of the black volcanic areas surrounding Flagstaff contributes materially to the high frequency of summer thunderstorms.

Two striking topographical features at Mount Shasta and at Flagstaff produce in the first case high northwesterly wind speeds, and in the case of Flagstaff a greater frequency of summer thunderstorms due to volcanic rock storing heat from the sunlight. If you will remember that dark objects store heat, and light or white objects (snow, ice, sand) reflect heat, then it is easy to deduce the reason for Flagstaff's inordinate number of thunderstorms.

If heating and the rise of heat—by convection—were alone chiefly responsible for cloud accumulation, then mountainous areas would receive summer showers during the average time interval less elevated areas around the country do—between about 2 P.M. to 4 P.M. But in mountain territory it takes less heating to produce summer showers due to orographic lifting— the upgliding process. Convection and orographic lifting combine to produce early showers in the mountains.

Whether it will rain or not depends on your own assessment of cloud conditions in mountain areas, or anywhere you may be camping or boating for that matter. Obviously, the cloud classification chart in Chapter 2 will be most helpful in identifying those clouds which have a strong rain potential, but three other rules can be quite helpful in forecasting the probability of mountain thunderstorms reaching you, and how soon they may do so.

From Chapter 3 we learned that wind direction and velocity normally change with height. This is caused by difference in temperature as altitude increases, resulting in turn in different atmospheres of pressure at given levels of altitude. This variation of wind aloft is called wind-shear and from what is known about the behavior of wind-shear these three rules will provide a valuable aid in predicting stormy mountain weather.

1. *Colder air aloft is moving in when the wind backs with increasing altitude.* Remember that high altitude air always comes to ground. In an earlier chapter, we discussed how to determine a backing wind, but it is pertinent to the rule above so we will review it here again. Station yourself in a position so that with your arm you point *at where the wind was before it moved.* The movement of your arm will describe an arc when you point it to where the wind is now. If the arc is counterclockwise, the wind has backed.

2. *When the wind veers with increasing altitude, warmer air is moving aloft.* If you follow the procedure given in rule 1, but your pointing arm makes a clockwise arc, then you'll know the wind has veered.

3. *You can judge reasonably accurately the distance away of a moving cloud, and what its speed is, by using your forefinger and a watch.* The finger method of judging distance is based on the principle that the distance between the average set of human eyes is about one-tenth the distance from one eye to the end of an extended arm with the forefinger held upright. The procedure works like this: With your left eye closed, align your upright forefinger with the left edge of a cloud whose length, in feet, you can reasonably "guesstimate." Keeping your finger immobile, close your right eye as you open your left; your finger will appear to jump to the right. Estimate the distance, in feet, that this jump appears to have covered along the length of the cloud. Multiply this by ten to get the approximate distance away of the cloud, again in feet.

With one eye closed, you can time the movement of a cloud past your finger for an estimated distance in feet in order to determine its speed. A typical example: You estimate a cloud is three miles long, or about 16,000 feet. On your finger distance ranging, the finger seems to move one fourth the length of the cloud—or 4,000 feet. Multiply by ten—the cloud is 40,000 feet away, or roughly eight miles.

By referring to the first two rules, the sports-man is in the position of making a reasonable decision about what the weather is going to be.

From a study of two decks of clouds, the observer may find this situation: Low-level clouds (stratus or cumulus) are moving from the southeast; cirrus clouds are flowing from the southwest. Generally it is true that the wind direction in the layer between the two cloud systems turns 90 degrees in an ascending clockwise manner. According to rule 2, this relative motion of the cloud systems would indicate that warmer air is moving in, signifying the approach of a warm front, with a tendency toward thickening clouds and the possibility of rain developing.

On the other hand, assume that low-level cumulus clouds are rolling in from the northwest, with an escort of middle-level altostratus or alto-cumulus clouds from the southwest. It is a fair certainty that the wind direction between the two cloud systems turns 90 degrees in a counter-clockwise manner. The wind backs with increasing altitude. Rule 1 would advise you that this is an indication of colder air moving in. Advancing colder air is the informer that tells us that a cold front has recently passed. Look for a clearing trend in the skies.

Reproduced in the Appendix is a Narrative Climatological Summary for Seattle, Washington. Along with it is a list of stations for which local climatological data are issued. While the Seattle summary does not include weather information about a mountain region, it is representative of the kind of information available from the Environmental Data Service, National Climatic Center, Asheville, N.C.

If for example you wished to know what is the time of day when maximum heating occurs on Mt. Shasta, you would not find it in this particular publication, but there are other publications available from the Climatic Center listing this information, or if you prefer from the National Weather Service office nearest the mountain locality you expect to visit. The great value of the Climatological summaries is that, with fine accuracy, they spell out what you can expect in the way of weather for any time of the year.

One other factor about weather generally should be mentioned—*forecast persistence.* Assuming the day is a bright sunny one with few or none of the signs of turbulence or atmospheric instability already discussed, you can be fairly certain that if you use the weather that presently surrounds you as a forecast, it will hold true for tomorrow. Percentagewise, your batting average should be about 75 out of 100.

Specifically, if on the morrow you notice less than 10% difference in cloud cover and a rise or fall of less than four degrees of temperature, a diagnosis of continuing fair skies would be safe. I've checked the validity of the *forecast persistence* method against rainfall records as far back as 10 years, and I've found it to be a good general indicator of weather for a three-day cycle.

Forecast Probabilities by Watching the Behavior of Birds, Plants, Insects and Animals

Broach this subject to some meteorologists and they will just laugh and say such portents belong to a category of Fur, Fish and Feather Falacies, adding that only insofar as a cold day may follow a cool one, or a cold winter a cool fall, can creatures dependent on existing conditions give any indication of the future weather.

Such an old-fashioned conviction would have been pardonable 30 years ago, for the science of the study of biological rhythms in animals was still quite primitive. But those who today ignore the massive amount of evidence that has been accumulated proving the instinctive ability of animals to sense the weather in advance are wearing blinders. But our forefathers were not afflicted with this tunnel vision. They studied the strange tides of the moon, observed leaves turn up their undersides, watched seabirds come to roost, and they may have checked on which side of the garden—the sun or the shade—an old ground toad chose as protection against a coming wet or dry spell. Then they finally made a guess about the weather.

I am not going to insult the reader's intelligence or test his gullibility by asking him to believe an old country proverb such as this one:

Bury a snake, good weather make,
Hanging it high brings storm clouds nigh.

This superstition is patently ridiculous and probably evolved from the practical purpose of keeping not the rain away, but the smell. Nevertheless, there are many quite reliable forecast probabilities indicating how nature responds to the various warnings and signatures of weather.

One atmospheric portent of rain is the condition of grass in the morning. Wet grass (dew) late at night or early in the morning indicates the evaporation-condensation cycle of high-pressure fair weather. Lack of dew means the mixing of unstable air, and rain soon. A cloudy sky is an obvious sign that there is an abundance of water vapor in the air, but it also blocks the radiation of the day's heat away from the earth's surface. Instead of cooling, the gound remains too warm for water vapor to condense as dew. Similarly, the wind at night which would accompany a storm will keep the air stirred up, preventing the local chilling at ground level which produces dew. So, it is true that if grass is dry when the sun comes up, you can expect rain, generally in about eight hours.

The scientific controversy has finally been settled that the low flying of certain birds and bats is an indicator of bad weather approaching. Swallows and bats have ears that "see" at night better than a human can with his eyes in broad daylight. Actually, the ears of swallows and bats are attuned to sound waves. Both creatures send out ultrasonic signals which, radar-like, bounce back as echoes from obstacles, such as insects in the air that may make a meal. When swallows are seen skimming along lakes and streams, you can be sure a rainy spell is ahead: Because the inside pressure of their extremely sensitive ears is different from pre-storm low pressure, swallows and bats fly as close to the ground as possible where air pressure is highest, more equal to that inside their heads. In fine weather swallows and bats fly high. Generally speaking, birds fly high when the barometer is high and fly low when it is low. Deductive reasoning would tell you that the heavier, denser air of a high barometer has more lift and sustaining capacity than low pressure air which is less dense.

Since thinning air is more difficult to fly in, birds sit it out before a storm. Without question, flocks of roosting birds do foretell a severe atmospheric disturbance. This was proven, to my satisfaction at least, when I was assigned by a magazine editor to write an article about Hurricane Buelah, which struck the South Texas coast several years ago.

An excerpt from that article demonstrates that birds, and in this case fiddler crabs as well, are incredibly sensitive to increases or decreases in electromagnification: Since any storm is a product of electricity, animals have been observed to take up certain defense postures or align themselves to a certain compass orientation away from a weather disturbance that is likely to disrupt normal feeding and sleeping habits:

By Tuesday afternoon the entire Southern Texas coast had a lonely, shipwreck look— desolate and abandoned. Few humans stirred; and even the seagulls had given up their tireless scavenger patrols of harbors and beaches, and had found perches from which they stoically gazed out to sea. A full two days earlier, hundreds of fiddler crabs had been observed scurrying for inland burrows. The wind was rising, and it was hot in spite of overcast skies and spells of drizzly rain. All South Texas, it seemed, had heeded constant hurricane advisory bulletins and boarded up.

Elk in the Pacific Northwest are infallible snow forecasters. Many times these animals have been seen to collect in the shelter of trees two to three days before a blizzard. Shellfish, housecats, marigolds, swallows and bears have all demonstrated an unusual sensitivity to the external pacemaker of weather. They have inherited a kind of inbuilt barometer which warns them of impending changes days, weeks, months, yes, even a year in advance of their occurrence.

Many animal behavioral strategems go unnoticed by sportsmen, unless they happen to be at a particular place when the creatures are reacting to a storm approaching. But birds flying low and flocks roosting are generally quite visible signs of advancing low pressure. Another certain omen of worsening weather is when you see a flock of migratory birds flying the wrong way in what you would assume to be fair weather. The following is just one example of the many cases of animal lore which demonstrate natural forecasting abilities:

On March 22, 1947, several large flocks of gulls, chimney swifts, and swallows were seen winging rapidly southeast near Houston, Texas. Two days earlier, the same flocks had surged northward on the wave of spring which surged over East Texas. But at the same time an unseasonable cold front flowed into the northwest corner of the United States, reaching Houston some 40 hours after the birds were observed flying south. Now, it is not possible that the birds could have gone northward, met the cold front, raced southward again and reached Houston that far ahead of the front. What really happened was that about 250 miles north of Houston the barometer was falling rapidly. The birds flew close enough to the low pressure area to know that it presaged freezing temperatures, and retreated toward the Gulf.

Watch the skies during early spring and fall. If migratory birds are winging in the wrong direction, they can tell you inclement weather is on its way before your barometer registers it.

INSECTS

The grasshopper is an excellent barometer of hot summer weather. When the weather is dry or the light is bright for a period of time, yellow, yellowish-red and green pigments in grasshoppers are destroyed. Melanin is produced and they take on a brown color. A moist climate encourages the lipochrome and the insects turn yellow. Brown grasshoppers tell the sportsman that the game is generally ranging toward the northern limits of its normal habitat. Animal coloring generally grows progressively lighter as temperatures rise. Also ponds and lakes are lower, and fly fishing is generally better.

If you want to know what the temperature is, count the chirps of a black cricket for 14 seconds, add 40 and you get the air temperature, within about one degree, where the cricket is located. The problem is on rather cold nights, crickets have a tendency to stop chorusing. However, it has only recently been verified that a cricket thermometer often reacts to temperature more rapidly than mercury in a glass.

TREES AND PLANTS

Leaves and plants on the whole are quite reliable weather indicators. Leaves that wither on the boughs of trees in late autumn instead of dropping normally, indicate that an extra cold winter will follow. Too, when trees are inclined to snap or crack in the autumn it is a sign that the atmosphere is lacking in normal moisture. Expect a dry season. Damp air softens the leaf stalks of trees, placing a strain on them and turning the leaves up, so that they exhibit more than usual of their undersurface. This indicates rainy weather approaching, and is particularly true of the poplar, lime, plane and sycamore. A tree that is a most reliable forecaster is the white poplar, which has a downy under-surface that shows its white side when rain is on the way. Biometeorologists ascribe the cause of this to be the upward vertical component in the air movement associated with a coming of rain, which makes the underside of the leaf visible.

In the following list, 10 Plant Prognosticators have been tested for their accuracy. You can confidently expect that the changes they make in response to various weather signatures are reliable. Remember, the science of phenology—the branch of meteorology dealing with the relationship of climate to flora and fauna—has been actively investigating light cycles, photoperiodism, suncompassing, etc., in plants since 1917, and as a result has compiled a great store of knowledge about rooted organisms.

The odor of flowers is more apparent just before a shower (when the air is moist) than at any other time.

Cottonwood and quaking aspen trees turn up their leaves before rain.

When the leaves of the sugar maple tree are turned upside down, expect rain.

Before rain the leaves of the lime, sycamore, plane, and poplar trees show a great deal more of their under surface when trembling in the wind.

Clover leaves turned up so as to show their light undersides indicate approaching rain.

When the pink-eye pimpernel closes in the daytime, it is a sign of rain.

The pitcher plant opens its mouth before rain. Trees appear dark before a storm.

When the leaves of trees curl, with the wind from the south, it indicates rain.

The rhododendrom and laurel close their petals according to the degree of coldness; the former, full extended at 60 degrees and above, but closed at about 25 degrees.

In 1805, Admiral Sir Francis Beaufort invented his now-famous scale (which is illustrated in Chapter 3). This is not, however, of much use to the average outdoorsman, so I have included here a table *Figure 8-5*, relating wind speeds to land conditions.

BEAUFORT NUMBERS

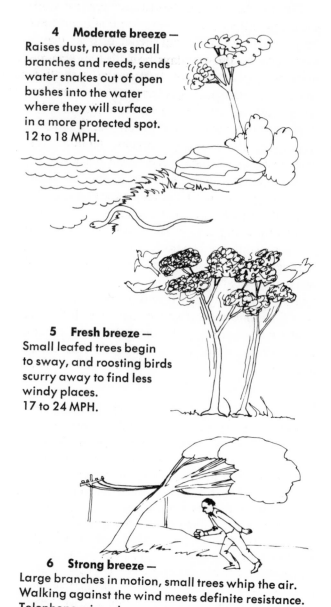

0 Calm — Smoke rises almost vertically. Less than 2 MPH.

1 Light air — Direction of wind determined by smoke. 5 to 7 MPH.

2 Light breeze — I can feel a breeze on my face and hear leaves rustling. 9 to 12 MPH.

3 Gentle breeze — Enough to send the fly fisherman home for the day, particularly if breeze seems to be amplifying. 10 to 14 MPH.

4 Moderate breeze — Raises dust, moves small branches and reeds, sends water snakes out of open bushes into the water where they will surface in a more protected spot. 12 to 18 MPH.

5 Fresh breeze — Small leafed trees begin to sway, and roosting birds scurry away to find less windy places. 17 to 24 MPH.

6 Strong breeze — Large branches in motion, small trees whip the air. Walking against the wind meets definite resistance. Telephone wires sing. 23 to 35 MPH.

Figure 8—5

CHAPTER NINE

Weather and the Skin Diver

I HAVE a friend, Craig Lawson, who possesses more than just a passing knowledge about skin diving and the habits of fish under a variety of weather conditions.

Craig is probably one of the most unusual commercial shrimp boat operators you'd ever be likely to meet: During times of inactivity when his trawler is anchored somewhere in the Gulf, Craig regularly retires to his cabin and starts writing poetry on a long, yellow legal pad. He's very good at it too, for one of the major greeting card houses has purchased hundreds of his verses and is continually after him to give up fishing and exchange his dungarees for a tailored suit, fat salary and a congenial office where he can devote all of his time to versifying.

But Craig is one of those disappearing individualists who finds his own company quite tolerable and he can't imagine forsaking all that elbow room in the Gulf of Mexico, between Tampico, Mexico and New Orleans, for a regular paycheck and a pretty secretary.

Craig, with 20 years of professional diving experience was the leader of a U.S. Navy Underwater Demolition Team for about six years, and has dived in a good many places, both as a frogman and as a private, pleasure-seeking citizen, including the waters off Korea, Greenland, Vietnam, Florida and the Bahamas. He knows more about weather, above and below, than he realizes, but until I asked him, had never put it into words.

I am indebted to Craig for some of the observations made in this chapter. I've simply given a scientific explanation for those observations of his I have recorded here.

Though not an oldtimer in years, Craig is like a lot of those savvy fishermen you see come to the same spot on a jetty year after year. On a morning that you might think is perfectly fine, you'll observe such a weatherwise ocean angler give the sky a searching glance, or he'll notice the sea is a bit oily on this day, and he shoulders his fishing rod and goes home. Why? Because he's read a weather sign that tells him something is going to happen that will spoil fishing until later.

The spearfishing skin diver is far more at the mercy of the inconstant weather than his counterpart on the surface with bait bucket and line. Accidents, attributed to weather factors, take the lives of many scuba divers annually, but they are avoidable. Evident in all the cases is the fact that the diver was either ignorant of a pending weather change, or ignored it. But a knowledge of how weather acts below, and how surface weather brings about changes beneath the skin of the water, can not only prevent tragedy, but guarantee more fun and better hunting and exploring for the skin diver.

Finally, I must point out that this chapter is not intended as a short course in skin diving. The subject would be out of place in a book devoted to the weather, and besides many excellent books have been published that describe safe skin diving techniques far better than I could. Rather, my purpose is to acquaint the beginner with weather problems and aids normally quite neglected in books on free diving, and to remind the experienced diver of facts he may already know as "hunches," without understanding their true basis.

The question might reasonably be asked, "How can the functions of bodies of water be included in the category of weather?" The an-

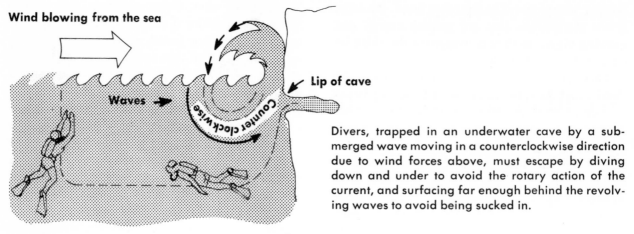

Lip of cave

Waves →

Counter clockwise

Divers, trapped in an underwater cave by a submerged wave moving in a counterclockwise direction due to wind forces above, must escape by diving down and under to avoid the rotary action of the current, and surfacing far enough behind the revolving waves to avoid being sucked in.

Figure 9—1

swer is that water, like air, is a fluid. In a motionless state, of course, you can't feel air, but it is treated as a fluid by meteorologists; the best example being the flow of cold air from a mountain high to a valley low. Like cold air, cold water is denser than warm and sinks.

A few years ago, Craig Lawson in the company of another experienced skin diver, decided to explore some of the caves off La Jolla, California. Craig's account demonstrates clearly the danger of sudden surface winds and submerged waves:

"It was a beautiful day, clear, with a blue sky, and a few possible thunderhead shapes on the horizon. We descended, and started looking around in a cave that was located in a cliff about 18 feet below the surface. I imagine the cliff probably extended above the water 60 feet or more. Our first indication that something was wrong was that our visibility was reduced to about 30 feet.

"Diminished illumination from the sun is one of the first things a diver should check. He should go topside to see what is going on. For all he knows, depending on where he's diving, he may have an ocean liner sitting on top of him. *We didn't surface,* and in a matter of minutes a gale had kicked up—we later learned with winds gusting to 55 knots. Yes, just that fast, a line squall had moved in. The action of the wind on top trapped us in the cave. When we tried to swim out through the mouth and over the lip, it was as if somebody had slammed a door in our faces. The turbulence banged our tanks against the roof of the cave, and we did experience a moment of panic.

"We knew what must have happened. The wind above was driving huge waves against the rock cliff above us. They smashed against the rock, then retreated, driving down counterclockwise into the water and pressing up against the lip of the cave, sealing it with tons of pressure. An inexperienced diver probably would have perished in that cave that day. If he had been down the same length of time we had and decided to try to wait out the storm, his air supply would have trickled out.

"We went straight down instead, swimming under the countercurrent, and surfaced a good 500 yards beyond the breakers, then swam for a beach area between the rocks (*Figure 9-1*). We knew if we had gone straight up behind the countercurrent we would have been drawn into it and crushed against the rocks."

Lawson's experience illustrates on an exaggerated scale the general behavior of breakers. The rule is that when the velocity of water at the crest of a wave exceeds the total wave velocity, the wave breaks. In other words, the crest has stretched out too far and has lost its stability. Now, what's important to the skin diver, who may find that he has drifted from his original entry point in the surf, is the depth at which waves break. There is a rule for this too: The depth at which a wave breaks increases with both wave height and steepness. So waves of *short-duration* break in deeper water than *long-duration* waves which have the same breaker height. The reason for this is that short-duration waves have greater steepness because their crests are closer together. The value of this relationship can be seen in *Figure 9-2*. In this illustration, notice that the smaller arrows marking the direction, and energy, of the wave crest heading inshore through the submerged canyon are spreading out, thus losing energy and growing smaller through divergence. On the other hand, the large arrow mark crests that are gaining energy and growing bigger as they converge on the ridge on either side of the trough.

There are many such valleys along parts of the Pacific and Atlantic coasts where waves passing over are, at best, just chop, or do not break at all. These troughs make good places to launch boats.

No one can predict tomorrow's weather infallibly. At the most a mistake in forecasting for a Sunday picnic will get you damp from sudden showers. Faulty calculations about diving weather, however, or ignorance of the interplay and effects of currents, waves, tide sets, turbidity and cold, can always be serious if not fatal to the skin diver. Thus, an important prelude to underwater exploration is to find out as much as you can about the submarine topography of an area you want to poke around in. Today, there are

hundreds of skin diving clubs in the United States. Every major diving area will have at least one, and, as I have found, the members are most willing to share information with visitors to their area. You might take down this list of questions to ask the locals:

What is the position and distance, in relation to the coastline, of the underwater bottom you are interested in exploring?

Ask for facts about the average weather conditions that prevail in the area during the month in which your visit takes place. Are there any unusual weather forecasts, such as sudden fogs, strange wind characteristics, or extra strong tidal currents you should know about? Generally tide tables are available, and these should be checked for tide heights and lows. However, you'd be better off to check coast and harbor charts which usually will contain information on the

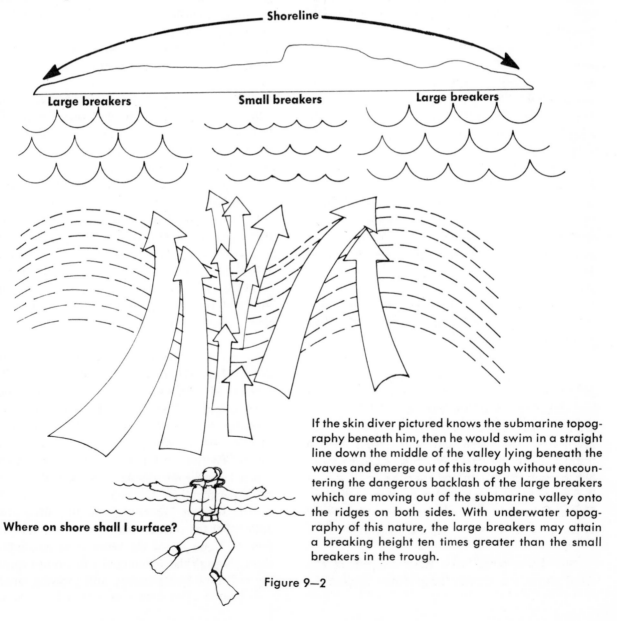

Shoreline

Large breakers   **Small breakers**   **Large breakers**

Where on shore shall I surface?

If the skin diver pictured knows the submarine topography beneath him, then he would swim in a straight line down the middle of the valley lying beneath the waves and emerge out of this trough without encountering the dangerous backlash of the large breakers which are moving out of the submarine valley onto the ridges on both sides. With underwater topography of this nature, the large breakers may attain a breaking height ten times greater than the small breakers in the trough.

Figure 9—2

normal range of tides and the variations from the charted depths that may be expected.

It is very important to remember that exceptional conditions—prolonged winds or extreme changes of barometric pressure—may come up at the time you're in an unknown area with the result that water depth may be much lower or higher than indicated on the charts.

What is the geological nature of the submarine land? Knowing some aspects of submarine geology can be important, for no one wishes to be visited by unexpected trouble. Suppose you are swimming along underwater with a faceplate and encounter a steep mud slope. If you stir the mud, you can start a process similar to a snowslide in the mountains, and divers have been known to get caught in the *turbidity current* that accompanies a submarine mud slide.

The snowball effect of an avalanche does not occur when a mud slope is disturbed. Instead, the stirred-up mud adds weight to the water and this mud-bearing water starts flowing down the slope, gathering more mud, and more speed as it grows heavier. The Dutch geologist Philip Kuenen compared the action of a large, thick mass of saturated sediment slipping down a submarine slope to the violent outpouring of deep water through a broken dam.

These mud slides are called *turbidity currents* because of their turbid color, resulting from the mixture of sediment and water. While they were first discovered in reservoir lakes—in Lake Mead, turbidity currents flow for miles, only stopping when they smack up against Hoover Dam—they are known to exist in shallow waters frequented by free divers, and great masses on the ocean floor. They have broken cables, and can reach, in the early stages of flow, a speed up to 80 miles per hour, or more.

There are several recorded instances of divers being caught in these dangerous currents. One of the things that can happen is that your face plate can be knocked askew and filled with mud or obscured on the outside with a thick film. In any event, visibility is reduced to zero in the swirling mud. Another, more perilous result, is that you can be caught in the dark current and forced down quickly below the level at which your compressed air tank will provide you with safety against increasing water pressure, without ascending decompression stages. For example, a push downward, from the maximum normal diving limit of 130 feet, of only 60 feet, would mean that you would have to ascend from that depth in stages to avoid the bends. And, depending on the length of time you've been down already, your diminished air might not be sufficient to take you to the top. The best advice is to avoid steep mud slopes, but if you do detect sudden movement in such a muddy one-way ticket to the other world, propel yourself immediately away from the descending current in a horizontal direction.

Another hazard to avoid is a coral reef rip-current. Similar in principle to rip-currents that carry away the piled up water from shore waves along a return path formed in a longshore bar, coral reef rips form in channels inside a reef. I had a particularly terrifying experience with such a rip in reef waters near the John Pennekanp State Park in Florida.

The reef I was exploring, like many, acted as a breakwater to the swells of the open ocean. Frequently large waves break over such a coral breakwater, ushering a flood of water into the channels inside the reef.

To find an avenue of escape, the excess water may have to flow for a long distance, depending, of course, on the length of the reef before it can find an escape gap in the coral barrier, through which it rushes out to the open sea. The problem is that these reef rip flows are intermittent and when wave action is light, the inner channel areas attract exploration.

In my own case, I suddenly found myself in the grip of a powerful rip that was returning water from waves that had broken over the reef for a distance of probably half a mile. Considering the force and speed that this amount of water would generate returning to the sea, I was lucky to grab hold of a coral outcropping in the channel and hang there for about three minutes, like a feather in a strong wind to avoid being swept into the treacherous breaker zone outside the reef. The moral of experience is, examine sea conditions before you start exploring in areas where reef rips are likely to be. Waves breaking strongly over a coral barrier are a sign that you'd better look for someplace else to dive. I must add, though, that generally reef rip currents are of short duration. Nevertheless, they are certainly strong enough to smash a diver against coral shelves, with resulting injury.

Before leaving the subject of currents, it seems appropriate to repeat one anecdote which was related to me by Craig Lawson, for it demonstrates that divers are helpless in some tide currents, but can survive if they know what to do.

Lawson's experience was with a 17-knot tidal

current which carried him like a submerged, bobbing cork far out into Wanson Harbor where he had been working as a member of a Navy crew inspecting the area for shipping obstructions. Lawson was tumbled like a rolling ball on the current, but made no effort to try to swim out of it, because he knew that it was much stronger than he. When finally, the current subsided and he was in placid water, he followed these procedures, which according to Lawson, can save a diver's life if he's suffering from vertigo as a result of being tossed around in a watery turbulence:

"When you are in quiet water again, after a ride in a tidal current or in a rip, your senses are disoriented. You are in a void. The first thing to do is to take out your mouthpiece—take out your mouthpiece and blow—and watch the bubbles. Even though your body may be suffering from vertigo and says to you the surface is up here, follow the bubbles. When you reach the surface, you can decide which is the quickest and safest route to shore."

A lot of fishermen and skin divers assume that fish are stupid. Many species are, but experiments have proved that fish can learn, and this means they have memories. So, for example, if you've found a favorite hole where the fish are abundant, and you keep returning with spear in hand, you may find your luck will eventually begin to sour. The fish will become wary of that haunt, particularly if there is no great ingress and egress of new fish to the spot.

One good area found all along the coasts, however, seems to provide an inexhaustible supply of marine life, and to me it is one of the most exciting adventures in spear fishing. It combines all the excitement, tension and camouflaging techniques the expert deer hunter must use to be successful.

This is fishing an interface. An interface is the clearly visible line that marks the edge of a tide as it moves out of a bay into the open ocean. My own luck in Apalachicola Bay, Florida—one of the many interface areas I've fished—serves to prove that when you can repeatedly find game, time after time, it ceases to be luck; it's just good old-fashioned strategy.

During certain seasons of the year, Apalachicola Bay has a muddy appearance due to the inflowing of water heavy with sediment from rains falling into the Apalachicola River. This tan coloring makes the tide line as easily indentifiable as a dye marker. As a matter of fact, I conducted some tide flow experiments, using various dyes, while investigating the phenomenon known as Red Tide in the bay a few years ago. If you are hunting in an interface where it is difficult to discern the tide line, a can of talcum powder is an excellent dye marker. Just sprinkle the powder along the vague interface and it will demarcate as sharply as a chalk line on a blackboard.

Oceanographers are a bit sensitive about the use of the word *interface,* so to clear up any misunderstanding as to the type of interface I am referring to, I propose this definition: A vertical interface is that junction where two separate

CROSS-SECTIONAL VIEW OF A VERTICAL INTERFACE

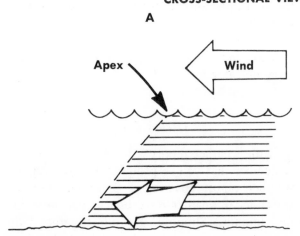

Tide current here is moving faster at the bottom than the combination of wind and tide current near the surface.

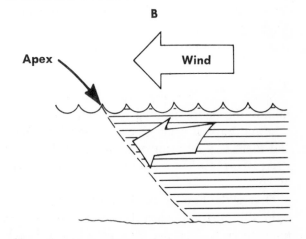

Here the wind is blowing faster at the top than the tide current is flowing at the bottom, causing a lag effect in the lower portions of the interface.

Figure 9—3

bodies of water meet, i.e., bay water and ocean water. The bay water may be brackish due to dilution by inflowing fresh water. Generally, such an interface will start traveling seaward from a bay as a vertical front but depending upon wind action the surface line of the interface may move slower, or faster than the lower point of the interface moving at the bottom.

In *Figure 9-3,* you can see how a cross-sectional view of an interface would look under different wind conditions. As the interface moves out beyond the seawall at Apalachicola, it encounters the green, shallow water of the Gulf, and begins to disintegrate as the water deepens and turns blue. Now, generally the interface carries an inviting load of nutrients—fish food composed of insects, decaying matter, all sorts of edibles—as a result of drainage of river into bay, and is denser, therefore darker, than sea water.

The smart skin diver stations himself in the murk just behind the line of demarcation of the interface and waits for the fish to come to him. In other words, as illustrated in *Figure 9-4,* he will be looking out of the murk into the clear water which the tidal interface is invading. In a very real sense he is camouflaging himself in the murk. Scientists have discovered that certain kinds of fish can detect the human odor, but the density of the murk behind an advancing interface will obliterate the human smell, and since no proof has been offered that a fish can distinguish a human from another fish—except that a skin diver's size might arouse fishy suspicions that he is a predator—the murk is excellent camouflage. There is another reason for lurking in the murk. The fish is in his natural habitat and can certainly defeat any skin diver in a swimming contest. Anybody, for instance, who chases a grouper with a spear gun in clear water is going to burn up a lot of air and retrieve a good many wasted spears.

Speaking of groupers, they are great about sniffing the debris floating in an interface. They stop and look at some object attractive to them, and there is a moment of hesitation before they strike. This is when the skin diver lets loose with his spear.

One of the best times to hunt the interfaces is right after a storm, when there is a heavy flow of mud, carrying food particles, off a bay or beach. The invading interface will be even denser than usual, creating a more advantageous water cover.

Clouds, the appearance of water, wind, set of the currents, odors—these are just a few of the

Figure 9—4

Skin diver stations himself in the murk of fringe behind the interface where he is less visible to curious fish who come to investigate the nutrients clustering along the line of the interface. He is employing the sound tactics of the deer hunter who selects natural cover to hide himself from the buck he is after.

surface signals the skindiver should be alert to identify if he is to enjoy the submarine depths safely. The Cloud Classification Chart and the Wind Directions in Chapter 2 are indispensable aids, but there are also other signs to look for; there are rules of topography which shouldn't be ignored and there are some basic precautions about safety in the water generally.

Following are some weather watch signs for skin divers. In Chapter 5, dozens of other weather portents have been examined, ones that the skin diver should not fail to heed. But those listed here are, in the opinion of many experienced divers and diving instructors I've interviewed, important enough to be placed in a separate category.

Greasy Water

If the weather report is for scattered showers, remember that you've probably heard a regional weather report covering a 250-mile area. But tricky local weather disturbances can arise in a few minutes. Suppose, at your favorite diving spot, the water, usually green or light blue, has a "greasy" slate gray look. This would, lacking other factors, indicate a falling barometer. Dive if you wish, but make it shallow and surface in 10 minutes or so to check conditions.

Strong Gasoline Fumes in Your Boat

If you detect strong gasoline vapors, first, of course, check for a fuel leak. But if there is none, and, based on past experience with your equipment, you can't account for a more pervading gasoline smell, the probabilities are excellent that a low pressure system is moving in. Remember, low pressure releases odors pent up by the high pressure of good weather. Odors are more distinct.

If You Just "Don't Feel Right" About the Weather

Quite often you'll arrive at a familiar area, but something tells you that things are not quite right—it's like coming home to your wife on certain days; there is something wrong, but you don't know what it is. The best advice is to delay a bit and see what the weather is going to do.

Topography Ashore a Strong Clue to Sub-surface Topography

Subsurface topography usually does not vary much from the topography above. For example, if the area around a lake is composed of sand hills rising to 50 feet, the lake will probably have a sandy bottom about 50 feet deep. If the shore is rocky, the adjacent bottom will probably be rocky. On these rock bottoms, generally, clear water exists, although there may be a layer of sediment or mud covering the rock. Shales, also called mudstones, siltstones or claystones, are the most common type of sedimentary rocks found in the northern seas. The limestones (and dolomites) are quite common in tropical and subtropical areas. The extensive spring and cave formations in Florida are limestones. Fragmented limestones or broken shells and fossil-cluster fragments are also numerous in the tropics. Usually shell bottoms are especially dangerous to heavily weighted divers who can sink into the soft mud quickly.

Watch Out for Muddy Bottoms

In the continental United States there are extensive areas of mud bottoms. Earlier, it was pointed out how dangerous *turbidity* currents can be. Mud bottoms are also treacherous. Most of the mud bottoms are composed of clay and silt sediments. These are classified by the area in which they are found. Shelf muds come from large rivers. Lagoonal muds occur behind barriers. Tidal estuary flats are caused by powerful tidal currents. Deep basin muds are washed from the lands. Wherever muds are found, they are dangerous to the diver. They impair visibility, restrict movement, and foul regulators. The novice diver should stay out of the muddy areas and off the bottom. Muds found in waves are especially dangerous because of the inability to ascend to air. Even the slightest movement in the water will stir up these sediment muds and create a hazardous condition quickly.

If you are going to dive in muddy areas, non-fouling regulators should be selected, of a type easily cleaned. The standard single-hose first stage is used most commonly by divers in the phosphatic muds of Florida.

Rain and Wind

If there is no, or very little, wind accompanying rain, the chances are very good that a cloud accumulation is emptying and the day will turn fair. But if winds are increasing, gusting, the prognosis is for bad weather. As the saying goes, "Winds don't blow for nothing."

Diving in Heavily Trafficked Waters

If you must dive in heavily frequented water, first notify the local harbor authorities before starting out. Do not use a boat which is painted a blue or blue-green color, since if visibility decreases, the boat will blend in with the surrounding seas, making it more vunerable to collision. Be certain, in any event, to hoist the white and blue "Alpha" flag of the International Code of Signals. This flag means "Diver down; Keep clear." Theoretically, this signal should warn off any other vessels. From a practical standpoint, it doesn't. There are too many amateur boaters around who wouldn't know this flag from the red "Bravo" flag which means "Dangerous Cargo," or "We have explosives aboard." A good idea is to have a buddy on board with a husky voice and a megaphone.

CHAPTER TEN

Weather Logs of Sailors

IN HIS exciting book, *A World Of My Own,* Robin Knox-Johnson, faithfully logged his famous 313 day solitary voyage around the world in a tiny ketch named Suhaili. The following excerpt from his book aptly points up the fact that weather was his ally, and his enemy. Had it not been for his sailing experience, knowledge of the vagaries of weather, and courage, Knox-Johnson's lonely ordeal may have ended in tragedy, instead of a great sea adventure.

"The scene that met my eyes was not quite what I had expected. Apart from a breakwater stretching out from the north shore of the channel the entrance to Otago Harbour was most un-harbourlike; instead of the wharves and cranes I had expected to see, there were green hills and sand dunes. I could see no point in hanging around at the entrance as I might wait for some time before anyone came along, so I started to try to sail up the channel. This was not easy as the wind was blowing down the channel and as I got more into the centre, I realized that the tide was ebbing as well. I tacked round and as I came back to Tairoa Heads, realized that I had made about ten yards progress. The current was definitely weaker on the south side though, and I found that the wind came round slightly close in by the cliff face so I headed nearer to the cliff to make what progress I could, and when the wind began to fall away put the helm over to come about. Suhaili was not moving very fast and she slowly began to come round, but the wind appeared to have veered and although this should have helped us, it meant, in fact, that we drifted farther into the sheltered bay instead of the sails coming aback and pushing us out into the channel again. The rocks were getting closer. I looked quickly astern to see whether I could gybe her round but the rocks were too close. Lashing the tiller hard over, I ran forward to back the jib manually, but even as I did I realized that it was too late. We were no longer moving, I need not worry about the rocks as we were aground. I was furious with myself. Thinking so hard about how to gain ground I had never thought that this litle bay, bordered by steep rocks, might be quite shallow."*

The "unexpected" factor in Knox-Johnson's experience above—his grounding in the little bay—only proves how true it is that deepwater salts and weekend boaters alike continually encounter weather situations that are unanticipated and perilous.

This may be an unpleasant note upon which to introduce this chapter, but facts cannot be ignored. In 1973—in that year alone—more than 60 percent of the boating fatalities reported by the U.S. Coast Guard in its annual Boating Statistics were weather related. In other words, more than 700 deaths were the result of an error committed by a boat operator who either failed to apprehend or ignored the warning signs evident in the sky, the state of the barometer, the motion of waves, or the pull of the tide.

However trite the old expression, "hindsight is better than foresight" may be, it sums up the purpose of Weather Logs of Sailors—professional evaluation of case histories of accidents which resulted in injuries or fatalities due to prevailing weather conditions. The reports printed here are factual, based on actual Search and Rescue missions of the U.S. Coast Guard in which distressed vessels were involved in some accident due to weather conditions. In addition to the official conclusions reported by the investi-

* From the book, A World of My Own, by Robin Know-Johnson. Copyright © William Morrow & Co., Inc.

gating Coast Guard officer, there are other comments offered drawn from a variety of sources, all authoritative, on navigation, weather and boat handling.

Relatively few of the 8,000,000 boaters skimming across our waters today give much thought to logging their weather experiences. I believe this is due to a general lack of appreciation of how fast a storm may brew up, even though all of us at one time or another have been subjected to an uncomfortable weather sequence. Without disparagement to boat owners, Rear Admiral R.A. Keating remarks that the optimistic creed of American pleasure boaters seems to be that "Perhaps the weather will change. They forget that weather imposes its own stalling speed."

Some storms do advertise themselves far enough in advance to give boating sportsmen time to think about what they will be like. Luckily, in most cases with the weather anticipation is worse than reality, or so we hope.

It is reported that the swimming pool on the estate of Jay Gould at Lyndhurst, at Irvington-on-the-Hudson, was so big that a lifeguard patrolled it in a rowboat. On a clear day he could see the diving board. If we all had a pool that size in which we did our boating, we wouldn't have to worry about unexpected changes in the weather. An examination, however, of the selected Coast Guard SAR reports may help develop some new insights about the stalling speed of weather.

I think it is important to stress that the Search and Rescue missions of the U.S. Coast Guard are, ipso facto, deductive. Most distress calls relayed to a patrolling Coast Guard vessel, reach the crew master *after the accident has happened.* In the event of an emergency call from a boat in trouble, a drowning or sinking, the task of the Coast Guard is to render immediate aid. Once survivors are safe, comes the arduous, often frustrating job of reconstructing the events leading to the accident.

My own experience as an observer on more than a dozen SAR missions is that while most boatmen are honest about their mistakes—if they knew in fact how they made them—they exercise that human failing to avoid responsibility for error.

Owning up to a mistake in judgment where weather was the determining factor does not take away from the skills of the boatman. Knox-Johnson was furious with himslf for his error in judgment when he sailed into Otago Harbor and went aground. Dutifully, he reported it in his log book. Hundreds of boat handlers with long experience guess wrong about weather-related conditions and learn from their mistakes.

The Coast Guard earnestly tries to piece together reliable information about the existing weather at the time an accident occurred. In the absence of full knowledge, investigators explore all the relevant factors that may have contributed to the trouble, question witnesses if there were any, then draw a report. This is formulated around the facts presented and analysis of the evidence that may be construed to be true at the time of the accident.

Thus, Coast Guard SAR reports are as scrupulously honest and impartial as any second hand report ever can be. Eventually, this information filters down to broaden the exegis of the U.S. Coast Guard Auxiliary's free public instruction program to promote boating safety.

I have made no attempt to classify the selected SAR Reports following according to a certain type of weather condition. Rather, I have chosen at random those SAR investigations that cover a broad area of mistakes in judgment—failure to apprehend the seriousness of prevailing weather conditions, or ignorance about what those conditions would portend within a few hours. Consequently, all the SAR Reports printed here have been reproduced, as written, with the exception that non-pertinent facts have been omitted. At the conclusion of the six cases presented here are comments on these investigations which expand on the Findings of Fact arrived at by Coast Guard authorities. All names of persons involved have been changed.

CASE I
BOAT COLORS BLENDING WITH THE SEA

From: Investigating Officer, MMIS, San Francisco
To: COMMANDANT (BBA)
Via: (1) Officer in Charge, Marine Inspection, San Francisco
(2) Commander, Twelfth Coast Guard District (orb)
Subj: S/B CROWELL, CF 000 XX; capsizing on 5 July 1969, Monterey Bay off Point Santa Cruz, with loss of life

FINDINGS OF FACT

On 5 July 1969, at approximately 1530 hours (all times zone +7), while participating in the Thistle Class Association District Championship race, the S/B CROWELL, capsized twice. In capsizing the second time, all persons on board were thrown into the water. The second capsizing took place in Monterey Bay off Point Santa Cruz, approximately 4 miles west of Moss Landing. The bodies of Robert Brown and Celia MacKinack were recovered and Frank MacKinack is missing and presumed drowned.

The S/B CROWELL, in this casualty was a 17 foot Thistle Class Sloop, of fiberglass and wood construction, of open design and flotation tanks integral with the seats. The boat utilizes a centerboard and tiller rudder for control and steerage. The bottom of the boat was painted medium blue with dark blue topsides. Owner of the boat is Frank MacKinack. The boat was equipped for racing and reportedly had three non-approved "Float Coats" aboard. No Coast Guard approved life saving devices were aboard.

The weather at the time of the casualty was strong gusty wind from the west at a velocity of 20 to 25 knots. The seas were choppy at about 8 foot crests. The sky was cloudy and the sea line was hazy. Earlier the wind velocity was 2 to 4 knots from the southwest and the seas choppy at about 5 foot crests. The wind shift occurred at approximately 1400 hours. No storm warnings were posted on Monterey Bay for the 5th or 6th of July.

On 5 July 1969, the Thistle Class Association of Northern California District Championship was scheduled for 1400 hours. However, a postponement was required because of poor wind conditions. The starting line was moved and at approximately 1435 hours the race began. At the start of the race the wind was less than 5 knots from the southwest. During what was termed a "drifting match" the wind began to haul around and increase in velocity. This changing condition existed while the boats were racing to the original weather mark, approximately a mile and a half from the starting line. At the time of the start, the air temperature had approached 80° F and most crews of the boats in the race removed life preservers and foul weather gear. The wind increased to approximately 18 knots by the time the boats were rounding the weather mark, the first race course buoy. Within a short time, a matter of a few minutes, the seas and winds had reached their maximum with 8 foot waves and chop, with driving 25–30 knot winds, both from the west. During the next leg of the race, a total of nine boats were capsized. All boats attempted to right themselves and several were successful, including the crew of the CROWELL.

During the transit of the mile between the first and second marks, the Coast Guard Auxil-

iary boats, who were on their voluntary rescue stations, were called to help pick up the overturned boats. However, all the participants in the race attempted to right the boats and continue. The water conditions were very bad, being both rough and cold. This forced many to abort the attempt to continue the race. However, the CROWELL's crew was observed to right their boat and continue. Of the four Coast Guard Auxiliary boats on safety patrol, the SO LONG DARLING was the first to come upon the many boats being capsized and damaged by the wind and water. There was some confusion during the rescue operation as the people involved tried to get the most seriously damaged boats in first. However, after a quick count of the fleet of Thistles, it was determined that one boat, the CROWELL, was missing. Coast Guard helicopters were dispatched to the area and searched through the night with negative results.

On 6 July 1969, at approximately 0038 hours, the Coast Guard Cutter CAPE HEDGE was on the scene and conducted the search for the S/B CROWELL and its crew. At approximately 0930 hours, some four miles distance to seaward in a southeasterly direction, one body was found. She had on a jacket type "Float Coat" that is reputed to provide buoyancy. At approximately 1555 hours, the CROWELL was found some two miles to the south of the point where Mrs. MacKinack was found. The boat was almost totally submerged with only the bow showing. The body of Robert Brown was found with the boat wearing a "Float Coat." Brown also was wearing a flotation racing vest. The vest was torn and waterlogged as the inner cells were no longer waterproof and the flotation panels were saturated with water. Neither the "Float Coat" or the vest were Coast Guard approved.

At the race meeting held on 5 July 1969, it was known that sea conditions and wind strength, clear of Point Santa Cruz, were rough and not the same as inside where the starting line was located. During this same meeting, life-saving equipment was noted as an optional item for crew clothing. In order to conduct the race it was determined that the two windward marks had to remain outside Point Santa Cruz.

Examination of the CROWELL, after it was recovered, revealed that both fiberglass seat tanks were flooded due to the tanks having unfilled 1/8″ diameter screw holes where the jib track fitting had been relocated. The stern foam block was missing which accounted for the boat being found floating down and the tip of the mast awash. Examination revealed that the stern foam flotation had not been reliably fastened to the hull.

CONCLUSIONS

1. It is concluded that the cause of the casualty was due to the S/B CROWELL proceeding into an area of rough water and gusty winds south of Point Santa Cruz, which caused the boat to capsize and flounder without sinking.
2. Contributing to the casualty was the defective buoyant flotation gear installed aboard the S/B CROWELL which precluded the persons aboard from using the capsized boat as means of survival.
3. It is concluded that the condition of the S/B CROWELL rendered it not seaworthy for the service for which it was used, that is, sailing in the rough water areas beyond the lee of Point Santa Cruz.
4. It is concluded that had the persons aboard the S/B CROWELL been wearing approved Coast Guard life preservers and had the boat been painted a contrasting color in lieu of two shades of blue, which blended with the sea conditions making detection difficult, and had the boat been in seaworthy condition, the three persons aboard may not have perished.

CASE II
ANCHORING ON A LEE SHORE RATHER THAN ON THE LEE SIDE OF AN ISLAND

From: Officer in Charge, Marine Inspection (LA-LB)
To: Commandant (BBA)
Via: Commander, Eleventh Coast Guard District (o)
Subj: Auxiliary S/B GOODHEART, CF 000 XF; capsizing on April 1970, Anacapa Island, Pacific Ocean, with loss of life Danger F. Westrom and Francis Bell

FINDINGS OF FACT

At approximately 1730 on 11 April 1970, the S/B GOODHEART, capsized in the surf in approximate position 1,000 yards, 085° from the west end of Anacapa Island. The owner, Mr. Danger F. Westrom, is missing; Mr. Francis Bell lost his life; and Mr. Harvey Carter received minor injuries. All times in this report are +8.

Vessel data:

Name .... GOODHEART
Number .... CF 0000 XF
Service .... Pleasure, uninspected
Type .... Auxiliary sail
Material .... Fiberglass
Propulsion .... Sail/auxiliary outboard
Horsepower 4
Length .... 21'
Width .... 6'10"
Mast .... 24', aluminum
Year built 1968
Owner/operator .... Danger F. Westrom

At the time of the casualty the weather was as follows: wind northwest at 15 knots; moderate northeast sea; long, moderate to heavy northwest swell; cloudy with excellent visibility; sea temperature 57°; air temperature 68°.

The GOODHEART departed Channel Islands Marina at approximately 1030 on 11 April 1970 with three persons on board. Their intentions were to sail to Anacapa Island and return that afternoon. Mr. Carter had sailed with Mr. Westrom on several previous occasions and considered him a competent sailor. It was Mr. Carter's first trip with Mr. Bell.

The GOODHEART proceeded on the starboard tack in a general southwesterly direction without incident until approximately 1400. The vessel was carrying a main sail and jib. The wind had eased off for approximately thirty minutes but was again up to 15 knots. At about 1400, Mr. Carter had to urinate. He proceeded to port side and balanced himself by holding onto a shroud. The GOODHEART was riding steadily, however, Mr. Carter suddenly found himself in the water. The aluminum mast had bent and went over the side. Mr. Carter pulled himself back on board and the three persons retrieved mast and sails from the water. Inspection revealed the stays and shrouds to be intact. The failure was confined to the mast.

The boom and sails were stowed below and the mast was lashed fore and aft on deck. The GOODHEART at that time was approximately four miles northeast of the west end of Anacapa Island. There were no radio or visual signaling devices on board. Sufficient approved lifesaving devices were on board. The outboard motor was started, however, it was running poorly and would occasionally stop. The three persons decided to head for a cove about 1,000 yards from the west end of Anacapa on the north side of the island. The seas were starting to pick up somewhat and the individuals involved hoped to find some kind of assistance at the cove.

Enroute to the cove at approximate speed of 1½–2 knots, the GOODHEART sighted another vessel about 1½ miles to the eastward. They tried to signal the other vessel by waving an orange lifejacket, however, they apparently weren't seen. The GOODHEART arrived at the cove about 1700 and dropped anchor. Mr. Carter stated the vessel was equipped with a small Danforth anchor and cable consisting of chain and hemp rope. The length of cable is unknown, however, the cable was observed to be at approximately a 45° angle when first anchored. The GOODHEART was anchored about 70–80 yards off the surf line in an estimated 5–6 fathoms of water. The chart of the area shows a sandy bottom. The GOODHEART, where anchored, received some shelter from the wind and sea, but not sufficient to prevent the anchor from dragging.

About 1715 Mr. Carter noticed an increase in the motion of the vessel and went topside. Mr. Carter observed the anchor to be dragging. The vessel was now more exposed to the weather. Mr. Carter went forward to look to the anchor. Mr. Westrom unsuccessfully tried to start the outboard. At one time, Mr. Carter had the anchor in and dropped it again in an attempt to find holding ground. The anchor continued to drag and the occupants all donned life jackets.

At approximately 1730, the anchor appeared to hold with the GOODHEART about 50 feet from the shore. Breakers were breaking over the vessel. At this particular area of Anacapa Island, there are no beaches as such. The shoreline consists of cliffs and rocky ledges. The occupants had also put their shoes on in the event they had to climb the rocks. Shortly after 1730, a larger breaker capsized the GOODHEART. The vessel then righted itself with Mr. Bell and Mr. Carter in the water and Mr. Westrom still on board in the cockpit. Mr. Bell and Mr. Carter started swimming for shore. Shortly thereafter, Mr. Westrom was observed to be in the water also swimming for shore. Mr. Carter is a strong swimmer; Mr. Bell and Mr. Westrom were good swimmers. All were wearing relatively light clothing.

Mr. Carter, by swimming and body surfing, reached shore and managed to pull himself onto a rocky ledge just out of the water. Mr. Westrom made shore directly under the ledge referred to above. Mr. Bell also made it to shore, but came in at a cliff area about 30 to 40 feet to the eastward. Mr. Carter removed his life jacket and lowered it for Mr. Westrom to reach. Mr. Westrom grasped a strap but it carried away at the stitching when weight was applied. An easterly current along the shore carried Mr. Westrom to the area of the cliffs and beyond. This was the last time Mr. Carter saw the other two persons involved.

Mr. Carter worked his way somewhat higher from the ledge and spent the night there. About 0800 on 12 April, an outboard spotted the wreckage of the GOODHEART, came in to investigate and observed Mr. Carter waving his shirt. The outboard managed to pick up Mr. Carter and get out of the cove. Another vessel in the vicinity with radio capability was asked to contact the Coast Guard and advise of the casualty.

At 0830, the Coast Guard dispatched the patrol boat CAPE HATTERAS and a helicopter to Anacapa Island to search for the two missing persons. Mr. Bell's body was recovered on 25 April near Anacapa Island by a National Parks Service boat. Mr. Westrom is still missing.

CONCLUSIONS

The primary cause of this casualty, in the opinion of the undersigned, was the dragging of the anchor due to insufficient weight of anchor and/or length of cable for the existing weather conditions and a sandy holding ground. Probably just as important was the decision to anchor on a lee shore rather than continue around to the lee side. Contributing causes are considered to be: erratic operation of the auxiliary outboard motor in that it could not be restarted when the anchor was observed to be dragging.

CASE III
IGNORING WIND-WAVE ACTION ON LAKE

From: Investigating Officer, Port Arthur, Texas
To: COMDT (BBA)
Via: (1) CG, OCMI, Port Arthur, Texas
Subj: Unnamed XXXX00, Motorboat Accident on Cedar Creek Lake, 31 May 1972, with loss of life

FINDINGS OF FACT

At approximately 3:00 P.M., CDT, 31 May 1972, a party of four persons was fishing on Cedar Creek Lake near Seven Point, Texas in Unnamed Motorboat. The boat capsized, resulting in the loss of life of Henry Gonzales due to accidental drowning.

Description of the vessel involved:

Name . . . . None
Official Number XXXX00
Built 1966
Service . . . . Recreational
Material . . . . Fiberglass
Length . . . . 14 feet
Breadth . . . . 4 feet (est.)
Depth . . . . 1.5 feet (est.)

104

Propulsion . . . . Outboard
Horsepower . . . . 40 H.P. Johnson
Lifesaving Devices . . . . 6 approved Life Jackets and 2 Ski Lifebelts

The weather at the time of the casualty was clear, with good visibility. The water conditions were rough with strong winds from the southeast.

A fishing party, consisting of Mr. and Mrs. Jackson and Mr. and Mrs. Gonzales, was engaged in running a trotline on Cedar Creek Lake approximately one-fourth (¼) mile north of Texas State Highway 85 Causeway across the lake. The boat became flooded by wave action on the lake, and capsized. Mr. Gonzales was not seen again until his body was recovered at 11:15 A.M., CDT, 1 June 1972. There were adequate life preservers on board the vessel, but Mr. Gonzales was not wearing a life preserver at the time of the casualty.

CONCLUSIONS

1. That the cause of the capsizing was flooding caused by wave action on the lake due to strong winds. A contributing cause of the casualty was disregard for the weather conditions on the lake at the time of the casualty.
2. That the loss of life of Mr. Henry Gonzales could have been prevented if he had been wearing a life preserver, and the boat had been returned to the bank of the lake when the weather conditions became adverse.

CASE IV
FAILURE TO CONSULT "SAILING DIRECTIONS" AND UNDERESTIMATING TIDE SET IN POOR VISIBILITY

From: Investigating Officer, Terminal Island, California
To: Commandant (BBA)
Via: (1) Officer in Charge, Marine Inspection (LA-LB)
(2) Commander, Eleventh Coast Guard District (o)
Subj: S/V WINDFALL, 000XXX; grounding and sinking on 25 May 1969 with loss of ten lives

FINDINGS OF FACT

Late on the 25th or early on the 26th of May 1969, the S/V WINDFALL grounded and ultimately sank on Sacramento Reef, approximately three miles south of San Geronimo Island, off the west coast of Baja California. As a result of this casualty, three persons died and

seven are missing, and presumed dead. All times in this report are zone +7.

Vessel data:

Name . . . . WINDFALL
Official Number 000XXX
Document . . . . Permanent enrollment and yacht license
Service . . . . Pleasure, uninspected
Length . . . . 138.4'
Breadth . . . . 30.1'
Depth . . . . 16.1'
Tonnage . . . . 299 GT; 203 NT
Propulsion . . . . Sail/300 H.P. diesel engine
Hull material . . . . . . Steel
Owner/Operator . . . . Southworth Heinz

No agency of the United States, Mexico, or any other organization obtains detailed weather information for the area where the casualty occurred and reliable weather information at the time of the casualty is unobtainable. The following are relevant descriptions of the weather in the area at the approximate time of the casualty.

The fishing vessel KAREN MARY, which communicated with the WINDFALL at approximately 1700 hours on 25 May 1969, estimated that at the time of her communication, she was approximately twenty miles south-southeast. At that time, the KAREN MARY was headed north toward San Diego. The KAREN MARY estimated that at that time visibility was approximately four to five miles, the sky was overcast, and the sea was sloppy.

A vessel which had spent the night of 24 May 1969 and the early morning of 25 May 1969 moored in the lee of Isla Geronimo described the weather as being overcast with a relatively good visibility with a slight mist falling and with a not uncommonly high sea.

When interrogated following the 1 June 1969 discovery of the wreckage on Sacramento Reef, the villagers on Isla Geronimo indicated that for approximately eight days prior to 1 June the weather had been sufficiently poor to prevent the villagers from going to the reef in their small skiffs in order to fish and dive near the reef. The villagers also indicated that during such weather conditions the light on Isla Geronimo was sometimes not visible from the reef.

The tide tables show low water in the area of Sacramento Reef was at 2307 hours on 25 May 1969.

As taken from the Sailing Directions, the prevailing winds along the coast are northwesterly and may be said to blow steadily from that direction for about eight months of the year. Rains are most frequent between May and October. Fogs occur at all seasons, but chiefly during the summer months, setting in at night or in the early morning and clearing away about 10 A.M. The currents near the coast set in the same direction as the prevailing winds and vary in strength from ½ to 1 knot. Near the land the influence of the tides is also felt; an easterly set should be guarded against at all times.

At the time of the casualty, the WINDFALL was enroute to Ensenada, Baja California, on the last portion of a voyage which commenced in San Diego on the 21st of February and which, through subsequent months, took the vessel to many Baja California ports. This final leg of the journey began on the 21st of May 1969 in Cabo San Lucas, the southern tip of Baja California. The voyage during which the casualty occurred was typical of many which had been undertaken by the vessel's owner during the period of his ownership. During this voyage and others, the owner, Southworth Heinz, invited various people to be aboard the WINDFALL during various portions of an extended voyage. These people would join the vessel at various distant ports after flying to the vessel's location. When the duration of an individual's invitation had been expended, the individual would leave by similar mode of transportation. Such a practice had been employed during the voyage in question.

It is known that the WINDFALL left Cabo San Lucas on 21 May 1969. The course which she followed between Cabo San Lucan and Sacramento Reef is unknown.

During the day of 25 May 1969, the wife of one of those persons aboard received a call from her husband via radio telephone and the Marine Operator. She indicated that the vessel would arrive in Ensenada in the afternoon of 27 May 1969. She did not arrive in Ensenada in the afternoon of 27 May 1969. She did not indicate whether the vessel was experiencing any difficulty. The only other reported contact with the WINDFALL, either visually or by radio, after subject vessel left Cabo San Lucas was a radio conversation between the WINDFALL and the fishing vessel KAREN MARY. At approximately 1700 hours on 25 May 1969, the KAREN MARY intercepted a radio communication from the WINDFALL. This interception led to a conversation between the two vessels. At this time the WINDFALL indicated that she was approximately fifty miles northwest of Cedros Island and was proceeding under power at approximately five knots toward Ensenada, where it was estimated she would arrive during the afternoon of 27 May 1969.

Although the WINDFALL is a sailing vessel,

throughout the voyage and upon her departure from Cabo San Lucas her sails were not rigged.

The vessel was first reported overdue on the afternoon of 30 May 1969. At dawn on 1 June 1969, aircraft from the Coast Guard Air Station, San Diego, began a search from Ensenada south. At 1055 hours on 1 June 1969, a wreck which corresponded to the description given of the WINDFALL was located on the Sacramento Reef approximately 3.8 miles southeast of Isla Geronimo, off the west coast of Baja California. Positive identification of this wreck as that of the WINDFALL was made on 2 June by a business associate of the vessel's owner who was transported to the scene by Coast Guard helicopter.

Sometime following the notification to the island villagers that a vessel had been wrecked on the reef, some of the villagers proceeded to the scene of the wreckage and did some diving. Later reports from the villagers indicate that the extent of these diving expeditions were limited due to the nature of the equipment possessed by the villagers. The villagers did, however, find, approximately fifty feet from the wreckage and on the ocean bottom, a body later identified as that of George Hazelrod, one of the passengers aboard the WINDFALL.

A second body was found on or after 1 June 1969 by villagers on the island, washed up on the island's shores.

CONCLUSIONS

1. That, the WINDFALL was proceeding toward Ensenada at approximately five knots and under power.

2. That, by dead reckoning ahead from the position given to the KAREN MARY, i.e., approximately fifty miles northwest of Cedros Island at 1700 hours on 25 May, the WINDFALL was at Sacramento Reef at approximately 2300 hours on 25 May 1969.

3. That, the sky was sufficiently overcast during transit between Cedros Island and Sacramento Reef to prevent use of celestial navigation.

4. That, due to the distance offshore and reduced visibility, the WINDFALL was not navigated by visual piloting.

5. That, the WINDFALL was being navigated by dead reckoning.

6. That, failure to make sufficient allowance for a southeast set of ½ to 1 knot current while navigating by dead reckoning probably caused the vessel to be set on shore, thereby placing it on a course that carried it onto Sacramento Reef.

7. That, the vessel carried a complete set of navigational charts of the area in which she was operating. The vessel carried sufficient navigational equipment for celestial navigation problems. The vessel also possessed a fathometer, however, it is reported by the previous navigator that while underway this instrument was rarely used. The vessel carried a radio direction finder which was believed to be in good working order. The vessel had a seven-inch, Navy-type magnetic compass, which was believed to be in excellent condition with virtually zero deviation. That, had the fathometer been in operation and the 100-fathom curve used as a danger sounding, this casualty could have been avoided.

8. That, the weather in the area of Sacramento Reef was probably unfavorable.

9. That, the light on Isla Geronimo probably was not visible due to the restricted visibility.

10. That, the cause of this casualty was faulty and/or an error in navigation on the part of the operator.

11. That, upon striking the reef the vessel's head was deflected to port, thereby accounting for a heading of 300° T upon entering the reef, in lieu of the more northerly heading the vessel would have been on while transiting the area between Cedros Island and Ensenada.

12. That, the vessel struck Sacramento Reef at low water.

13. That, on the following high water, the bow section of the vessel was pushed around by the seas to a heading of 065° T, its final position.

14. That, as a result of this casualty ten persons lost their lives.

15. That, the action upon the vessel when it entered the area of the reef at a speed of five knots with the momentum which would likely be generated by a vessel of that size and in an area where the wave action is extremely violent, would probably be sufficient to prevent those persons aboard, who were caught unaware, from providing for their own rescue. And, even if persons were able to become clear of the vessel without incurring debilitating injury, their escape from the violent waters might have been impossible.

16. That, no person on board the WINDFALL was the holder of a license issued by the U.S. Coast Guard.

17. That, there is evidence of violation of a law administered by the U.S. Coast Guard, in that this vessel is greater than 200 gross tons, and under Title 46, U.S. Code, Section 224a, she is required to carry licensed officers.

CASE V
INEXPERIENCE WITH ONSHORE WIND AND EBBING TIDE

From: Investigating Officer, Marine Inspection, Miami, Florida
To: Commandant (BBA)
Via: (1) Commanding Officer, Marine Inspection, Miami, Florida
(2) Commander, Seventh Coast Guard District (obs)
Subj: Death of Ainsley Pruit in Boca Raton Inlet, Florida on 27 December 1970

FINDINGS OF FACT

On 27 December 1970 at approximately 1353 EST, while entering Boca Raton Inlet in choppy seas and during an ebbing tide the operator of the M/B X00X0 lost control of the vessel. The vessel broached and overturned throwing its three passengers into the water. Ainsley Pruit, one of the passengers, was drowned.

The M/B X00X0 was an open boat of fiberglass construction, 16 feet long, 5'6" wide, powered by a 33 HP Outboard Motor; year built not known. It was owned and operated by a Deerfield Beach, Florida, resident.

The weather at the time of casualty as reported by the U.S. Coast Guard Station, Fort Lauderdale, Florida, a reliable source, was clear with scattered cumulus cloud cover; visibility 6 miles; an East Wind (090° T) was blowing directly up channel at 15 to 18 M.P.H. with seas choppy.

The afternoon of 27 December 1969, the M/B X00X0 with Marion Fowler at the helm was capsized by the very choppy water in Boca Raton Inlet, Florida. The occupants were thrown into the water. Ainsley Pruit was last seen swimming but is believed to have panicked and drowned. The death certificate listed cause of death as drowning.

CONCLUSIONS

1. Ainsley Pruit was thrown into the waters of Boca Raton Inlet when the motor boat M/B X00X0 capsized and that he was drowned.
2. The casualty was due to the operator's inexperience with handling a boat in a hazardous condition caused by an onshore wind blowing up the channel and on ebbing tide.

CASE VI
COMPLETE LACK OF JUDGMENT WITH SURF AND TIDE CONDITIONS

From: Investigating Officer
To: Commandant (B)

Via: (1) Officer in Charge, Marine Inspection, Seattle
      (2) Commander, 13th Coast Guard District (o-6)

Subj: Unnamed, unnumbered 12 foot rowboat, capsized at the mouth of the Raft River near Queets, Washington on 19 April 1969; two men missing and presumed dead

FINDINGS OF FACT

A 12′ rowboat with three persons on board was carried by the current into the surf and capsized at the mouth of the Raft River, 4½ miles south of Queets, Washington on 19 April 1969. George Hall and J. J. Martin are missing and David Reimer made it safely to the beach.

The only vessel involved was an abandoned, wooden hulled rowboat. This boat was 12′ long with a 4′ beam.

The weather and sea conditions were described as overcast, 12′ high surf, strong current in the river, tide flooding, WSW wind at 20 knots, visibility 12 miles.

At approximately 1025 PST on 19 April 1969, David Reimer, George Hall and J. J. Martin arrived near the Raft River. They had planned to see about locating some land for investment. When they arrived the three men walked down the beach to the Raft River. On the river bank they found an old abandoned rowboat and used driftwood as oars to paddle across the river. They stayed on the south side of the river for about 1½ hours and started to cross back at about 1200 PST. The downstream current in the river carried the boat into the surf. The three men jumped from the wildly lurching boat just before it capsized in the surf. Reimer made it to the beach safely. He saw the other two men in the water; one just north of the rock at the mouth of the river, the other being swept to the west side of the rock. Both men soon disappeared. Reimer stayed there about 15 minutes and then went to seek help. He could find no help as this area is very sparsely populated. He then returned to the beach and found the boat on the beach, but could find no sign of the two men. About an hour later he started walking the road to Queets, and in a few minutes he was picked up and taken to the National Park ranger at Queets. The Park ranger notified the Grays Harbor County Sheriff and the Coast Guard.

A helicopter from the Coast Guard Air Station at Astoria, Oregon was dispatched at 1347 and arrived on scene at 1456 PST. The helicopter conducted a search of the beach, surf and sea in the area until 1540 PST, with negative results. Conditions at the mouth of the river precluded the use of scuba divers.

All three men were inexperienced boaters, but they did know how to swim.

CONCLUSION

1. From the above facts it is concluded that:
   a. This casualty was caused by the strong current in the river.
   b. Contributing causes of this casualty are that the men were inexperienced and used inadequate equipment.

Authoritative Comment on Conclusions of Fact on SAR Cases Reported

For each of the Coast Guard investigations reported here other Coast Guard, naval and weather authorities were consulted to the purpose of briefly amplifying the explanations for the accidents ending in tragedy. Some of the weather mistakes are quite obvious. But even for the experienced boatman it is helpful to be reminded of basic rules of boat handling in various weather situations.

Case I: The colors of the boat in the Thistle Class Association Race so blended with the sea that detection of her location was severely impeded. The selection of boat colors generally should be made with water coloring in mind. Even a white stripe or band around the boat's middle would have made her easier to see. Another important reason for choosing clearly visible colors is that when visibility is poor, the chances of collision with other boats are greatly enhanced. Coast Guard Boating Statistics list dozens of cases where collision could have been avoided, even in poor visibility, had the weather and coloring of the struck boat not camouflaged her presence in the water.

Case II: The Coast Guard findings of fact make clear the reason why it is always best to anchor on the lee side of an island, rather than on the lee shore.

Case III: Sudden squalls or a quick rise in the wind occur unexpectedly on lakes, particularly during the summer in the afternoon when the convection process is usually at its greatest. Remember, heat transference spawns wind. When lake waters begin to ripple with little wavelets, it's a good idea to head in for shore until you see whether or not the situation will worsen.

Case IV: The tragedy of the S/V WIND-

FALL teaches the important lesson of why dead reckoning plots are so important. The Coast Guard report in this case was unusually detailed.

The questions that inevitably must be asked is: why wasn't the fathometer in use? With visibility so poor, it certainly would have warned the operator piloting the WINDFALL that he was approaching shallow waters. Assuming that it was out of order, lead line soundings should have been made.

Perhaps the most serious offense was the apparent failure to consult the Sailing Directions which would have warned of the kind of shore terrain along the WINDFALL's course. Also, the operator would have been able to plot a corrected dead reckoning course against the tide set which also would have been described in Sailing Directions.

As it was, a one-knot tide set would have equaled 20 percent of the WINDFALL's assumed speed of 5 knots. As an example, a tide set of one knot at about 45 degree angle S.E., would have created a three-quarters offset of the WINDFALL's course—equaling at her presumed speed a 14 mile off-course error.

This tragedy, again, is a grim reminder of the urgency of consulting the available navigational data for any sailing area—data that describes average wind and water conditions.

Case V: A wind blowing onshore, with a tide coming out creates two opposing factors that can be extremely dangerous, especially to a small boat. A twisting effect is created by the wind waves clashing with the opposite current waves. Now, if these two forces were exactly 180 degrees apart, the problem would not be so critical. In Case VI, following, a description of Flood and Ebb Tides is given, which, while applying to the Pacific Northwest, nevertheless should be carefully noted, for similar conditions do exist along some areas along the Atlantic Coast.

In any event, in this case it was obvious that a passenger met a tragic end, because the boat operator was unaware of the wind and water conditions.

What could he have done, given this set of circumstances, to offset the terrible twisting movement of the wind-wave forces? He would have had a better chance of keeping his boat afloat if he had kept facing into the wind, since the wind most probably was exerting the stronger of the two effects. In a situation of this sort it is very important to maneuver in such a fashion as to avoid having the wind or current on the beam. This boatman was experiencing the force of one or the other, or a combination of both, on his beam.

Case VI: To say rowing across the river in an abandoned boat, using driftwood for oars is foolish, would be redundant. It was obvious that these men demonstrated extremely poor judgment and two of them paid with their lives. Boaters in the Pacific Northwest particularly should be aware of the velocity of river currents at turning of the tides. The Marine Service Chart—Ereka, California to Canadian Border—warns of these conditions. Extracting briefly from advice on that chart, we learn: On the Coast of the Pacific Northwest there are roughly two tides each day. As the tide rises and falls, the tidal current *floods* and *ebbs*. The movement toward shore or upstream is the *flood;* the movement away from shore or downstream is the *ebb*. The period between the change when there is no horizontal movement is called *slack water*. In Oregon and Washington rivers these currents gain considerable velocity, particularly when the ebb current is reinforced by the river runoff. When a swift ebb current meets heavy seas rolling in from the Pacific at the shallow river entrance (the *bar*), the two opposing forces cause the seas to pile up and break. This is the most dangerous condition. Even on calm days a swift ebb may create a bar condition which is too rough for small craft. Boatmen should be tide-conscious and cross from harbor to ocean on slack or flood, or when the sea is calm. If you are inside the bar when rough conditions exist, the obvious thing to do, of course, is remain inside. If you find yourself trapped outside a rough bar on an ebb, it would be wise to wait a few hours until the flood (in-flowing current). There also exist, in many of the river entrances, shallow areas called "sands," "shoals," "splits," "flats" or other names, on which the waves build up to the point where they are extremely dangerous to small boats. These areas should be avoided at all times.

WEATHER RULES FOR SAFE BOATING

The foregoing six cases from the Search and Rescue files of the U.S. Coast Guard are representative of hundreds of casualties casued by ignorance or failure of pleasure boaters to heed wind and sea conditions. Weather rules for safe boating have been published by various agencies of the U.S. Government. The excellent ones below are based on Safe Boating Tips compiled by The National Weather Service, The Eighth Coast

Guard District, New Orleans Squadron of The U.S. Power Squadrons, and the U.S. Coast Guard Auxiliary, Division IV, all of New Orleans.

1. Carry some type of radio receiver on your boat, and while afloat keep tuned to a radio station for the latest weather advisories.

2. If an emergency develops while you are in the water, keep calm. Panic spreads easily, and a well-found boat is capable of surviving nicely in bad weather if handled calmly and correctly.

3. Your raised and grounded fishing pole provides lightning protection during a thunderstorm.

4. If a thunderstorm is approaching, you should be sure to lower your radio antenna, unless it is a type that can be rigged to provide a zone of protection. Most boat antennas of fiberglass construction do not afford adequate protection even though they may be properly grounded.

5. Should your motor fail in rough seas, or, if the sea is so strong, that you cannot make headway attach a sea anchor from the bow to keep the boat heading into the waves. A bucket, or shirt with the sleeves knotted, attached to a line from the bow will do the job in an emergency.

6. Keep a weather eye out for the approach of dark threatening clouds which may foretell a squall or thunderstorm. Any steady increase in wind or sea or any increase in the velocity of wind opposite in direction to a strong current may cause dangerous wave conditions or a rip tide that may broach a small boat.

7. Don't depend on a casual look at the weather before starting out. A late afternoon thunderstorm can brew up in a surprisingly short time— in some cases less than an hour. Added to gusty winds and heavy rains is the threat of lightning seeking the easiest path to earth, which could be you. If you see a thunderstorm coming your way head for shore quickly; if you wait until you hear thunder it may be too late.

8. If you are hunting water fowl or fishing in what you might estimate to be protected waters, don't fail to heed "Small Craft Advisories." A sudden shift in the direction of the wind may cause the water to lower rapidly and leave you high and dry. Check the weather before starting out, or, if practical, keep posted on developments by carrying a portable radio with you.

9. Developing the habit of observing the sky, wind and water, and recognizing the changes in the offing, will make you a better boatman, knowingly prepared for the storm that may be just over the horizon.

10. Should a person fall overboard, throw a ring buoy or buoyant seat cushion near to, but not at, the person. Tear pages from a book or magazine to help mark his location. For nighttime emergencies a waterproof flashlight should be attached to the ring buoy or buoyant cushion. It is important to be prepared in advance for all emergencies. In effecting the rescue of a man overboard, approach him from the leeward (down wind) so he will drift to the boat. Should another man go into the water to assist with the rescue he should have a life preserver on and be attached to the boat by a line around his body.

11. Make a boating plan before starting out. Inform your family or friends where you plan to go; then, if you are overdue returning, someone will be able to notify the Coast Guard. If you are delayed because of a breakdown or for other reasons, this information will greatly speed up search and rescue assistance from the Coast Guard.

12. If you are in a small boat and caught in a squall, have everyone on board put on life preservers and sit on the floor of the boat. This will improve the stability and handling of the boat and afford a better safety factor for survival.

13. Should you run aground, check the tide conditions immediately. If the tide is rising, wait until your boat is free and back off slowly. Otherwise shift passengers and load to heel the boat in order to break it loose from the bottom, then back off slowly. If feasible, carry an anchor into deep water and kedge off with an anchor winch or block and tackle.

14. When operating in shallow and unfamiliar waters take frequent soundings with a boat hook or an oar. If you must explore do so going upstream slowly. If you proceed downstream the current will probably carry you into whatever trouble that may lie ahead. Study the action of the water. The surface will tell you many things. The riffles over a submerged wingdam; the swirling water around a sunken log or obstruction; the appearance of your wake when you reach shallow water—these signs tell a story to the weather-wise boatman.

Earlier in this chapter, I quoted a phrase used by Rear Admiral R. A. Keating: "Weather imposes its own stalling speed." Admiral Keating's remark stems from his 30 years of naval navigation and a particular rule that the Navy has practiced for years—when the wind reaches one-half stalling speed of an aircraft, the pilot may not take off.

This seems to make a good analogy for boaters: If the stalling speed of the wind approaches 15 to 20 knots, and the seas are nearing force 4, common sense says to stay out of the water unless you have a very large vessel, capable of facing a probable increase in wind and water conditions.

As the selected SAR Reports published here have clearly shown, the stalling speed of weather can be deadly.

Appendix A

Addresses of Weather Service Marine Centers and Port Offices

ATLANTIC AREA

Weather Service Office
30 Rockefeller Plaza
New York, N.Y. 10020
971-5561

Weather Service Airport Sta.
Portland City Airport
Portland, Maine 04102
775-3235

Weather Service Airport Sta.
Municipal Airport
New Haven, Conn. 06512
HO 7-1540

Weather Service Airport Sta.
Terminal Bldg., International
Airport
Philadelphia, Pa. 19153
SA 6-4275

Weather Service Airport Sta.
Washington National Airport
Washington, D.C. 20001
628-9149

Weather Service Airport Sta.
Imeson Airport
Jacksonville, Florida 32229
EL 3-7370

Weather Service Office
U.S. Coast Guard Base
427 Commercial Street
Boston, Mass. 02109
CA 7-8139

Weather Service Airport Sta.
East Boston, Mass. 02128
567-4670

Weather Service Airport Sta.
Bridgeport Municipal Airport
Stratford, Conn. 06497

Weather Service Forecast Center
FOB 4, Suitland
Washington, D.C. 20233
736-3070

Weather Service Airport Sta.
Norfolk Municipal Airport
Norfolk, Virginia 23518
UL 3-4368

Weather Service Airport Sta.
Municipal Airport
Charleston, S.C. 29411
SH 4-3207

Weather Service Office
U.S. Customhouse, Rm. G-6
101 E. Main Street
Norfolk, Va.
23510

Weather Service Airport Sta.
T. F. Green Airport
Hillsgrove, R.I. 02886

Weather Service Airport Sta.
National Aviation Facilities
  Experimental Center
Atlantic City, N.Y. 08405
MI 1-4325

Weather Service Airport Sta.
Friendship International Airport
Baltimore, Maryland 21240
SO 6-2434

Weather Service Airport Sta.
Wilmington, N.C. 28403
RO 2-3240

Weather Service Airport Sta.
International Airport
Miami, Florida 33159
634-7687
634-3915

GREAT LAKES AREA

Port Meteorological Officer
Marine Services Unit
Weather Service Airport Station
Cleveland Hopkins International
Airport
Cleveland, Ohio 44135
267-3900

GULF AREA

Weather Service Office
701 Loyola Avenue
New Orleans, La. 70113
525-4064

Weather Service Airport Sta.
Tampa International Airport
Tampa, Florida 33607
877-3617

Weather Service Airport Sta.
Bates Field
Mobile, Alabama 35608
342-2423

Weather Service Office
515 Post Office Bldg.
Galveston, Texas 77550
SO 5-9479

Weather Service Airport Sta.
Ryan Airport
Baton Rouge, Louisiana 70807
357-4740
357-9943

Weather Service Office
146 Federal Building
Mobile, Ala. 36602
433-3241

Weather Service Airport Sta.
Fort Myers, Florida 33902
WE 6-2057

Weather Service Airport Sta.
Lake Charles Air Force Base
Lake Charles, La. 70604
477-5214

Weather Service Airport Sta.
Corpus Christi International
Airport
Corpus Christi, Texas 78408

Weather Service Office
1002 Federal Office Bldg.
Houston, Texas 77014
228-4265

Weather Service Office
Post Office Building
Pensacola, Florida 32503
HE 2-5534

Weather Service Airport Sta.
Jefferson County Airport
Beaumont, Texas 77627
RA 2-4922

Weather Service Airport Sta.
International Airport
Brownsville, Texas 78520
LI 2-8802

PACIFIC AREA

Weather Service Office
2544 Custom House
300 So. Ferry Street
Terminal Island
San Pedro, Calif. 90731
831-9281 ext. 239

Weather Service Office
Box 3650, Pier 2
Honolulu, Hawaii 96811
588-869

Weather Service Airport Sta.
Municipal Airport
Juneau, Alaska 99801
AT 6-3640

Weather Service Airport Sta.
Eureka, California 95503
HI 2-6594

Weather Service Forecast Center
5651 West Manchester Ave.
Los Angeles, Calif. 90009
776-2201

U.S. Weather Service Office
Guam, Mariana Islands 96910
55-102

Weather Service Airport Sta.
Lindbergh Municipal Airport
San Diego, California 92101
293-5609

Weather Service Office
703 Federal Building
Seattle, Washington 98104
583-5447

Weather Service Airport Sta.
Clatsop County Airport
Astoria, Oregon 97103
WA 1-4131

Weather Service Airport Sta.
San Francisco International
Airport
San Francisco, California 94128
761-2521

Weather Service Airport Sta.
Honolulu International Airport
Honolulu, Hawaii 96820
852-102

Weather Service Office
Rm. 219A, Custom House
San Francisco, Calif. 94111
556-2490

Weather Service Airport Sta.
International Airport
Anchorage, Alaska 99502
BR 7-0801

Weather Service Airport Sta.
5420 N.E. Marine Drive
Portland, Oregon 97218
AT 2-8600

Weather Service Airport Sta.
Oakland Municipal Airport
Oakland, Calif. 94614
562-8573

Weather Service Airport Sta.
Lindbergh Field
San Diego, Calif. 92101
293-5065

Appendix B

Narrative Climatological Summary

The Seattle-Tacoma International Airport is located 6 miles south of the Seattle city limits and 14 miles north-northeast of the city of Tacoma. It is situated atop a low north-south ridge lying between Puget Sound on the west and the Green River-White River Valley on the east. The terrain slopes moderately to the shores of Puget Sound 2.2 miles west of the field. The Olympic Mountain Range rises sharply from the west shores of Puget Sound and is about 50 miles distant from the airport. To the east about 2.5 miles rather steep bluffs border the Green River Valley. The foothills of the Cascades begin 10–15 miles east of the field and the Cascade Range is some 40–50 miles east.

The middle-latitude west coast climate of the Seattle-Tacoma area is modified by the imposing barrier of the Cascade Range on the east and to a lesser extent by the comparatively short Olympic Range to the west and northwest. It is characterized by equable temperatures, a pronounced though not sharply defined rainy season and considerable cloudiness, particularly during the winter months.

The Cascades are very effective in excluding continental influences from the Seattle-Tacoma area, particularly in keeping cold air from draining westward during the winter. Occasionally the pressure distribution will result in a southward flow of cold air from Canada west of the Cascades and it is only under these conditions that extremely cold weather strikes the southern Puget Sound area. The prevailing southwesterly circulation keeps the average winter daytime temperatures in the forties and the nighttime readings in the thirties. Summertime temperatures are predominately modified by the relative proximity of the ocean. During the summer months the nighttime readings are very consistently in the lower or middle fifties. On what may be called a typical summer afternoon the readings hover in the seventies or possibly lower eighties.

Occasionally during the warm season, even as early as April and as late as September, a weak elongated area of low barometric pressure develops along the immediate coast and rather dry hot continental air moves toward the lower pressure, spreading over the sections west of the Cascades. It is under these conditions that Seattle-Tacoma and vicinity gets its few hot days. These hot spells are only of a few days duration and almost invariably "break" or end with a sharp drop to temperatures of 70° or so, as it only takes a small change in the general pressure pattern to bring cool maritime air back in over the coastal lowlands.

The agreeable temperatures along with the light precipitation characteristic of the warm season give the Seattle-Tacoma area a very pleasant summer climate.

The dry season is centered around July and early August. July is the driest month of the year normally and December the wettest. However, the precipitation is rather evenly distributed through the winter and early spring months. Better than 75 percent of the yearly average falls from October 1 through March. The rainfall of Seattle-Tacoma and vicinity comes almost entirely from the moving storms or areas of low barometric pressure common to the middle latitudes. These disturbances are most vigorous during the winter and through this season follow paths that bring them close to western Washington; whereas in the summer the storm tracks shift northward and the weaker individual storms are not the wind and rain producers that they are during the winter months. Local summer afternoon showers and a few thundershowers do occur in the Seattle-Tacoma area, but they are not sufficiently common to contribute materially to the average precipitation.

The occurrence of snow in the Seattle-Tacoma area is extremely variable and very often when it does fall it melts before accumulating measurable depth. There are winters on record with only a trace of snow and on the other extreme as much as 21.4 inches have fallen in a 24-hour period (January 1950). This is understandable in view of the fact that the air brought in over the area by the winter storms usually has had a long trajectory over the ocean. In fact, it is only when a storm is so oriented as to enable it to bring cold air out of Canada directly or over only a short water trajectory that deep snowfalls occur in the southern Puget Sound area.

Since the southern end of the Puget Sound trough is open to the southwest winds generated by the storms moving in off the ocean, the prevalent wind for the eight months encompassing the storm season is southwest. The Puget Sound trough also is open to the north. Hence, the occasionally severe winter storm that develops to the south or moves inland to the south of the Seattle-Tacoma area will result in strong winds from the northerly quarter.

Winds are relatively light during the summer months. During the course of a typical summer day the winds will be light and variable at night, becoming northerly and picking up to 8 to 15 m.p.h. during the after-noon, the proximity of the Sound resulting in a form of land-and-sea breeze.

Fog or stratus that forms over the Sound due to radiation and advection very seldom closes the field for more than a few hours in the morning. This also is true of fall, winter, and spring stratus with northeast winds from Lake Washington which is 6 miles east-northeast of the field. The steep bluffs along the Green River Valley tend to contain the fog until after sunrise when circulation increases and the fog drifts in, decreasing visibilities for a short time. Fall ground fogs frequently are deep enough to close the field during mornings; otherwise ground fogs are generally unimportant. Most of the summer stratus moves into the area from the southwest quadrant.

The most important smoke source is the extensive Seattle industrial area 6–10 miles north to northwest. Visibility is occasionally 1 mile in stable air and light northerly winds, otherwise seldom less than 3 miles.